PIONEERS OF
RUSSIAN SOCIAL THOUGHT

PEASANT SCENE IN A GREAT-RUSSIAN VILLAGE

From a nineteenth-century woodcut

PIONEERS OF RUSSIAN SOCIAL THOUGHT

STUDIES OF NON-MARXIAN FORMATION IN
NINETEENTH-CENTURY RUSSIA AND OF ITS
PARTIAL REVIVAL IN THE SOVIET UNION

BY

RICHARD HARE

Geoffrey Cumberlege
OXFORD UNIVERSITY PRESS
LONDON   NEW YORK   TORONTO
1951

Oxford University Press, Amen House, London E.C.4

GLASGOW NEW YORK TORONTO MELBOURNE WELLINGTON
BOMBAY CALCUTTA MADRAS CAPETOWN

Geoffrey Cumberlege, Publisher to the University

PRINTED IN GREAT BRITAIN
BY SPOTTISWOODE, BALLANTYNE AND CO. LTD.
LONDON AND COLCHESTER

PREFACE

NUMEROUS studies of social and political thought in nineteenth-century Russia have already been written. Most of them try to find a certain coherent and progressive sequence in the medley of Russian radical ideas. My purpose is somewhat different, and more restricted in scope. I have neither attempted to exhume and rekindle controversies long since decided and forgotten, nor to retrace in detail the multifarious tendencies or ideas which were then competing for mastery over the minds of Russian intellectuals. I have, instead, confined my selection to a small number of distinctly representative Russian personalities, and related them to the significant manner in which they have since been revalued or devalued in the Soviet Union. In this way I have tried to focus attention on a few salient features drawn from the mental history of that earlier period, chiefly on those which have most stubbornly survived the test of time. Moreover, a bare analytical sketch of transient schools of thought is apt to make them look more insignificant and dated than they really are, unless it links them closely with their emotional background and points to a recurrent interplay and clash of powerful temperaments and characters. There is little trace of accident or caprice about the psychological peculiarities of the people assembled in this book; for they faithfully embodied corresponding peculiarities ingrained in their Russian environment, though to a limited extent they also helped to shape and colour it.

It will of course be obvious to any reader who gets beyond the opening chapter that the Russian reformers I have chosen do not fall neatly into any category merely because they were pre-Marxian or because they never became disciples of Marx. They include so-called conservatives, social-minded but non-political figures, and the more complex radicals. The extreme adherents of both right and left (e.g. Leontiev and Chernyshevsky) even share some traits in common which are not far removed from the authoritarian element in Marx. Though many Russian statesmen and officials did their utmost to behave like liberals, and honestly strove to make Western institutions work, we must by now admit that what is called the liberal outlook never struck root in Russia. The determination of Nicolas I to isolate his country from foreign revolutionary infiltration simultaneously cut her off from some healthier elements of Western growth. On the intellectual plane there is no Russian equivalent, not even a remote approximation, to Locke or Montesquieu. Herzen, to whom I have devoted one chapter, has sometimes, but quite unjustly, been called a liberal thinker. That only provides us with one more object-lesson in the fallacy of trying to measure even the most Westernized Russian thought by the yardstick of European or American counterparts.

Since international Marxism is such a well-ploughed field of study in its own right, I have deliberately omitted any account of the early Russian Marxians, though I deal with the impact of Marx on several Russian original thinkers (notably on Herzen and Bakunin) who strenuously opposed him. Some more specific reactions to Marx by his Russian contemporaries, including Bakunin, and by others who lived after him, will be included in the sequel to this volume which carries my study up to the 1917 Revolution. None of the personalities figuring in this volume turned into constructive statesmen or active professional revolutionaries. But they played their part as intellectual pioneers by providing more than enough ideas for later statesmen and revolutionaries to save, destroy, or transform the Russian Empire, in so far as ideas were able to promote the accomplishment of these objectives.

Not only have most of the works referred to here never been translated into English, but a number of them are not easily available even in Russian. I have therefore, so far as space permits, let my protagonists state their more unfamiliar arguments in their own words, and responsibility for the English rendering of them rests with me. Where I have mentioned dates of events in Russia prior to February 1918, they are given in the 'old style' of the Julian calendar, prevalent till then. Subsequent dates conform to the Western calendar.

I am deeply indebted to the Rockefeller Foundation for having given me access to the collections of rare Russian books and periodicals which belong to American libraries. I also wish to take this opportunity of thanking the various librarians, scholars, and others, who have given me help and advice.

June 1951.   R. H.

CONTENTS

LIST OF ILLUSTRATIONS

CHAPTER I

EARLY WESTERNIZERS

I

EUROPEAN civilization first assumed a coherent shape in Russia during that vigorous monarchical age when Peter the Great founded, and Catherine II elaborated, a Russian version of enlightened despotism, relying on a select aristocracy for intelligent and zealous service and on a multitude of serfs for blind obedience. The superstructure so rapidly erected was dazzling, eclectic, and fantastically cosmopolitan, for it drew contributing elements not from neighbouring Germany or fashionable France alone, but from every country in Europe which had any remarkable speciality to offer. Yet the foundation supporting this glorious castle in the air remained the ancient Russian Empire, physically enlarged by further military conquest, and with new windows opening on to Europe, but in many enduring features far more Asiatic than European, and still securely set in the hieratic Eastern mould of Byzantine Christianity, which it had forcibly imposed on a loose congeries of pastoral and nomad tribes.

No wonder that a haunting sense of instability pervaded every layer of this complex and unprecedented society. The spiritual bonds uniting the upper strata with the lower ones were tenuous and strained; the rift between them was slowly but surely widening. But strange to say, the French Revolution and its aftermath, which cracked the foundations and social structure of all the major European countries, left Russia virtually unscathed. In the aggressive guise of Napoleon's onslaught, that Revolution, far from hastening the disintegration of the Russian Empire, appeared to consolidate its divergent classes and races more firmly than ever before. Their internal strains and conflicts proved then to be less irreconcilable to one another than they were jointly opposed to the French democratic mission and its culmination in Napoleon. 'An unforgettable time,' Pushkin recorded of the 1812 campaign, 'a time of glory—with what unanimity we then all shared the feeling of national honour with that of love for the Emperor.'

The Russian national poet claimed further that his compatriots, once they were put to the test, had demonstrated that
they already outshone their Western neighbours in moral and
physical courage. 'On the ruins of smoking Moscow we did not
bow to the impudent will of him who made you tremble, but
with our blood redeemed the freedom, honour and peace of
Europe.' So Russians were encouraged to think, not only that
their country had borne the brunt of the Napoleonic Wars and
overthrown Napoleon, but that she alone had saved her weaker
allies from ignominious defeat.

To Catherine's mind the French Revolution had seemed
neither more nor less than a hideous and deplorable earthquake
which disturbed but failed to engulf the magnificent ceremonial
march of an improving social order, led forward by energetic,
benevolent and cultured sovereigns, supported by a brilliant
aristocracy. Her successors sincerely maintained a similar
edifying conception, but they paid far more attention to fortifying its material basis than they did to promoting its spiritual
growth. Would-be enlightened despots quickly degenerated
into crazy martinets, like Paul, infected by that megalo-
maniac fever which seems to unhinge the minds of those who
wield absolute power. Nevertheless, after Napoleon's final defeat in 1815, the Russian Empire, the granite rock of Eastern
Christianity, standing at the head of the Holy Alliance, occupied much the same position of preponderance and apparent
impregnability as the Soviet Union displays in Europe today.

What lay behind that imposing external façade, whose air of
monumental grandeur partly overawed and partly mystified
the outside world? That was the question uppermost in the
minds of many cautious and apprehensive European statesmen,
who wondered how long the Vienna settlements would last.
Soon one portent after another appeared, as if in answer,
making it plain to discriminating observers that the internal
state of Russia belied its outward show of calm and unified
strength.

First came the Decembrist Revolt (1825). Russia was evidently seething with dissension and doubt. For the first time her
Westernized aristocrats systematically challenged the principle
of autocratic rule as distinct from the person of the autocrat.
Their revolt was different in kind to the palace revolutions
of preceding centuries. The Decembrist leaders were army

officers, noble-minded but politically inept, fired by a mixture of humanitarian French, constitutional English, and federal American ideas. An extreme group, notably Pestel and Speshnëv, favoured following the example of the French Revolution, and aimed at something like a republican dictatorship. The majority, however, wanted to transform the autocratic Empire into a limited monarchy protected by a legal system, approximating to the English model of an aristocratic oligarchy. Neither group sufficiently realized that, for a political revolutionary, successful seizure of power, at any price, is more important than the best intentions. But they taught this dubious lesson to their successors.

In its initial stages the Decembrist movement had gained the sympathy of many wise and enlightened Russians. Its ideal aims seemed unquestionably right; its methods sounded feasible (a military *coup d'état* to replace the Tsar by his brother); for the unconventional Grand-Duke Konstantin, who had renounced his rights to the throne after making a morganatic marriage, had the makings of a good constitutional sovereign, whereas the brutal barrack-room mentality of his brother, Nicolas I, was already a notorious menace. But the more realistic brains admitted later that the means they chose were wrong, that their abrupt leap into armed rebellion had been a premature and misguided act, entailing the ruin of the cause they had at heart.

When Pushkin deplored 'the intoxicating and dangerous dreams which had such a terrible effect on the finest flower of the last generation', he obviously referred to his former friends, the ill-fated Decembrists. Another initial sympathizer, Nicolas Turgenev, later recommended in his choice French style, that sensible Russians, instead of letting themselves be swept off their feet by their insatiable craving for novelty, should begin to study more soberly the underlying principles of education and the distribution of wealth, in order to recognize 'le néant de toutes ces utopies', and to break away in time from 'ces funestes doctrines' which were progressively leading people backwards 'vers la barbarie'. The one-time Decembrist M. Fonvizin, went so far as to write a pamphlet entitled *Communism and Socialism*, where he denounced the 'proletariat' as 'the plague of Western Europe encouraged and led by demagogues with self-seeking motives'. But, he concluded with hopeful self-assurance, 'This terrible crisis does not threaten Russia. If Hegel's philosophical idea that every historical people represents in turn the world spirit and must develop and fulfil it in its own period, for the benefit of mankind . . . if this idea is not an empty fiction, then the Russian people must be called upon at some time as a historical people, and destined to create out of its own native elements a new world idea.'[1]

Among all the intellectuals of that period, the influential poet and court pedagogue Zhukovsky was the most emphatic in denouncing both the French Revolution and every political aspiration which sprang from it, including the 'constitutional' Decembrists. He fully admitted that monarchs, especially in Germany, had failed in their duty to the people they ruled—but when the belief in what is sacred has vanished, he asserted, only egoism and cold material calculation can reign in its stead. 'In the idea of the social contract, of the autocracy of the people, the first step is a constitutional monarchy, the second democracy, the third Socialism and Communism; perhaps there is a fourth and last step—the annihilation of the family, the exaltation of man—freed from every obligation limiting his personal independence—to the dignity of complete and unimpeded bestiality.'[2] That retrograde movement, for Zhukovsky, represented the rake's progress of modern Europe. 'Leave constitutions in Europe for ten years, and the result will be everywhere democracy, which in less than ten years will spread into Socialism and Communism. . . . I am an enemy of license and every kind of despotism, but I am convinced that only autocracy can do good and lead human beings forward. Autocracy should be (and more easily *can* be than any other form of government) surrounded by a wise and moral aristocracy.'

Of course Zhukovsky's warnings fell on deaf ears. He spoke too late to divert the sweeping course of events, too figuratively to be understood either by the rigid Emperor or by his enemies. When Nicolas I suppressed the amateur military revolt, and with quite needless cruelty sentenced its leaders to death and its mildest helpers to the Siberian mines, he simultaneously crippled the independent-minded, energetic and gifted aristocracy of early nineteenth-century Russia. Their *élan*, enterprise and exuberant originality, finding no broad constructive

[1] P. Sakulin: *Russkaya Literatura i Sotsialism*, p. 454, Moscow, 1924.
[2] *Ibid.*, p. 457.

outlet, ran wild or sank into paralysis. It became a conspiracy to speak a word, treachery to show initiative, a rebellion to exercise one's powers of judgement. Gradually the nobility faded out, and their place was taken by a cautious, narrow-minded, prosaic and servile officialdom. The brilliant European-minded generation of Pushkin took refuge in agriculture, in dissipation, or in the freer but more exacting sphere of the arts, where several proved to be supreme. The unwieldy Empire began to wilt under the exasperating control of civil servants and policemen. Yet the majority of its subjects, who knew nothing better, endured this rule with stoic fortitude. When in 1839 de Custine gazed with a mixture of horror and awe at the features of this 'pre-historic giant', he instinctively exclaimed: 'Il faut être Russe pour vivre en Russie . . . D'autres nations ont supporté l'oppression. La nation russe l'a aimée; elle l'aime encore.'[1]

II

The life of Peter Chaadayev (1793–1856) is at once a worthy commentary on Nicolas I's oppressive reign and a portent of the darker future. His political and social analysis, with its peculiarly conservative but constructive Western bias, forms the starting-point for that intense fermentation of thought which deter-mined the conflict between Slavophils and Westernizers throughout the nineteenth century.

It has been customary to equate Westernizers with liberals and revolutionaries, and Slavophils with conservatives. This classification is both inaccurate and superficial. It ignores the fact that influential Westernizers, like Chaadayev, were poli-tically conservative, and that many Slavophils—Bakunin is an extreme example—were violently radical. It misses the more important point that Westernizers were frequently disappointed in the West, and at that stage were apt to turn Slavophil. Both Ivan Kireyevsky and Herzen, whose first love was a richly idealized Europe, passed over to a mystic faith in the future of the Russian *moujik*. Besides, the spiritual conflict went far deeper than a political tug-of-war between groups of left and right. It amounted to a fundamental divergence between East and West over dual claims set up by organized society and free

[1] Marquis de Custine: *La Russie en 1839*, vol. 3, p. 295.

conscience—a divergence which assumed new and sinister shapes among the intellectuals of a huge Eastern Empire partially Europeanized in the seventeenth and eighteenth centuries. It was further complicated by the Russian discovery of History in the guise of Hegel's conflict of opposites.

Chaadayev was a talented but frustrated aristocrat, a thorough Westernizer, who spoke and wrote French better than Russian, and better than many Frenchmen. Apart from their political colour, Russian intellectuals usually belong by temperament to one of two main groups, and sometimes to both. One uses argument and analysis in order to obscure the truth or to dress it up in alluring disguises; the other is determined to discover truth, whether its nakedness is pleasing or horrible. Chaadayev belonged to the latter, less popular, group.

He was the first Russian who scientifically ascribed the wretchedness of Russian society to a disease of stunted and one-sided growth, due to insufficient intake of nourishment from the life-giving sources of European culture. His diagnosis, though honest enough, was dismal, and it horrified many Russian patriots. But he followed it up by proposing a bold and highly imaginative cure. There remained only one way by which the Russian Empire could escape rapid decomposition and death; namely, by setting out to incorporate within herself the whole *past* process of European culture, which she had hitherto missed through her provincial backwardness. After assimilating all these fruitful elements, the assiduous pupil might turn the tables on her teacher, and in the end repay her moral debt by rescuing the creative Europe of enlightenment and progressive religion from the suicidal Europe of socialist materialism and moral chaos. 'The people of Europe are strangely mistaken about us. Impelled by a sort of national instinct, they insist on pushing us towards the East in order to avoid meeting us any more in the West. Let us not be the dupes of their involuntary artifice; let us discover our future for ourselves, and without asking others what we ought to do. . . . Do not laugh; you know my intimate conviction. One day we shall place ourselves intellectually in the heart of Europe just as we are now politically the focal point of Europe. We shall be more powerful then through our intelligence than we are today through our material force. That will be the logical outcome of our age-old solitude. The greatest things emerge from the desert.'[1]

But—at this point Chaadayev's warning grows emphatic—Russia could not hope to steal a march on nature. She must serve a long period of humble apprenticeship before she could rise out of the barren and savage isolation to which she had condemned herself, before she could beneficially exercise that moral leadership, which she falsely imagined was already hers. Such was the positive and widest aspect of Chaadayev's message. But he is more generally remembered for the letter of denunciation which made him famous overnight by its 'succès de scandale' in Russian society.

Chaadayev started his career by winning distinction as a Guards officer in the Napoleonic Wars, and he entered Paris with the victorious Russian armies. In 1821 he was offered the dazzling position of adjutant to the Tsar. Much to everyone's surprise, he spurned the promotion, and shortly afterwards he resigned from the service. He informed his aunt sardonically that he thought it in every way more admirable to reject such a signal favour rather than to take advantage of it. 'I found a real satisfaction in thus showing my own contempt for people who themselves despise everyone.' Pushkin, who became his intimate friend, warmly admired his talents, and wrote about him: 'In Rome he would have been Brutus, in Athens, Pericles—but here, he is just an officer in the hussars.' Both as young men had shared the aspirations of the Decembrists, and it was to Chaadayev personally that Pushkin addressed his glowing exhortation:

> Keep faith, my friend, that day will break,
> The dawn of radiant happiness,
> Russia will leap refreshed from sleep,
> And o'er the wreck of tyranny
> She will inscribe our names.

Witnesses have recorded that a red flag, with these verses flamboyantly inscribed on it, was found draped over the Pushkin monument in Moscow during the early fervent days of the March Revolution (1917). It appears that the exploit was not repeated during the October Revolution.

After retiring from the army, Chaadayev travelled in

---

[1] P. Chaadayev: *Sochineniya*, vol. i, p. 188, Moscow, 1913.

England, France and Italy. Though he was impressed by the 'immensity' of London, he wrote more enthusiastically about Brighton, 'la plus jolie ville du monde', where he spent his time walking and bathing in the sea. On his return to Russia, he made repeated attempts to obtain other government employment, but they were all rebuffed. In the end he resigned himself to the rôle of a leading figure in Moscow's intellectual salons.

Pushkin's friend, Prince Vyazemsky, described him as an eminent professor with a movable chair which he carried with him from one salon to another. His own modest study, where he held an informal reception every Monday, became a centre of life. Impassioned rivals, like Herzen and Khomyakov, met and disputed there on almost neutral ground, and the most distinguished foreigners, such as Prosper Mérimée, Liszt, Berlioz, and Michelet, visited him there when they travelled to Moscow. His contemporaries bear witness to the stimulus of his keen conversation, which roused their minds like the prick of a spur on a sensitive horse, and rescued them from their habitual bondage to trivial daily gossip and routine. He was specially renowned for his mordant 'bons mots'. 'In Moscow,' he used to say, 'every foreigner is taken to see the great Cannon and the great Bell—a cannon which is incapable of being fired, and a bell which fell to the ground before it could be rung. Surprising city, in which the most notable sights are so remarkable for their ineptitude—or is that bell without a tongue perhaps a hieroglyphic, a key to the true meaning of our huge mute country?'

III

Had he confined his activities to discourse, Chaadayev would have survived like Stankevich, only as a legendary inspirer of a devoted circle of admiring friends. But he took the bolder step of giving more permanent shape to his thoughts in a series of *Philosophic Letters* which he wrote in French to a friend. The first is by far the most original and compact; the others are more random reflections on the philosophy of history, ranging from Homer to Moses and Mahomet. He told A. Turgenev plainly that the first letter 'was not written for the general public, with which I never wished to have any dealings, as is clear from every line of it'. Yet the editor of *The Telescope*, apparently with Chaadayev's approval, secured a copy of it (first written in 1829) and wishing to make a 'scoop' for his rather humdrum journal, published it there (No. 15, 1836) in a Russian translation. He succeeded beyond his wildest expectations, for Chaadayev's letter not only created a public uproar, but it roused to a fury the slumbering hornets' nest of officialdom. Herzen, who read it with a thrill of admiration while living in exile at Vyatka, called it, 'a shot resounding suddenly through the dark and silent night, a signal, a cry for help, a herald of dawn—or was it a sign that dawn would never break? Be that as it may, it was time to wake up.' *The Telescope* was promptly suppressed by the Ministry of the Interior, and the censor, who had passed the offending article, was dismissed. The indignant Nicolas I declared Chaadayev to be a raving lunatic, and gave express orders for him to be placed under the supervision of a doctor. One might form a more topical picture of the hectic situation by visualizing what would happen in the Kremlin today if an impassioned article denouncing some tenets of the Stalinist régime as contrary to the interests of true Soviet patriots, had somehow slipped its way through the mesh and appeared in one of the highly serious Soviet monthlies.

Chaadayev's letter, written under an imaginary but significant address, *Necropolis* (City of the Dead), was almost entirely devoted to a ruthless diagnosis of the ills of Russian society, and it rose into a kind of funeral dirge over the blank and inescapable barbarism of Russian life as a whole.

'We never marched forward in step with the other nations of the world; we belong to none of the great families of the human race, neither Western nor Eastern, nor have we managed to incorporate any of their traditions. We stand segregated, as if condemned to banishment outside the passage of time, and the universal education of the human race has passed by without touching us.

'Look around us; everything seems to be in motion; we are all like wanderers. Not one of us belongs to a definite sphere of existence; nothing stable or indispensable holds us together. Life flows past us without leaving a single trace either on our surroundings or on ourselves. Our very homes are more like temporary lodgings; we are strangers in the midst of our own families. We merely camp in our towns, even more fleetingly than the nomad tribes that move across our steppes, for these

B

tribes are more intimately attached to their barren country than we are to our towns. . . . All peoples experience periods of vigorous passionate activity, periods of youthful growth, when their poetry, creative ideas, and happiest memories arise, the source and foundation of their subsequent history. . . . Only we have nothing of this kind. We began in the wildest barbarism, followed by crude superstition; then came the cruel humiliating rule of the Tartar conquerors, whose effects have not yet vanished from our way of life. That is the painful history of our youth. . . . We have no enchanting memories, no vital edifying examples in our national tradition. . . . We are still obliged to hammer into our heads what others do by instinct or have learned from experience. . . . We are involuntary vaga-bonds on the broad high road of history, and the intelligent life of the West is not for us.

'So long as societies are floating in the void, unformulated, without convictions and rules, even for regulating routine matters, there is bound to be a chaotic fermentation in the moral sphere. . . . We are still at that stage. In the West the child in its cradle is already penetrated by ideas of duty, justice, law, and order. These are integral elements of European social life, where religion is the moving force of history. . . . Foreigners who start to admire Russia as an exciting new phenomenon have not observed that the same characteristic which makes us so bold and reckless also deprives us of tenacity and persever-ance; they fail to see that what makes us so indifferent to the risks of life makes us equally indifferent to all good and evil, truth or falsehood. And that is precisely why we lack those sustaining motives which push other nations along the road to improvement.

'Alone in the world, we have given nothing to it, and we have learned nothing from it. Whatever has reached us out of the progress of the human mind, we have disfigured and dis-torted. Even the best ideas, through lack of co-ordination and consistency, get muddled up in our brains, like empty ghosts. The experience accumulated throughout the ages means nothing to us. Christians though we are, the fruit of Christi-anity did not ripen within us. Are not the Abyssinians also Christians? Isolated from the European family, we sought our moral code in miserable Byzantium, and while the world was being built anew, we remained as before cowering in our hovels of mud and straw, cut off from that universal movement in which the social idea of Christanity was formed and developed.'[1]

No wonder that the Russian government was shocked and infuriated by this unorthodox thunderbolt. But when the answering official storm burst over him, Chaadayev did not prostrate himself in abject recantation; moreover his punishment turned out to be surprisingly light—a mild rebuff compared with the grim fate which would have befallen him if he had deviated from the orthodoxy of a later age. He frankly admitted to the Tsar and Count Benkendorf that he had expressed himself with some impatience and exaggeration in his letter, but he maintained that his honest criticism was fundamentally more useful to his country than the self-satisfied complacency or boastful nationalism which his letter condemned.

Indeed, in his whimsically entitled *Apology of a Madman* (1837) he was still bold enough to assert; 'Patriotism may make heroes, but love of truth makes wise men. Patriotism divides people against each other and nourishes national hatreds. I cannot love my country with closed eyes, a bowed head, and deaf ears. To my mind a man can only be useful to his country if he sees it distinctly. . . . Though Russia covers a fifth part of the world, from the point of view of history she is nothing but a geographical fact. Buried in an immense tomb, Russians have merely been living the lives of fossils. The truth is that we have never yet considered ourselves and our history from the philosophical point of view. . . . That is why we indulge in all these strange fantasies, all these Utopias of the past, all these dreams about an impossible future that today torment patriotic minds. . . . It is on these poor relics of an insignificant empty past that a Chauvinism, which consents to be blind, wishes to lay the foundations of an unattainable and deceptive future.' Moreover, in its hasty ardour, the latest school of patriotism had turned against Peter, and taught Russians to see themselves as children of the East. 'Certainly we are situated in Eastern Europe but for all that we have never formed part of the East. Asia has a long history which has nothing in common with that of our country. . . . We are simply a Northern country, both in our ideas and in our climate equally remote from the perfumed valley of Kashmir and the sacred banks of the Ganges. True, some of our provinces border on the Eastern Empires,

[1] Letter to A. Turgenev : *Sochineniya*, pp. 77 ff.

but our centres are not there, our life is not there, and they never will be, unless some astral revolution displaces the axis of the globe.'[1]

It has been suggested, not without some foundation, that Chaadayev was trying to inspire Nicolas I to revive the Western Empire-building programme of Peter the Great. He hinted at this when he commented on the preponderant rôle of individual leadership in moulding modern Russian history; 'The most profound trait of our historical physiognomy is the absence of any spontaneity in our social development. Every important trait in our history is imposed on us from above, every new idea is imported. Peter the Great found at home in Russia only a blank sheet of paper. With his powerful hand he wrote on it, "Europe and the West"; since then we have belonged there. . . .'[2] It is enough for us that a sovereign will should declare itself among us, and all previous opinions will be wiped out, all minds opened to the new thought which is given to them. And', he added significantly, 'without Peter the Great who can guarantee that Russia would not have succumbed and turned into a Swedish province?' That daemonic Tsar was not for nothing at war for twenty-eight consecutive years.

IV

Arguing from the natural malleability of the Russian character and the pure unspoiled nature of Orthodox Christianity, the extreme Slavophils deducted that Kiev Russia had started a new and separate era of civilization. Chaadayev, on the contrary, felt convinced that the very same racial character and type of religion were largely responsible for the spiritual paralysis of Russia and for the misery of her past.

Roman Catholics, while singling out Chaadayev for favourable mention, have slurred over his hostility to unadulterated Christian teaching and his express belief that political Christianity had no longer any part to play in educating society. 'The reins of world guidance have naturally to fall from the hands of the Roman pontiff; political Christianity has to make way for a Christianity that is purely spiritual, and in that

---

[1] Letter to A. Turgenev: *Sochineniya*, p. 228.
[2] *Ibid.*, p. 223.

sphere where earthly powers have dominated for so long, there will remain only the symbol of unity of thought, the high example and memorials of past ages.'[1] (Letter to N. Turgenev, 1837.) It is true that he expressed a decided preference for the Catholic Church, because it had previously proved itself to be a much more potent civilizing agent than the Orthodox Church had ever been. But he bluntly asserted that the crushing weight of unrelieved Christian influence had stifled civilization in Russia.

In Western nations, he observed, the art and science of their pagan heritage had blended fruitfully with Christianity, especially in the Renaissance. Without these vital Graeco-Roman strains they might easily have ossified as completely as Byzantine Russia did, and produced the same gloomy theocracy, renouncing fresh impulse and experimental endeavour.

'We must always remember one thing, namely that there hardly existed in our society any moral principle apart from religion. To it must be attributed everything we have, the good as well as the evil. But the religious system of the West was much more favourable to social development than the religion which fell to our lot. The Western nations owe their success to fertile combinations, not petrified by any narrow spiritualism. Look at our social history; it is nothing but a long series of blunders, leading to the gradual enslavement of our whole rural population. In all other countries, slavery had a different origin—namely foreign conquest. With us one fine day the majority of the country found itself enslaved to its own native rulers through some imperious need of the country, without abuse on the one side and without protest on the other.'

Those who correctly picture Chaadayev as a staunch fighter, both against the official imperialism of Nicolas I and against the misleading Schellingian dreams of the politically-minded Slavophils, are at a loss to explain what freak of fancy impelled him to compose a memorandum to Count Benkendorf, pleading for the ban to be lifted from I. Kireyevsky's semi-Slavophil journal, *The European* (suppressed in 1832). On the face of it this step seems to be either a self-contradiction or a sure sign of his own conversion to the more intelligent parts of the Slavophil credo. To my mind it comes nearer to the latter, but it is easier to understand as a natural switch of emphasis in Chaadayev's own interpretation of the Russian Empire. If the Russian past

[1] *Sochineniya*, vol. 2, p. 211.

was dreary, and its present hideous, the only alternative to despair—for Russians—was to pin all hopes on a tantalizingly different Russian future. The memorandum undoubtedly reveals an evolution in Chaadayev from frank political pessimism to a qualified optimism about this cardinal question. In certain matters he finds that he wholeheartedly agrees with Kireyevsky. His own main thesis is not generally recognized as Slavophil because it contends that, far from doing without Europe, a civilized future for Russia depended on her finding her own missing links, by going through all the higher phases of the European past, which Russia had never reached and which the French Revolution had already betrayed in Europe. 'Whatever may be the special merit of European laws, they are like all social forms, the result of a mass of antecedents to which we have remained strangers. They could not possibly be adapted to us as they are at present. Besides, since we lag so far behind Europe in culture, and since our own institutions contain many elements which obviously repel all imitation of European ones, we must devise a way of drawing on our own resources in order to reap those benefits which one day we are destined to enjoy. Above all we must try to give ourselves a serious classical education, *a mental discipline which is not borrowed from the surface of that civilization which we find today in Europe, but rather from what underlies and preceded it, from what has given birth to all that is really good in the civilization of today.*

'At a moment when the sad results of the spirit of confusion are so deplorably evident among peoples more advanced than us, but who owe their progress to an earlier period when intelligence ripened in peace and security, how could a man who loves his country not desire to see tranquillity at home? One would need to be strangely blind not to admit that there is no country where sovereigns have done so much for the advance and enlightenment of their peoples as in Russia; all that we are, all our civilization, we owe to our monarchs. Everywhere else governments have followed, and still follow, impulsions started by their peoples, whereas with us the Government has always been in advance of the nation, and the impetus proceeds from the former.

'It is to the old Europe, where such great deeds were accomplished in which we never participated, where so many great thoughts arose which never found their way to us, it is to them that we should look for our examples.' (Memorandum to Count Benkendorf.)[1]

It has been said that Chaadayev wrote this memorandum with his tongue in his cheek, hoping thereby to rehabilitate his reputation in official circles. It seems more probable that he expressed his sincere convictions. For the tenor of the memorandum conforms with what he wrote elsewhere, notably in some of his private letters. Moreover, had his sole object been to regain the Emperor's favour, he would hardly have risked pleading for a journal which Nicolas I had just banned for political unreliability. It is none the less true that Chaadayev was trying hard to get himself accepted as a 'useful person'. He had previously sent in a petition asking to be allowed to serve in the Ministry of Public Instruction. This request had been refused, though with a frigid counter-suggestion that a post might be found for him in the Ministry of Finance—but Chaadayev felt totally at a loss in finance, and so the matter appears to have been dropped.

In his memorandum about *The European*, he availed himself of the opportunity to hint to Benkendorf that the Emperor had misunderstood the principal aim of his first *Philosophic Letter*. In the midst of his heavy preoccupations how could Nicolas I have given more than fleeting attention to this fragment: 'I tried to show how the human mind, after deviating from its legitimate road by following the absurd and impious eighteenth-century philosophy, has now returned to a wiser understanding, that faith is recovering its rights while the claims of science become more sober and moderate. I characterized the revolutionary principle as one of destruction and blood. . . .'

But Chaadayev's judicious appeal had no more effect on Tsarist officialdom than a gentle tap on a prison wall. He reluctantly abandoned his last hopes of influencing events through personally converting Russia's rulers, and his thoughts turned more and more towards a long-term assessment of the Russian Empire's future rôle. He began to persuade himself that if Russia had appeared on the scene later than the Western nation-states, divine providence intended her to do better than her predecessors, and therefore to avoid their worst mistakes. Why should Russia clumsily repeat that long series of follies which other nations had committed, and pay the same crippling

[1] Letter to A. Turgenev : *Sochineniya*, pp. 336–9.

penalties? Her primitive culture preserved at least one positive
merit, a vigorous virginity of mind, an eagerness to learn.
Chaadayev reformulated the nineteenth-century dilemma in the
following terms. If Russia followed the beaten track of the
West, she would condemn herself to the same deceptions and
subsequent misery as Europe had suffered. But if she turned
aside and ignored Western experience, she would continue to
stand still. Peter the Great had shown the right way (no half-
hearted compromise) by boldly picking out from pre-revolutionary Europe only what seemed to him most useful and strong,
and therefore valuable for Russia. Eventually the most invigo-
rating European ideals might be fulfilled in Russia more completely than in Europe itself, but not unless Peter's example
was improved on by wise and determined successors.

V

Chaadayev's cautious and guarded patriotism irritated most of
the Slavophils—except the Kireyevskys—as much as their
unbalanced exaltation disturbed his sober common sense. Yet
he unwittingly presented them with a new idea which they
quickly turned to their own advantage. The Slavophils felt, and
virtually argued, that Orthodoxy must be the most genuine and
universal religion because it was the most important attribute of
Russian national character. This amounted to a fantastic semi-
racial mysticism, but it could not fail to charm a number of
ignorant or depressed Slavs, however absurd it might appear
to other races. Meanwhile Chaadayev paid more attention to
the international non-racial and morally progressive character
of the true Christian religion, and frankly give credit to the
Catholic Church for having till then done far more than
Orthodoxy to promote it. This argument, however, instead of
acting as a cold douche on the Slavophils, opened their eyes to
the prominent part they might begin to play as the latest
champions of Christian historical philosophy, especially if they
could discredit the Catholic Church, demonstrate that its
mission had been corrupted, and that its mantle had now fallen
on 'Holy Russia.' The development of this notion culminated
as an *idée fixe* in Dostoevsky's feverish mind.

By means of a two-way link with past and future, first,
Russia as the heir of Byzantium and Rome, then, as the

incarnation of an expanding universal theocracy, the fossilized Orthodox Church could be regenerated and fitted into the ancient Christian plan of universal movement towards the goal of a 'Kingdom of God on earth' (whatever such a nebulous goal might mean). Chaadayev's religious views and his controversies with the Slavophils retain more than academic interest. Since the Russian Communist party has evolved into the exclusive priesthood of a compulsory state religion, it has been able to intensify its appeal by playing on many habits of mind cultivated by the activists of the nineteenth-century Orthodox Church. For the nineteenth-century Pan-Slavs already emphasized community of religion more strongly than that of race. Their gross political perversion of a purely devotional religion already filled Chaadayev with gloomy forebodings.

Most discerning historians agree that, after Peter abolished the Patriarchate, the Orthodox Church lost its last shreds of independent moral authority. It degenerated into a kind of Christian Caliphate, leading an army of civil clergy, abjectly subservient to every whim of the temporal power. Such a servile religion could bear no fruit of its own unless it was in the rarefied stratosphere of the remote monasteries. But the Church could best be judged as a more or less efficient government department. It had ceased to be either independently adventurous or frankly conservative. True religious conservatism had been better preserved by the Old Believers and the Sects, whose survival under severe and unremitting persecution was the surest proof of their vigorous faith. Nevertheless the sectarians, with all their personal virtues, remained eccentric zealots, devoid of any patriotic or civic sense.

Turning his mind to the West, Chaadayev thought he had found there most of the enviable qualities which the Churches at home so conspicuously lacked. He was fascinated by the active and social-minded Catholic policy, by the Papacy's impregnable independence, by the efficient and yet centralized organization of this truly international and simultaneously supernational Church. Did Chaadayev think seriously about the union of the Orthodox and Catholic Churches? V. Solovyëv later interpreted some of his remarks as if he did, and it seems that Chaadayev in later life was counter-influenced by the Slavophils into acknowledging the emergence of some unique merits in Russian orthodoxy. Yet he never wholly abandoned his belief that the Catholic Church, in spite of its deplorable worldly vices, was much better adapted than his own to take the lead in any international mission of moral education. In a letter to his French Catholic friend, the Comte de Circourt, he complained that proverbial Russian humility had been pushed too far by the triumphant tyranny of those in power; the congregation of the Orthodox Church reflected the resigned despair of simple and kindly people forced to abandon their natural craving to make earthly life more tolerable. Perhaps there was a strain of rare spiritual nobility in this hopeless self-sacrifice. 'Our Church is essentially an ascetic one', he wrote; 'yours is essentially a social one; hence the indifference of ours to everything which happens outside it, and the lively interest taken by the other in everything that goes on throughout the world. They represent the two poles of the Christian faith, revolving round the axis of their own unconditional actual truth. It was a disaster for Russia that she derived her Christianity not from the republican monarchy of the early Caesars, but from the oriental despotism inaugurated by Diocletian, from the Government of Constantine, where the Emperor in fact ruled the Church councils, which were apostolic only in name.'[1]

Chaadayev is even more outspoken in some notes on a religious brochure, discovered among Khomyakov's papers after the latter's death.[2] Here he stated that not only Catholicism, but any European version of Christianity, not excluding even the heretic Protestant sects, would have benefited Russia far more than her own sterile Byzantine cult. 'No, it was not a living faith which stopped the Protestant heresy when it came to establish itself on the border of the greatest Orthodox country; it was an oriental despotism supported by an oriental cult, entirely shut up in sterile ritual, and which for that reason alone could not open its frontiers to a religion which repudiated all outward pomp. Itself an idea, Protestantism stopped short where the reign of ideas came to an end, and where the reign of brute force and stereotyped ceremonial began. That is all. The truth is that Protestantism penetrated into Russia more than once (through the Anabaptists) in different shapes. It found itself faced by that odious and absurd persecution which transforms even our own sectarians, originally quite inoffensive

[1] *Vyestnik Evropy:* April 1906, p. 568.
[2] Khomyakov: *Polnoe Sobranie*, vol. 2, p. 510, Moscow, 1911.

people, into enemies of public order. Thus it was obliged to retreat from a temporal power founded in the Mongol school, seconded by a religious power equally intent on exploiting that fatal heritage.'

From the evidence available it would seem that the pro-Catholic interpretation of Chaadayev has sometimes been wishfully exaggerated. Clearly he was always more concerned with the visible and living social consequences of various religious organizations at different times than he was with establishing the undeniable superiority of any single religious cult. On this ground he praised the religious life of ancient Egypt and India as well as the work of the Catholic and Protestant churches, as all superior to Orthodoxy. In one of his letters he urged that priests should speak a language addressed more to the hearts and imagination of people than to their intelligence. 'That Christian art, flower of the purest religious feeling, was much more valuable to society than any number of volumes of cold sermons will ever be.'

VI

The last fifteen years of Chaadayev's life were spent in an uninterrupted struggle against the national self-deception and conceit which the official vulgarization of early Slavophil thought was breeding throughout Russian society. Realizing that the fashionable craze for the Berlin school of philosophy was partly to blame for this deplorable state of mind, he wrote a plaintive letter to Schelling in 1842: 'The prodigious elasticity of that philosophy which lends itself to every possible application has created among us the most bizarre fantasies about our future rôle in the world. Its fatalistic logic which almost suppresses free will, while in a way constituting it, in turning towards our past, has reduced our whole history to a retrospective Utopia, an arrogant apotheosis of the Russian people. It has nearly reached the point of depriving us of the best inheritance we received from our fathers, that modesty of mind, that temperance of thought, which a religion strongly impregnated with contemplation and asceticism had brought into our being . . . . But fevers are infectious. You know that in philosophy we are still mere beginners; we must therefore discover whether we are going to abandon ourselves to an order of ideas provoking every excess of human infatuation, or whether we can revive our faith in the path which we have followed hitherto, religious humility, modesty, always the most distinctive trait of our national character, and the most fertile principle of our unique development? Pray continue, Sir, to triumph over a vain philosophy which claimed to supplant yours.'[1]

Certainly Russians had rarely shown less Christian humility than since that time when all the clubs, *salons* and government departments buzzed with vainglorious talk about the native genius and soaring claims of Russian Christianity. Chaadayev found in Gogol's *Correspondence with Friends* a depressing example of that same patriotic arrogance—so alien to the finest Russian personalities. Even that pitilessly truthful writer had sunk to the low level of courting national popularity; the clouds of adulatory incense which rose before him had made his head begin to swim.

Worst of all, these national megalomaniacs cared nothing for their country's internal prosperity and well-being, made no genuine effort to improve her standard of living and inward spiritual culture. For them all was well, provided the government was spectacular and powerful and the people self-consciously 'Russian'. 'In the depths of our rich nature they claimed to discover all kinds of miraculous qualities distinguishing us from the rest of the world. They began to repudiate all the serious and fruitful lessons which Europe had taught us, and they wanted to set up on Russian soil a completely new moral order, which would throw us back to some fantastic Christian East, thought out exclusively for our own benefit. They could not see that by separating ourselves morally from the European nations, we should simultaneously alienate ourselves politically, that once we had severed our brotherhood with the great European family, not one of those peoples would stretch out a helping hand to us in the hour of danger. . . . The government, too ignorant or too careless, failed to grasp the import of these learned hallucinations, though it hardly encouraged them. Occasionally it lashed out against the most advanced or impudent members of this crazy cohort. But it knew none the less that the day it threw down its own gauntlet in the face of the impious and decayed West, it could not fail to enlist the sympathy of all these new patriots, who take their unfinished studies, their inarticulate cravings and vague hopes,

[1] *Sochineniya*, vol. i, pp. 245–6.

for the real national policy—just as it could count on the docile
following of the crowd, always ready to share patriotic dreams
dressed up in the banal idiom of current usage. And that was
how one fine day the leaders of Europe found themselves in
the Crimea.'[1]

One of the many important differences between the Russia of
Nicolas I and the Russia of Stalin is that a Soviet intellectual
opposed to Russian Communist expansion may be reduced to
silence before he can speak, whereas a far-sighted bold critic
like Chaadayev managed to put up a long and stubborn fight
against the policy which culminated in the Crimean War. For
being a truer patriot, with more concern for his country's culture
and welfare than any of his opponents, he was officially declared a madman, and all the doors of government service were
slammed in his face. Perhaps he found some bitter satisfaction in
living to witness the humiliation of the Crimean War, when his
country succumbed to the needless sufferings which he had
persistently foretold but remained powerless to avert.

At the height of the nationalist hysteria aroused during that
campaign, Chaadayev wrote the following lines, which would
be a worthy epitaph to him even if he had written nothing
else. 'We sought our country's well-being and better institutions, we even wished she might have a little more liberty, if
that was feasible. But we were far from imagining that Russia
represented some kind of abstract principle comprising a definite solution of the social problem, that she herself constituted
a whole world apart, the direct and legitimate heir of the
glorious Eastern Empire, of its titles and virtues, that she had a
special mission to absorb all the Slav peoples in her breast, and
thereby to work out the regeneration of the human race. Above
all, we did not think that Europe was on the point of falling
back into barbarism, and that we were called on to save the
world with these few rags of that same civilization which had
drawn us out of our ancient torpor. We treated Europe with
civility, nay, even with respect, for we knew that she had taught
us many things, among others our own history. When it happened to us by chance to triumph over her, like Peter the Great,
we said : "Gentlemen, it is to you we owe it."[2] Then one day

[1] *Sochineniya*, vol. 1, p. 309.
[2] Peter the Great's words to the Swedish generals taken prisoner after
the Battle of Poltava.

we reached Paris, and they gave us the welcome that you know of, forgetting for the moment that we were really young *parvenus*, and that we had as yet put nothing into the common stock of nations, not even a poor little solar system like the Poles, our subjects, not even some miserable algebra, like the Arabs, those infidels whose absurd and barbarous religion we are now combating. They treated us well because they found we had the manners of decently brought-up people, because we were polite and modest as befitted newcomers without any title to public esteem except the advantage of their large stature. Now you have changed all that—so be it. But allow me, I beg you, still to love my country in the way of Peter the Great, of Catherine and Alexander.'[1]

Unfortunately for Chaadayev, neither the Government nor public opinion showed any response to his discriminating brand of patriotism. The Government did its best to rouse the country's war-morale by promoting the crudest anti-European Chauvinist clamour. Of course results fell short of their expectations, and even among the Slavophils the more discerning refused to be whirled off their feet to join the pan-Slav campaign. Here Chaadayev found a few kindred spirits. The Slavophil, A. Koshelëv, probably hit the mark when he observed about the internal effect of Russian military disasters : 'The Battles of the Alma and Inkerman, the siege of Sevastopol, grieved us but little, for we were convinced that the defeat of Russia would be less intolerable and prove more beneficial to her than a continuation of that state in which she had been living for some time. The feelings of society and even of the common people, though partly inarticulate, were of the same kind.'[2] If Koshelëv was right, this state of feeling, in the midst of Russia's struggle against a coalition of European powers, afforded tangible proof that Chaadayev had many silent supporters, who agreed that Russians could gain more from defeat than from any pan-Slav pan-Orthodox victory. Though Chaadayev veered towards the Slavophils in the thirties, he stuck to his contention that Russia must grow much more Europeanized (in traditional culture, not necessarily in technique) before she could launch out on any successful independent course, must go two steps backwards before she could take one step forward, and learn to walk before

[1] *Sochineniya*, vol. 1, p. 308.
[2] A. Koshelëv : *Zapiski*, pp. 82-3, Berlin, 1884.

she could run. Otherwise the much-discussed Russian mission would lose its bearings, run amok and turn into a suicidal mission of destruction.

Perpetually opposed to all the prevailing currents of Russian political opinion, Chaadayev left no influential disciples. But he was one of the first in that long line of isolated citizens whose persistent efforts, agonies and prayers failed to deflect the course of the Russian Juggernaut, and who could barely save themselves from being crushed under its weight. At least among the discerning minority he awoke and stimulated minds, even where he failed to convince them. He set in motion powerful impulses which continued to work their way out among the later leaders of political and social thought, most markedly perhaps in V. Solovyëv, who enlarged on Chaadayev's theme that Oriental and Western Christianity could fuse and supplement each other, if the former deliberately allowed her more experienced partner to take the lead.

Chaadayev prided himself on being a Christian philosopher. It did not worry him that neither his philosophy nor his Christianity conformed to any recognized denomination or school. Many of his compatriots never forgave him for his devastating criticism of the Orthodox Church. He valued the friendship of the ultramontane Joseph de Maistre, yet he never became a Catholic, though the legend persists that he did. One of his contemporaries said of him : 'He wants to make Catholic converts, without joining them himself.' Christianity always appealed to him less as an organization, or a doctrine, than as an active historical ferment. The more versatile efficiency of the Catholic Church at that time, compared with other Churches, impressed his pragmatic mind. But he observed that Catholicism might be a temporary phenomenon which had already exhausted its beneficial functions. And he warned against the horrors of neo-Catholicism organized under an Orthodox disguise. In attempting to transfer the old religious centre of gravity into a more sober historical philosophy, he began to attach a novel religious significance to the rôle of Russia in the world, to the problematic future of a vast amorphous entity, belonging neither to Asia nor to Europe, yet emerging irresistibly into powerful life, 'with one foot on Germany and the other on the Pacific Ocean'.

It would be surprising if his evolutionary but anti-nationalist (and still more, anti-national socialist) cast of mind had not consigned him to a well-earned oblivion in the Soviet Union. And so it very nearly has. But the Bolshevik passion for transmuting prominent figures of the Russian past into heralds of their own régime has even found a place for Chaadayev. One enterprising critic, N. Alekseyev,[1] called him 'a precursor of the Russia radicals', and by a bolder flight of fantasy he discerned in the first *Philosophic Letter* 'the whole Russian Revolution, the whole of Communism and the International in embryo'.

An *opponent* may turn into a *precursor* if he stimulates his enemies and their successors to take drastic counter-action, especially if they borrow some of his ideas in order to transform them into a weapon in their fight against him. The single element of pan-Orthodoxy, torn from the conditional context, to which Chaadayev confined it, provided the radical wing of the Slavophils with just such ammunition. To that limited extent Chaadayev may plausibly be claimed as a 'precursor' of Russian socialism, unless we see in the practice of Russian socialism nothing more than a logical extension of the military and industrial dictatorship inaugurated by Peter, one of Chaadayev's favourite sovereigns. But the latter interpretation would be a monstrous heresy in Soviet ideology, apart from being an oversimplification of the dual strain which runs through Soviet policy. One may assume that most of the readers of Mr. Alekseyev's book were protected from the shock of access to the original works of Chaadayev. In any case his dashing attempt to portray Chaadayev as a budding Bolshevik seems to have faded out and produced no serious sequel. From time to time Soviet critics unearth these startling and suggestive parallels between conservative 'revolutionaries' and the more recent radical ones. But, in so doing, they run the risk of being challenged or shot down by the party sentries who guard this dangerous ground.

VII

V. S. PECHERIN

No study of the early Westernizers should omit to mention the astonishing but almost forgotten story of V. S. Pecherin, (1807–1885) who outdid Chaadayev in his spectacular renunciation

[1] N. Alekseyev: *Russkoe Zapadnichestvo*, Moscow, 1929.

of all that official Russia stood for. As an exceptionally brilliant student of classical antiquity, he had received permission to travel in Europe in order to complete his education, and at the early age of twenty-eight he became Professor of Greek at Moscow University. His vivid and beautifully polished Russian translations from the Greek Anthology attracted the attention of the Minister of Public Instruction, the cultured Count Uvarov. His public lectures were packed with attentive listeners and applauded by connoisseurs. Thus established in such a distinguished position in Russian intellectual life, relatively sheltered from the storms of political intrigue, it would seem that Pecherin had embarked on a stable, prosperous and useful career.

Despite all this he found his life in Moscow intolerable. The self-satisfied and banal vulgarity of Moscow society tormented him. Its atmosphere was so pervasive, that it wrecked even the haven of refuge he had hoped to find by living alone and undisturbed among the spirits of his ancient Greeks and Romans. After one single year in his university post, he found a pretext for going abroad again (1836) and firmly decided that he would never return to Russia.

In a strange explanatory letter to Count Stroganov, the Rector of Moscow University, he wrote: 'Hatred became my daily bread. I lived alone with my hatred as others live with a beloved woman. When I went out into that horrible world, I always showed a calm and cheerful face. I even earned its smiles.' Then one night he had a dream in which the voice of God spoke to him reproachfully: 'What are you doing? There is no future here. Take up my heavy cross, and carry it, if need be to Golgotha.' He felt impelled to obey that voice. The indulgent Count sent Pecherin a letter of credit to enable him to pay for his return fare through any Russian Consulate abroad. But Pecherin never used the letter. Nikitenko and Pogodin both said he had gone mad, and the incident had a damping effect on Stroganov's liberal policy of allowing more young Russian scholars to study abroad.

During his previous sojourn in Italy Pecherin had listened sympathetically to people who spoke about the Russians as Huns, menacing Europe with a new period of barbarism. And on his last journey back to Moscow he had seen in a vision, written over the Russian frontier, an inscription which read

c

'Abandon hope, all ye who enter here'. Moscow ladies said of him; 'Il a le mal du pays', which was then a veiled expression for the yearning to escape from Russia and travel in Europe—a feeling far more acute than vague dissatisfaction. Thus Pecherin abandoned a secure and honoured position in his own country, and voluntarily exchanged it for a life of cruel hardship in exile, wandering from place to place, a penniless vagabond, homeless, sometimes on the verge of starvation. Passing through Liége during a religious festival, he entered a brilliantly lit church filled with smartly-dressed local notabilities. He recorded the edifying thought that he, a vagrant from the road, clad only in dusty rags, could freely enjoy that wonderful music and gorgeous spectacle together with the 'beau monde'. It impressed him deeply with the truly democratic character of the Catholic Church.

But this was only one portion of the picture. He did not become a monk till four years later. His Swiss tutor had filled him with burning ideals of social improvement, and during his stay in Lugano and Zurich he assiduously cultivated the society of international revolutionaries. Gradually he grew bored with their empty futile talk, and disgusted by their dissolute lives. He records the sobering effect of his conversation with a Polish apostle of Communism, who raved about the 'approaching republic', when there would be free banquets in the taverns for everyone, rivers of wine, and naked girls dancing over the tables. The prospect of these mass Bacchanalia did not appeal to him. When he decided in favour of the Catholic Church, he went the whole way and took his vows as a Redemptorist monk. This was an action which his intelligent Russian contemporaries, including Herzen, could neither understand nor forgive. Herzen in his memoirs writes about Pecherin with an amazed but hostile curiosity. While pitying and admiring him for his bold self-imposed exile, he could not commend a Russian renegade who had forsaken his country solely in order to embrace a living death. How could such a brilliant cultured man, filled from boyhood with hatred for every kind of tyranny, choose that most terrible tyranny of all, the bondage of Catholic monastic vows?

Pecherin's exchange of letters with Herzen throws a lurid light on his own inward conflict. He retaliated vigorously against Herzen's eloquent reproaches. 'Nations do not live by reason, but by sacred traditions and legends. Why did you forget that, Herzen?' Every time intellectuals undertook to rebuild the social order, argued Pecherin, the result was brutal despotism. 'Look at the philosopher kings of Greek antiquity and of eighteenth-century Europe. The socialist "phalanstery" is nothing but a disguised barracks and communism is tyranny in a new shape.' But, curiously enough, Pecherin agreed with Herzen's social prognosis in one very important respect. He agreed that Russia, together with the United States, would start a new cycle of world history. Moreover, Russia would probably establish and successfully develop a Socialist society before any other nations could do so, since nature had given the Russian Empire immense resources, 'enough to provide a feast of material well-being for her elect'. Scientific technique, in the hands of an omnipotent and brutal government which rode rough-shod over national character, culture and tradition, would do the rest. But the thought of this approaching civilization, as prosperous and efficient as it was soulless, far from attracting Pecherin, filled him with repulsion and horror. 'Will anyone be able to escape from the tyranny of this colossal materialist civilization? Even as they used to drag Christians into the Roman arena and expose them to the mockery of a crowd revelling in spectacular displays, so will we men of prayer and silence be dragged into the public market-place and asked : "Why do you try to escape from our society? Come and work in our factories. Join us in spreading electricity and steam. The garden of Eden is here on earth." '[1]

In 1861 Pecherin left the Redemptorist Order. He spent the remaining twenty years of his busy life as a priest, attached to the Catholic chapel of one of the large Dublin hospitals, perpetually ministering to the sick and dying, and filling his leisure hours with the study of oriental languages and botany. But a curious homesickness oppressed him.

In the sixties he corresponded from Dublin with Ivan Aksakov, and the Moscow intellectuals began to discuss him publicly. The extraordinary story of his life sharpened their curiosity and he became again for a brief period as much a *cause célèbre* as he had been after he first fled from Moscow University in 1835. Katkov suggested that, so long as Pecherin was a sincere Christian, he ought not to be blamed for his

[1] A. von Schelting: *Russland u. Europa*, p. 235, Berne, 1948.

misguided conversion to Catholicism, and should be encouraged to return to Russia, Pogodin poured cold water on this suggestion and urged that such a talented renegade as Pecherin should never be allowed to preach in Russia, where he might easily make more converts to the scheming church of Rome than he had formerly made to the study of Greek.

In a letter to I. Aksakov, Pecherin closed this controversy by making his own attitude unmistakably clear: 'The Editor of the *Moscow News* hopes for that sort of freedom of conscience which will benefit the Russian Government; *i.e* he would be glad to find Catholic priests serving the Russian autocracy. For myself at least I can answer this; I never was, and never will be, an obedient citizen. I sympathize warmly with the heroic deeds and sufferings of the Catholic clergy in Poland. Were I in their place, I would act as they do, if God granted me a share of their energy and faith. I never upheld that the Catholic religion in any country should serve as a support for autocracy and so help Nero to punish disobedient Christians. I fully share the opinion of that most noble representative of Catholicism, Montalembert; I desire that boundless freedom of conscience which he so eloquently defended, and with him I believe in the future alliance of democracy with Catholicism. No Catholic priest persuaded me, or ever had the smallest influence over my mind. . . . I voluntarily sacrificed to God what I valued most of all—my liberty. "To the West, to the West," an inner voice called to me, and to the West I went, whatever it might cost me. The Catholic faith came much later. It was only the conclusion to a long logical process, or more properly it was the last refuge left for me after the general destruction of European hopes in 1848.

'Now with deep concern I stretch out the hand of brotherhood to that young generation, to dear Russian youth, which I want to embrace in the name of the future, of freedom of conscience, and the Assembly of the Land.'[1] (Letter from Dublin, 7 September 1863.)

Pecherin showed rare courage in burning his boats, while managing at the same time to preserve his critical judgement intact. From some marginal notes he left it is evident that, although a Catholic priest, he strongly disapproved the dogma of Papal Infallibility and hated the papal régime for its worldly

[1] M. Gershenzon: *Istoria Molodoi Rossii*, p. 163, Petrograd, 1923.

intrigue and lying prelates.[1] But he hated governmental Russia more wholeheartedly, never expressed regret for the hard course he had taken, and pinned his faith in the future (equally for Russia and Europe) on the gradual triumph of those orderly European ideals which were simultaneously alien to autocracy and revolution. No one but a Russian intellectual could have cultivated that peculiar blend of burning anger and impersonal love, which the self-exiled Pecherin expressed in these uncompromising lines,

> How sweet it is to hate one's native land,
> And eagerly await its utter ruin,
> And in its ruin to discern
> The dawn of a new life for the world.[2]

VIII

NICHOLAS OGARËV

The name of Nicholas Ogarëv (1813–1877) is chiefly remembered as that of Herzen's staunchest friend and disciple, his companion in exile, and his collaborator on *The Bell*. But he deserves some independent consideration apart from, and prior to, his voluntary self-effacement in Herzen's service. He then played a quite notorious part in Russia as a progressive-minded Westernizing landowner, who made valiant though unsuccessful attempts to apply French social doctrines to the thorny problems of Russian estate-management.

At the early age of twenty-two, when he was first sentenced to exile, he was already a charming lyrical poet and an aspiring philosopher, a good-natured Sybarite and a somewhat spoilt child. His term of exile was far from harsh, but it tore him away from the stimulating life of Moscow, and from the congenial circle of friends, who like him had played with the fire of Saint-Simon and Fourier. Whereas Herzen was banished to distant Vyatka, Ogarëv went no further than the Penza province, where he was placed under his own father's benevolent supervision. There he could continue to write wistful verse, and to work spasmodically at the outline of an all-embracing new philosophical system, while his father tried to smother his

---

[1] M. Gershenzon : *Istoria Molodoi Rossii*, p. 174, Petrograd, 1923.
[2] *Ibid.*, p. 108.

graver thoughts by plunging him into a giddy round of local pleasures and obligations.

His father's death left Ogarëv a wealthy independent land-owner, and the possessor of four thousand *souls*. In 1838 he put some of his ideas to the test of practice by freeing all the serfs on his main estate in the Ryazan province. He made over all the agricultural land to them in perpetuity, partly under separate deeds of private ownership, but leaving the woods, fishing-rights etc., under the control of the *mir* (village commune).

Waving the wand of liberation over them, and providing them with land would, he fondly believed, suffice to fill his former serfs with an unpredictable access of zest and incentive. But he found, to his consternation that, on the estate where he had freed them, the peasants continued to plough their own land with exactly the same haphazard inefficiency as when they had worked for their landlord. Every exhortation to do better they countered with the sole response that, 'if God gave a harvest, there would be bread'. After due reflection, he drew up a project for founding an *école polytechnique* to grapple with rural backwardness. And here he noted ruefully under a series of headings 'what the people do not know'.

The specific list he made is all the more instructive, since it was compiled, not by a tough backward-looking slave-driver, but by the most conscientiously liberal landowner of his day. It constitutes a withering indictment of communal land-owner-ship by a former well-wisher of that system. Ogarëv thus enu-merates what he had found to be the most tenacious peasant characteristics and their baleful consequences.

'(1) No sense of honour, no idea either of law or of any duties attached to citizenship. This partly accounts for their inertia.

'(2) Immutable observance of routine. They will admit no scientific explanation of any natural phenomenon. Whether his clothes are in rags, his hut filthy, or the soil badly tilled, the peasant is in no hurry to make any improvements, since every-thing happens as God wills.

'(3) Peasant faith in the arbitrary will of God amounts to a servile terror of power. Even as this fatalistic faith gives them a formal religion without any moral substance, so does the habit of slavery, recognized by the legislator, provide a formal legality without positive laws . . . I do not know how else to call equal-ity in liability for taxation combined with inequality of personal ability, equality in allotment of land together with inequality of working capacity and capital. *Our mir really consists of equality in slavery.* Our communal administration is an assembly in which every member is at once executioner and victim, an "envier" and one who fears to fall a prey to the envy of other members.

'If in the West the idea of equality demands that all people should live equally well, in the commune it demands in fact that they should all live in equal wretchedness. The result of this whole communal structure is that the peasant (one might say the Russian man altogether) is by nature unable to grasp how any man can exist on his own without belonging to something or somebody. Thus all the improvements which plain common sense ought to contribute to our social life are forced to break through on the sly, in circumventing the law and the commune by the exercise of deceit and fraud. . . . For the common people the idea of a literate man is merely that of a man who has acquired the skill to forge documents'.[1]

Still cherishing his faith in Fourier, Ogarëv next founded a paper factory, employing serf labour under his personal supervision. The experiment failed abysmally, and it cured him of Fourier's optimism about the panacea of 'co-operative labour groups'. He observed that the wage-earning peasant, even if he earns more money than before, 'knowing that he can no longer be dismissed for slackness, has no incentive to do his utmost. Worst of all, he has no desire to raise his standard of life!' When this factory was finally destroyed by fire, Ogarëv decided to abandon further social experiments.

In 1856 he shook the dust of Russia off his feet forever, and went to join Herzen in England. This working partnership was his most fruitful period. But his married life had been disastrous, and after Herzen's death, left rudderless, he sank into a drunken torpor, relieved by lengthy lucid intervals. His last flickerings of reforming zeal found an outlet in educating the prostitute, Mary Sutherland, who lived with him, and in a keen correspondence with the exiled *narodnik*, Lavrov, exploring untried means of making Socialist propaganda more intelligible and less misleading to its readers.

[1] M. Gershenzon: *Istoria Molodoi Rossii*, 285 ff.

CHAPTER II

VISSARION BELINSKY

I

THE FORMATION OF THE RUSSIAN INTELLIGENTSIA AND OF ITS SOVIET COUNTERPART

THE Concise Oxford Dictionary, with a touch of possibly unconscious irony, defines the word _intelligentsia_ as, 'that part of a nation (especially the Russian) which aspires to independent thinking'. It does not tell us that in pre-revolutionary Russia the word acquired a narrower meaning, for it came to denote, not the educated and professional classes as a whole, but its more vociferous and politically-minded members, and chiefly those with burning radical convictions. Two major misconceptions sprang from this peculiarity. They still distort our understanding of the real Russian intelligentsia, and of those major authors of the nineteenth century, who did _not_ belong to it. One is a readiness to believe that all outstanding Russians were politically militant, and such fanatical crusaders against the entire existing social order, as both Tsarist and Bolshevik pundits have alleged them to be; the other is the assumption that a brutal and exasperating censorship perpetually dimmed their brightest ideas, and clipped the wings of every aspiring critic, philosopher or imaginative writer.

The latter is the more plausible judgement of the two, and would be truer, had it been less exaggerated by hostile radical prejudice in the past and by partisan prejudice today. Tsarist censorship never promoted fulsome hymns of praise to the Tsar, such as the Communist Party produces for the deified Stalin. It was deliberately negative, curbing but rarely strangling thought, except when thought infringed some clearly-defined political or religious articles of faith, which the Government held sacrosanct. Yet even so blasphemous a document as Chaadayev's _First Philosophic Letter_ managed to see the light of day before it was condemned. And outside that carefully guarded but restricted area Russian talent could roam as the spirit moved it, warbling 'its native wood-notes wild' to a small but intensely appreciative audience, which was all the thirstier for mental

VISSARION BELINSKY

From a portrait by I. Astafiev

stimulus because its normal life was often stuffy and dull. If political notes rang out from time to time, they sprang spontaneously from a deeper spiritual concern; they were authentic, not carefully 'inspired' by the plans and promptings either of conspirators or of public-spirited committees.

It would be absurd to suggest that censorship was not a curse to many writers, and inconclusive to argue that its severity roused minds which might otherwise have lain complacently dormant. It is none the less noteworthy that its most cramping phase, imposed by Nicolas I, coincided with the publication of some of the finest creative and critical writing ever brought forth in Russia. Pushkin, Lermontov, Gogol, and Belinsky, managed to reap an abundant harvest from that seemingly barren soil. The justice of this observation has been confirmed by Soviet critics, who somewhat plaintively compare their present journalistic literature with the genius of the past, but manage to put the blame on their incompetent literary colleagues who have merely failed to immortalize in art a life so infinitely richer in stirring events and heroic characters.[1]

Radical convention still demands that we should study the history of the Russian intelligentsia as an epic struggle of brave and enterprising reformers against an obtuse tyranny which went on crushing them until successful revolution crowned their efforts to crush *it*. The psychosis bred by Nicolas I, and its hang-over in the minds of nineteenth-century Russian publicists, are partly responsible for this one-sided approach. Many of the latter were so obstinately obsessed by the newly-discovered panacea of political liberalism, that they could no longer appreciate their eminent men of letters, unless they were also surrounded by the rosy haze of what turned out to be a bleak and illusory dawn. Every writer, in order to become worthy of consideration, must prove his credentials as a preacher with a clear-cut urgent message. In spite of Belinsky's testimony to the contrary, pure artistic talent remained suspect, unless it pleaded an ulterior civic motive. The public was taught to tolerate everything—except original genius. Even Pushkin and Turgenev, in order to be made socially respectable, had to be camouflaged as schoolmasters of the Russian people.

Bolshevik intellectuals, naturally enough, characterize still more rigidly those predecessors whom they single out as worthy

[1] *Komsomolskaya Pravda*, 13 May 1944.

of remembrance. Moreover in their strict separation of sheep from goats, of 'progressives' from 'reactionaries', they endeavour to build up the former as more intrinsically *Russian* than the latter, by virtue of their revolutionary initiative. A recent policy-making article,[1] which impertinently begs this complex question, begins by quoting the pontifical directive announced by Zhdanov earlier in that year: 'It is well-known that Leninism incorporated all that was best in the traditions of nineteenth-century Russian revolutionary democrats.' We are not told *what* was best or *why*. Soviet readers are next abruptly informed that 'the great Russian thinkers have been quite falsely represented as pupils or imitators of Western writers'. It was high time to recognize them as pupils who had far outstripped their former masters. The latest school of criticism—which is nothing if not exacting—demands in addition that all pre-Bolshevik Russian writers (including equally poets and political economists) shall be categorically regraded according to the political camp to which the Party now assigns them. For instance, despite his firm stand against the revolutionaries, Tolstoy is admitted to the 'progressive' camp, because he showed boundless faith in human nature, but especially in the nature of the downtrodden Russian peasant. Had he preferred Greek peasants, as Leontiev did, he would probably have been less favoured. Dostoevsky, on the contrary, is tossed without more ado into the 'reactionary' limbo, because he painted such horrifying pictures of human degradation and vice, derived from Russian models, and in so doing, is said to have grossly misrepresented and blackened 'characteristic features of the Russian people.'[2] But their imaginative insight, mastery of verbal expression, the enduring qualities for which the outside world still values these two writers, sink into minor 'formal' side-issues tacked on to the serious business of promoting class-warfare.

In this respect the Soviet critics of today have reverted to the methods of their mid nineteenth-century Utilitarian ancestors. Both try to hammer into Russian heads the *idée fixe* that a literary work is valuable solely for the social utility of the

---

[1] *Our Relationship to the Literary Heritage of the Past. Bol'shevik*, No. 10, 1947.
[2] V. V. Yermilov: *Against Reactionary Ideas in the Work of Dostoevsky* (lecture delivered to the All-Union Society for the Propagation of Political and Scientific Knowledge), pub. *Modern Quarterly*, vol. 5, No. 2, 1950.

the superficiality and meanness of political controversy, and avoided it like the plague. He found his arch-enemy in the spiritual stagnation which he saw creeping over Russian society in the reign of Nicolas I, a society partly smug, partly apathetic, tormented by bullies and parasites wearing military or official uniforms, and choked by a relentless flow of government circulars and regulations. Belinsky felt that too heavy a price was being paid for the moderate degree of peace and order which temporarily prevailed throughout the Empire. He recoiled in horror from that 'peaceful harbour, where only the mould is green, where the frogs are croaking under the soft mire—Away from that to any place where the waves roll freely under an open sky!'

In such a humdrum philistine society, intellectual talents, when they could not be canalized into existing official channels, quietly decayed or wildly ran to waste. Belinsky, despite his honesty and vigour, was mortified to find himself a 'superfluous man'. The rigid hierarchy of Russian ranks and functions held no niche for him and his unconventionally gifted contemporaries. They were driven out to find their lonely fulfilment in art or critical thought. Against the dark oppressive clouds surrounding them the fiery sparks of the superfluous men flared up and died away; but the brief brilliance with which they shone, even when magnified or coloured by its Russian surroundings, was none the less a reflection from the major light of Europe. As Belinsky observed in 1834: 'We discussed and argued about every new idea imported from abroad, but we never grew, fostered or created anything of our own. Others worked before us. We merely took the ready-made product and exploited its use. Hence the secret of our quick successes, but hence also the cause of our incredible instability.'

The lack of any solid or admirable traditions which Russians could call their own, plus a healthy yearning to improve (though only among the educated) had made them assiduous imitators and borrowers from abroad. Belinsky approved of much that had been borrowed, and he urged that the borrowing process should continue; but, he asked, need it be so haphazard in choice, so crudely misapplied to Russian life? Most repugnant to him was the medley of new-fangled intellectual fashions, derived from European countries, where they hung together on some kind of *point d'appui*, but then transferred in disembodied forms to Russia, where they hopelessly enervated and distorted the growing educated class. Pushkin's friend V. Küchelbecker, wrote with a touch of exasperated humour about the debilitating effect of these European fashions on Russian men of letters: 'With us everything is a *dream*, a *spectre*, everything seems to be or tries to be, everything is *as if*, *somehow* or *something*. We long ago ceased to feel any spontaneous emotions; despondency swallowed up all the others. We all continuously bemoan our vanished youth, we still chew and ruminate on that misfortune. . . . Our images are everywhere the same—the moon, which is of course melancholy and pale—dizzy cliffs, impenetrable thickets—in places where they never need to be —sometimes mysterious shadows and visions—but chiefly *mist*, mists over the water, over the pine-forests, over the fields, and most of all, *mist in the author's head*.'

Belinsky's clear and vigorous mind detested this morass of melancholy affectation, mental muddle, apathy and wasted talent. Resolutely refusing to be dragged down by it, he resisted its clinging destructive power with the desperate energy of a drowning man struggling to keep his head above water. Why had the source and sense of a natural way of life dried up in Russian society? 'We are people without a country,' he complained bitterly; 'worse than that, we are people whose country is a ghost, and we are ghosts ourselves. Yet we are people who make enormous demands on life, capable of any sacrifice, though forced to stand still like idle spectators. . . . Without a goal there is no activity, and without activity our life withers away. The source of interests, purpose and activity lies in the substance of our social life.' (Letter to Botkin, 8 September 1841.)

He soon came to the conclusion that a so-called civilized social life led nowhere unless it obeyed a stern but clear ideal of patriotism. A Russian patriot—so we are constantly reassured by eloquent Russians—is infinitely more generous, humane and broad-minded than the petty nationalist or fanatically racial patriot produced by all the other nations of the world. Belinsky was one of the first to harp on this ticklish theme. At least he never degenerated into a servile 'my country, right or wrong', type of patriot. He never urged obedience to national leaders unless the tune which they called could be harmonized with his own exacting demands of social duty. Before he could bow the knee in loyalty to her, he insisted that his country should be worthy of his personal respect. This guiding motive, more than any other, ran through all the convulsive spasms of his self-contradictory temperament, and introduced a note of purely emotional coherence in his short unsettled life.

'The fate of his country must lie heavy on the heart of any vigorous and healthy person. He is bound to be ill with its illnesses, hurt by its sufferings. To love one's country really means a passionate desire to see in it the realization of human ideals, and to promote them as far as one's strength permits. Any other kind of patriotism turns into a Chinese thing, love of one's own merely because it belongs to one. Peter the Great blasting his own son with curses, declaring he would rather have a stranger's son but a good son—than his own, but a worthless creature—there is an enviable example!' (Article on Lermontov's Works, 1840.)

III

Belinsky's father was a drunken provincial doctor, who envied and hated his son's intellectual gifts, and missed no opportunity to bully and humiliate him in every way. His mother appears to have been an irritable, empty-headed woman, indifferent to her son's fate, but permanently soured by her husband's failure to rise higher in the social scale. Belinsky escaped from this family hell by winning a scholarship at Moscow University. He lived there in the utmost squalor on a miserable pittance, but he studied with all his might. In 1831 he wrote a quite conventional romantic tragedy containing some abstract tirades in praise of Liberty. The university authorities heard about the manuscript and pounced on this offence as a pretext to expel him from the university for what they termed 'poor capacities and no application'. But a few years later this penniless outcast, without an atom of worldly influence, without even a university diploma, became the most powerful intellectual force in Russia. This is an extraordinary tribute to sheer personal ability buoyed up by unflagging enthusiasm, and it happened in the much-abused reign of Nicolas I.

From 1831 until his death Belinsky lived on his earnings as a journalist. His first substantial critical articles *Literary Dreams* (published in *Molva*, 1834) expounded Schelling's view of national character, and the way in which it ought to unfold in

every major nation which manages to grow beyond the vege-
table stage. But he wrote of course in terms of Schelling's
applicability to Russia, and his articles, circumscribed by this
urgent sense of purpose, had the merit of being much more
lucid and concrete than much of Schelling's cloudy philosophic
jargon. He admitted as a regrettable fact that Russia had so far
achieved no civilization of her own and no native literature,
though the latter showed healthy signs of sprouting. He casti-
gated empty-headed Petersburg dandies who chattered about
the latest European fashions and applauded any nonsense,
provided it was expressed in French; he denounced literary
charlatans who prostituted literature by their mercenary and
cynical verbal exploits in pandering to the lowest popular
instincts. As a saving grace, he warmly commended the younger
generation of educated Russians for their manifest dissatisfaction with the existing state of culture, for the sound sense they
showed in their deliberate reluctance to bring into the world
more and more superficial second-rate and immature work, for
the way in which they preferred to plunge instead into the preliminary study of science and philosophy, thus 'tapping the live
water of knowledge at its ultimate source'.

Belinsky's early articles denounced so boldly and so much,
that they made him many mortal enemies, but they also won for
him a small following of devoted and loyal friends. Moreover,
the positive side of his appeal provoked a surprisingly rapid
response in the more sensitive sections of Russian society. Bored
and dissatisfied young dandies abandoned ballrooms and card-
tables in order to bury themselves in libraries; dashing guards
officers and bucolic country squires vied with each other in
ordering thousands of volumes from abroad, in a rush to become
conversant with the latest products of European philosophy,
history, economics and *belles lettres*. Schiller, Byron, Goethe,
Schelling, but above all Hegel, soon became household words
in Russia, and the Shibboleths of the educated class.

Meanwhile Belinsky, aided by the philosophic circle of
Stankevich, had switched over from Schelling to the ethical
metaphysician Fichte, though not to Fichte, the German
nationalist doctrinaire. 'Acquaintance with Fichte's ideas first
convinced me that the inner life of the spirit is the only real positive concrete life, and that the so-called real life is a negation,
a mirage, futile and empty.' This phase of ultra-individualist

self-assertion, verging on insanity, luckily only lasted for a year. The next philosopher to captivate Belinsky was the inevitable Hegel, through whom he fell into the opposite extreme of anti-individual state-worship. For a Fichtean the outside world could merely be an insignificant muddle, hardly worth worrying about, since nothing but the ego was real. Only when the self-asserting ego happened to be embodied in a German citizen Fichte simplified the problem by arguing that this happy coincidence rendered Germans superior to all other races. Such a philosophy sounded sweet to German ears, but it could hardly be expected to appeal for long to nationals of other countries.

For a Hegelian, on the contrary, the outside world, and not the ego, became the incarnation of reason. The most perfect and highly organized form of reason, according to Hegel, reached fruition in the nation-state. To do him justice, Belinsky never felt at all at home either in Hegel's Logic or in his Philosophy of Law. But he fell completely under the thrall of Hegel's Philosophy of History, by virtue of which—though for no apparent reason—world affairs advance and improve by objectifying Hegel's categories in a dialectical process. According to Hegel, that process had started from rudimentary Pure Being in China, and was growing more and more perfect as it approached the realization of the Absolute Idea in the German nation. But Hegel had rudely excluded the Slavs from his list of 'historic' races, and this was an awkward stumbling-block for his Russian admirers, who might reasonably have thought him guilty of national prejudice in not suggesting that Russia's turn might come after Germany's. Hegel would have none of this. He called the Slavs 'a sombre mass of tribes, without initiative'. If the nineteenth century belonged to the Slavs, he said, it would be a ghastly century. If Germany did not succeed in finally embodying the Absolute Idea, the burden of world history would surely be taken up elsewhere, perhaps by America—perhaps in a bloody contest between North and South America. In every age one nation alone could be charged with the mission of carrying the world through whatever particular stage of the Hegelian dialectic it happened to have reached. Schelling, however, redressed the balance by prophesying a great future for Russia. This partly accounts for his immense popularity among the Russian intelligentsia. Belinsky was one of numerous Russians

D

who made Hegel palatable to his compatriots by sugar-coating his historical logic with Schelling's more flattering prediction.

Apart from the fascinating dialectic, Belinsky was at first impressed by that aspect of Hegel's doctrine which taught that the ordinary citizen ought not to meddle in public affairs, and should know how to leave the complicated business of politics in the hands of trustworthy and skilful experts. Belinsky was delighted by the idea that disinterested individuals living under a stable Government, protected from the tedious and distracting demands of political intrigue, should be able to devote their whole energy to productive work, and to serving the more important tasks of civilization. He seems to have blissfully overlooked the danger that Hegel's state, being a law unto itself, could also indulge at will in every internal tyranny and every external aggression. In such a state, even if its rulers were occasionally wise and benevolent, civilization could at best flourish precariously under a sword of Damocles.

In one of his confidential outbursts Belinsky told Bakunin that his whole life was in his private letters, meaning of course that he could unburden his soul in them, free from the cramping fear of censorship. A long letter which he wrote to a young friend in 1837 completely unveils his state of mind at this stage of his career. It contains much of his future in embryo and certainly deserves a place (which it is far from having received) among the major historical documents in the formation of the Russian intelligentsia. 'Drown yourself', he writes, 'lose yourself in science and art, love them as the goal and necessity of your life, and not as mere instruments of education and winning success in the world—only then will you be blessed! . . . Can you understand the result without knowing its causes? Can you understand the history of mankind if you are ignorant of what makes a man? That is why philosophy is the source of all knowledge, and why without philosophy every science is dead, incomprehensible and absurd. But it is no good beginning with philosophy. You must prepare for it by means of art. . . . Art strengthens and unfolds within you love; it fortifies you with true religion; for religion is truth in contemplation, whereas philosophy is truth in reasoned knowledge. Without a prior sense of truth in feeling, it is impossible to acquire it in knowledge. . . .

'Above all, avoid politics and steer clear of any political influence on your cast of mind. Politics in Russia are senseless, and only empty heads can busy themselves with political questions. Love what is good, and you are bound to turn out useful to your country, without thinking or striving to be useful to it. . . .

'If you want to understand the history of Russia—read the history of Peter the Great—he will explain everything. All great sovereigns of other nations are inferior to our Emperor Peter. They all developed their peoples, leaning on the past, on traditions. Peter tore Russia from her past, broke her traditions, and now it is absurd to watch our muddle-headed learned men and poets who search for our national character and art in that antediluvian period of our history from Rurik to Aleksei. Peter alone provides clear proof that Russia derives her civil rights and freedom not from herself but from her Emperors, even as she has received so much else from them. Of course we still have hardly any rights, we are still slaves, if you like, but that is because we deserve to be slaves. Russia is still a child who needs a nurse, on whose breast her heart beats. The nurse is full of love for her charge, but holds a rod ready to punish it when it misbehaves. To give the child unlimited freedom would merely ruin it. To give Russia a constitution in her present state would be to ruin her. Our peoples' only idea of freedom is licence—and licence is mischief. A liberated Russian people would not take its place in any parliament that was started. They would rush off instead to carouse in the vodka-shops, to break windows, and to hang all noblemen who shave their beards and wear suits instead of kaftans—though for that matter most of these noblemen are neither educated nor wealthy. The whole hope of Russia lies in education, and not in upheavals, not in revolutions nor in constitutions. . . . How many tyrannical landowners are there left in Russia? And those who remain, are they not despised by the others?' Even our military hooligans now are "quieter than water, lower than grass". And nowadays a student who drinks a bucket of wine, and can still manage to stand upright, no longer earns the astonished respect of his comrades. Rather, he arouses contempt and disgust. What is the reason for all this?

' It is the establishment of some kind of public opinion, thanks to the spread of our education and perhaps even more thanks to the power of autocracy. This autocratic power gives us complete liberty to think, if only a limited liberty to talk aloud and intervene in its affairs. It allows us educated people to bring books from abroad, which may not be translated or published in Russia. This is a legitimate and laudable precaution on the part of autocracy, for ideas which may help you can easily ruin the peasant, who is bound to misunderstand them. . . . What we ought to realize is that the boundary of Russia on her European side is not a boundary of thought—because thought passes freely across—but it is a boundary against political tendencies harmful to Russia, and in that I see not the slightest oppression of thought. . . .

'To be apostles of enlightenment, that is our destiny. So let us imitate the early apostles of Christ, who hatched no con-spiracies in secret or open political societies, but boldly spread their doctrines in the face of Emperors and judges, and feared neither fire nor sword. . . . In the sphere of thought all national differences must disappear, and only the human being will remain. So to the devil with the French! Their influence brought us nothing but ill. We imitated their literature and killed our own. Germany is the Jerusalem of the new humanity. Yes, German philosophy is a clear and mathematically distinct development of Christian teaching. But we are the rightful heirs of the whole of Europe. And therefore our destiny is already clear. We young people ought to initiate that alliance with Germany. . . .' (Letter to D. Ivanov, 7 August 1837.)

A year later Belinsky wrote to his mentor Stankevich that he was beginning to suspect either that philosophy must be non-sense or that people were quite incapable of understanding it. 'Art is closer to me', he wrote, 'and a good cast of the Venus of Medici is worth more in my eyes than that stupid satisfaction which I once sought in the solution of moral problems. The moral point of view ruined for me the whole flower of life, all its imagination and charm . . . We should be thankful that the poisonous breath of analysis did not touch Pushkin, and thereby deprive us of a great poet.'

IV

In 1839 Belinsky obtained through the editor Kraevsky a permanent post on the newspaper *Fatherland Annals*. He hated journalistic work, which, he complained, blunted his brain and sucked his blood dry; he pictured himself 'like Prometheus in a caricature; *Fatherland Annals* is my rock, Kraevsky is my vulture'. If only he were not obliged to write more than three articles in a year, he said, he could guarantee they would all three be worth reading. But he stuck to journalism solely in order to earn a living, and this explains quite adequately why so few of his writings are readable today. His best articles, he declared, were those which he worked out in his head, but which were neither written nor published.

By 1840 he already showed distinct signs of revolt against orthodox political Hegelianism, against 'the real is the rational', against the absolute primacy of any organization, whether governmental or social, over its individual constituent parts. 'I curse my desire to be reconciled with disgusting realities', he declared. 'The hangman exists and his existence is rational, but it is none the less horrible and revolting. For me the human personality is higher than history, than society, than mankind itself.' By 1841 his *volte-face* was complete. He candidly noted that in the previous year he had thought the diametrical opposite of what he thought now, and cautioned himself thus: 'Evidently one should avoid fanaticism.' He confessed to his friend, the amiable tea-merchant Botkin: 'You know my nature. It always runs to extremes, and never stays in the centre of an idea. With pain and labour I part with one idea and pass on to another with all the enthusiasm of a proselyte. Thus now I have switched over to a new extreme—the idea of socialism, which has become for me the idea of ideas, the essence of being, the question of questions, the Alpha and Omega of Faith and Knowledge. . . . Everthing derives from it, exists for it, and goes towards it. It has (for me) absorbed history, religion and philosophy. . . . Society lives through a definite sum of definite convictions, in which all its members are welded into one, like the rays of the sun focused in a burning glass, and they should be able to understand each other without needing to speak a word. That is why in France, England or Germany, people who have never met, complete strangers, can feel their kinship. . . . But we are people without a fatherland—no, worse than that, we are people whose fatherland is a ghost. . . . Social solidarity (*Sotsialnost'*) or death! that is my motto . . . what good is it to me that a genius on earth lives in heaven, when the crowd wallows in filth? What do I gain if the world of art, religion and history is open to me, when I cannot share

it with all who should be my human brothers, my neighbours
in Christ, but who are strangers and enemies to me—on account
of their ignorance. My heart bleeds and beats convulsively when
I look at the crowd and its representatives. . . . I know that
the Middle Ages were a great epoch. I understand the sacred-
ness and grandeur of its religious feeling; yet the eighteenth
century is dearer to me, the age of religious decline. In the
Middle Ages they burned at the stake heretics, free thinkers,
and sorcerers—in the eighteenth century they beheaded aristocrats, priests and other enemies of God, reason and humanity.
But the time will come, I ardently believe, when nobody
will be burned, and nobody will be beheaded, when the
criminal will beg to be punished for the sake of mercy and for
his own salvation—and he will not be punished, but life will
then be his punishment even as death is now.' (8 September
1841.)

Belinsky's faith in feats of human conscience compels respect,
even from the sceptic, but he seems to have naïvely taken for
granted that all his 'human brothers' pined for the same lofty
satisfactions as he did, and that their ignorance alone prevented them from realizing it. We find him repeating these
protests in a feverish tone of self-denial. In their blend of fierce
challenge with would-be submissiveness they sound like a persistent echo of his Christian upbringing modified by a strident
note of Hegelian intellectual arrogance. Nevertheless a few
months previously he had formally renounced Hegel root and
branch, and what is more, the Hegelian dialectic—as another
letter to Botkin clearly shows. It is a characteristically impassioned
and sweeping denunciation, but it seems to have received inadequate attention from Hegel's Marxian disciples in Russia. 'I
suspected a long time ago that the philosophy of Hegel was only
a moment, though an important moment, that the absolutism
of its conclusions is worthless, and that it would be better to die
than to be reconciled with them. Out of living phenomena he
has made phantoms, who cling to each other with bony hands
as they dance in the air over a graveyard. The "subject" for him
is no end in itself, but a mere means for the momentary expression of a general idea, which treats the subject like a Moloch,
playing with it for a while, and afterwards throwing it away like
a pair of worn-out trousers . . . I have weighty reasons to be
angry with Hegel, for I realize that I was faithful to him (in

feeling) when I accepted the existing state of affairs in Russia. All his talk about morality is utter rubbish, for in the objective domination of abstract ideas there can be no morality, even as there can be none in an *objective* religion (*e.g.* in Indian pantheism where Brahma and Shiva are equal gods, *i.e.* where good and evil hold equal sway). The fate of the subject, the individual, the personality, is more important to me than the fate of the whole world, more important than the well-being of the Chinese Emperor (*i.e.* the Hegelian Absolute). . . . With all due respect to your philosophical philistinism, I have the honour to inform you that even if I succeeded in climbing to the highest rung of the ladder of development—there too I would ask you to render me an account of all the victims of caprice, superstition, of the Spanish Inquisition, Philip II, etc. Otherwise I would rather throw myself down head foremost from the topmost rung of that ladder. I do not want happiness even as a gift if I cannot have a quiet conscience about every one of my blood brothers! They say that a certain amount of disharmony is a condition of any harmony; maybe that is profitable and melodious for masters of music, but it certainly is not for those on whom falls the lot of fulfilling the idea of disharmony.' (Letter to Botkin, 1 March 1841.)

After his healthy and sweeping revulsion from German philosophers, Belinsky seems to have found temporary refuge in the study of French socialists. But a Russian proverb says : if you have burned your mouth on milk, you will blow even on water. Belinsky had swallowed the bitter pill of Hegelianism and afterwards spat it out. This chastening experience seems to have stopped him from ever again linking his flexible ideals with any new pattern of social organization. Admittedly he wrote that Louis Blanc's *Histoire des Dix Ans* was a revelation to him, and that Louis Blanc's personality filled him with reverent devotion but that went no further than an outburst of sympathetic feeling for another man. Later on he found fault with Louis Blanc, whom he described as suffering both from a swollen head and a swollen heart. He read the fashionable Saint-Simon and Fourier, but his own frequent changes of faith, though they had not dimmed his ardour, had made him wary of dogma. He observed with relief that he had already shed romanticism, mysticism and all -isms. Moreover he shared the experience of the most rabid Russian Westernizers as soon as they became travellers in Europe. Europe's charms were most alluring when seen from a great distance.

After visiting France and Germany he began to reproach Europe, as if she had failed to fulfil her secret promises to him. Simultaneously Russia rose in his esteem. 'Real pauperism—the authentic proletariat—' he wrote, 'can only be seen in the West, especially in miserable Silesia.' In France he found 'a syphilitic sore running through the French body . . . the bourgeois who ruins children labouring for his gain, grabs the shirt from a beggar's back in order to secure payment of his debt, encourages vice because he derives financial profit from it.'

Unlike many Russians who revelled in sweeping generalizations about the West as a whole, Belinsky drew clear distinctions between the better and worse features which struck him so forcibly in different parts of Europe. Odd as it may seem (but Belinsky was a bundle of contradictory enthusiasms) he expressed profuse admiration for the English parliamentary constitution, especially for the system of bicameral government which enabled the middle class to counterbalance the aristocracy. 'As a result of this,' he proclaimed, 'the English government is as civic-minded, generous and magnificent as the French government is base, vulgar, petty and shameful.' Belinsky's friend Botkin was a confirmed Anglomaniac, and this factor may have swayed his judgement.

About the time of his extensive journey through Russia (1846) Belinsky's social religion seems to have cooled down. A closer knowledge of actual Russian conditions led him towards a more sceptical estimate of the French Socialists, and simultaneously to a soberer view of their limited applicability to Russian reform. 'The problems of this age are ours, only so far as they apply to our own situation; everything else is foreign to us, and we play the part of Don Quixotes when we get excited about such ideas. In this way we earn the scorn of Europeans rather than their respect. *At home, in ourselves, around us*, that is where we should seek both the problems and their solution.' Even among the French, the historically distant Voltaire and Rousseau seemed to Belinsky far more lasting figures than the contemporary French socialists, whom he described as a well-intentioned party, making a lot of noise, but weak and trivial. There is some evidence to show that towards the end of his life he had reverted to a rather more complicated version of his old faith in enlightened despotism as the only way out for Russia. In a letter to Kavelin (22 November 1847) he wrote, 'For me Peter—is my philosophy, my religion, my revelation in everything that touches Russia. He is an example to great and small who want to get things done.' He told Annenkov that the Russian liberals were enemies of all success, for they irritated the government by their impudent stupidities, making it nervous, and ready to suspect revolutionary plots where there was nothing of the kind. Yet his contempt for liberalism in Russian politics was clearly founded on his diagnosis of Russian peculiarities. It did not prevent him from finding progressive virtues in that same industrial middle class which is still the backbone of liberal movements in Europe.

The peculiar vision of a new Peter the Great, driving a picked team of bourgeois technicians in the industrialization of the Russian Empire, emerges again in one of the last letters he wrote. 'My believing friend [Bakunin] and our Slavophils have helped to cure me of any mystic belief in the people. Where and when did a people ever free itself? Always everything was done by individual leaders. When arguing with you about the bourgeoisie, I upbraided you for being a conservative, but I was then an ass, and you were a wise man. The whole future of France is in the hands of the bourgeoisie. Progress depends on them alone, though the people can play at times a passive and co-operative rôle. When I announced in the presence of my believing friend that a new Peter the Great was necessary for Russia, he attacked my idea like a heresy, saying that the people should do everything for themselves. What a naïve Arcadian thought!... He went on to argue, God save Russia from European bourgeoisie! But now it is clearly visible that the inner process of social development in Russia will not properly begin till the Russian nobility has been transformed into a bourgeoisie. . . . The best Slavophils idolize the common people just like my believing friend; but they derived their ideas from the socialists, and in their articles they quote George Sand and Louis Blanc.' (Letter to Annenkov, 15 February 1848.)

V

The political thread which runs through Belinsky's thought, though persistent and definite enough, never took first place in his mind. Fundamentally he cared little about the state and its forms, except to the extent that they helped or hindered the civilized life of society. He was the first Russian thinker to suggest how it was possible to stop the incessant tug-of-war between governmental authority and individual desires. Nothing but wisely directed power could eliminate the causes of their conflict, but power must come from above. An intelligent government (kept up to the mark by a resolutely independent intelligentsia) would learn how to stimulate and enrich personality instead of stifling or tormenting it to death. The Russian government had nearly reached this stage, since it had adopted officially a recommendation made by the intelligentsia—*i.e.* that the state and all classes of society could be reconciled in the common cause of developing national character as an ideal of international culture. The gravest flaw in this hopeful programme was the government's own interpretation of what national character should be. Official *narodnost'* hardened more and more into a blatant and repressive military Chauvinism, which not only flatly contradicted Belinsky's personal ideal of Russian character, but trampled down the nascent intelligentsia who were struggling to express their version of it.

Like most Russian intellectuals who temporarily succumbed to the German spell, Belinsky wrote some rather banal rhetoric in praise of universal moral qualities, but he remained shrewdly aware of the sticky morass to which a pursuit of humane cosmopolitanism could lead. That explains how in theory, at least, he found himself at one with the government when he took refuge in national character as the main motive force of modern civilization. Yet his interpretation of national character, unlike that of Nicolas I and Uvarov, became and has remained a source of inspiration to intelligent Russian citizens. For him Russian national character was neither a lyrical tribute to the static peasantry nor a nebulous reflection of Schelling's romantic philosophy in a few effervescent Russian minds. It was a lively embryo. Although it was only just starting to peck its way out of the shell, it already revealed a wider range of positive human qualities than had yet emerged in any other major European nation. In short, the essence of Russian *national* character turned out to be its power of *international* synthesis on the human plane.

Let Russians therefore beware of tying down their broad

expansive natures under the strait-jacket of any wretched one-sided philosophy. For had they not already proved themselves to be refreshingly versatile and eclectic compared with the more developed but horribly self-centred French, Germans or English? Russia was not such a weak and sickly growth that she needed to built a Chinese wall to preserve her national identity from being obliterated by foreign incursions. She did not need to be frightened of new European ideas. On the contrary, she throve best of all on acquisitions imported from abroad, provided she knew how to adapt them for her special needs. 'We take from the English', he wrote, 'their industry, their general business ability, but in so doing we need not become mere industrialists or business men.' And on the negative side : 'Everything European which is not humane we should reject with as much energy as everything Asiatic which is not humane.' Only Russian national character could be so rich and many-sided because the Russian Empire was already the most multinational of states, the most inherently international of nations, drawing from West and East alike, and what is more, setting the values of humane culture higher than political conquest or economic power !

Such was Belinsky's nearest approach to a coherent ideal after he had cut himself free from his temporary bondage to a succession of German philosophers. Unfortunately he never managed to disentangle his emotions from a subconscious veneration of the nation-state ; worse still, he continued to confuse human society with the state, and the state with individual rulers just as fatally as Hegel did.

This fluid habit of mind blurred his judgement. It led him to identify all human culture with the social expression of national character—an error to which one egocentric country after another has since fallen victim—and which culminates in the modern *reductio ad absurdum* of rival *de facto* 'national socialist' states, great and small, boosting their unique perfections under a variety of pretentious names. Yet he warns us that national character is no more than a foundation for personal character. 'Personality without a nation is a phantom, but so is a nation without personalities' ; Belinsky informs us : 'The one conditions the other. The nation is the soil, preserving the living sap of every growth, personality is the flower and fruit of that soil. What personality is to the human being, nationality is to the human race. Without nationality mankind would be a lifeless logical abstraction, a word without content, a meaningless sound.' He failed to see that the absolute primacy of national over personal character must sooner or later strangle the latter, while appearing to lend it shape and colour, and ultimately thus destroy itself. This is what started to happen under Nicolas I.

He then tries to justify his own passion for Peter the Great by telling us that great men are always and inevitably 'national' like the people to which they belong. Thus the struggle between an active genius and his sluggish environment turns out to be, not a duel between human initiative and the bondage of national institutions, but a fight *within* the nation-state between its vital elements and its dying ones, between the advance of reason and the stagnation of habit and prejudice. And since the masses always live by habit and follow the line of least resistance, the strenuous opposition of genius to the masses is a necessary stimulus to both, and simultaneously a test of the mettle of genius. 'The life of a people is not like some little boat, which any insignificant man can push in the direction he wants by a light movement of his oar.'

Belinsky became uneasily aware that the more his outlook on Russian society ripened, the nearer he drew to his old enemies the Slavophils, who had attacked him so bitterly when they founded the *Moskvityanin* in 1842. They were barely kept apart by his love of Peter the Great (whom most of them abominated) and by his lasting hatred of the Orthodox Church which to him stood for 'darkness, chains and the knout'. But in romantic patriotism the Slavophils were, as Herzen said, 'nos ennemis, les amis'. In 1846 Belinsky had joined the staff of *The Contemporary* and moved from Moscow to St. Petersburg. His *Survey of Russian Literature for 1846*, written for that journal, stated unequivocally his latest version of the way in which the embryonic Russian national character could grow up into an adult civilized society. Though it reads more like a confession of faith than a programme of action, it shows a measured judgement and restraint which is rare in Belinsky's stormy utterances. 'The Slavophils were right in many ways, but none the less their rôle is negative, though useful for a time.' In a private letter to Kavelin he seized the opportunity to enlarge on this idea: 'You accuse me of Slavophilism. That is not entirely without foundation. Like you, I love the Russian personality and believe in the great future of Russia, but like you I build nothing secure on the foundations of that love and hope. I do not use them as irrefutable demonstrations of something which is bound to happen. You have entered into the idea of personal development as the substance of the history of the Russian people. We want to go through this process quickly, but history is in no hurry. In our country personality is only just emerging from the shell, and what is why Gogol's types are still the truest Russian types. . . . I can't bear enthusiastic patriots . . . hardened sceptics are a thousand times better, for hatred is sometimes only a special form of love, but I must admit that quiet sceptics are wretched and unpleasant to me, abstract people, passportless human wanderers. . . . Enthusiasts often make mistakes, seeing in the object of their love qualities which are not there at all, but sometimes love alone can discover beautiful and great things which are hidden alike to ordinary observation and to the intelligent mind.' (Letter to Kavelin, 22 November 1847.)

VI

Belinsky's rather accidental contribution to the present Russian brand of national socialism has been inevitably singled out by Soviet critics as his principal asset. His rare political utterances have thus been torn from their context, and his essentially *a-political* outlook has been almost ignored. Often it has been imputed to the rigours of censorship, rather than to his own temperamental preference for non-political themes. In fact his whole life was devoted to the promotion of literature, philosophy and art, and to the painfully difficult task of bringing the *best* literature and art closer to the daily life of educated Russian citizens, before they were corrupted by the *worst*. 'In speaking of the successes of our social education,' he wrote, 'we really speak about the success of our literature, because our education is derived from the immediate effect of our literature on the ideas and conduct of society. Literature created the temper of our society, has already transformed several generations, sharply distinct from each other, and has thus set up a method for the internal reconciliation of all classes.

'It has formed a kind of enlightened public opinion, and brought forth something like a special social class, which differs from the middle class in not being composed solely of commercial or tradespeople, but of people from all classes. Thus they are able to approach each other through the medium of culture, which with us is exceptionally concentrated in the love of good literature.' (*Thoughts about Russian Literature*.)[1]

Influential Soviet critics, while rightly paying tribute to Belinsky's educational zeal, have laboured conscientiously to build him up as the forerunner of 'Socialist realism', as the far-sighted revolutionary who had preached the subordination of literature and art to the needs of the 'progressive state'—*i.e.* to the social imperatives of the ruling intellectuals. In fact this attitude appears to be the exact reverse of what Belinsky wanted. Over and over again in his articles he castigates the official critics, the dry moralists, the anti-aesthetic wooden rationalists, who were so busy blocking the living springs of Russian thought with dust and ashes. The last long article he wrote before his death (Survey of Russian Literature for 1847) returns to this theme with a parting flash of ardour. 'The scientist proves, the artist reveals, but both, if they succeed, convince people, the one by logical demonstration, the other through images and pictures. But whereas the first is heard and understood by few, the latter can be understood by many. . . . What *pure art* is, even its advocates cannot explain. An idea of purely German origin—for no such art exists—it is a bad extreme of another bad extreme, *i.e.* dialectical, didactic, cold, dry, dead art, whose creations are nothing but a rhetorical exercise on given themes. Beyond doubt art must first of all be good art, and after that it can express the spirit and direction of society at certain periods. *No one can disobey with impunity the intrinsic laws of art. A poet works wonders, can set the whole of literature moving in a new direction, so long as he instinctively and unconsciously obeys the call of his own talent. But the moment he begins to reason and search for a philosophy he will stumble and fall. The giant is suddenly weakened, like Samson shorn of his hair.* Being more sensitive than others, no artist can possibly escape being influenced in his work by the society around him.'

Belinsky had no doubt that an artist who tolerates a clique of intellectual pundits who tell him what to do, or to explain in rational terms what he has done, is either a charlatan or a miserable nonentity. 'At present many people are carried away

[1] V. Belinsky : *Sochineniya*, vol. 4, p. 293, 1900.

by the magic word "trend", and take it as the root of the matter, without being aware that in the sphere of art no tendency is worth a brass farthing without talent, and secondly that the trend, if it has any substance, must exist not only in the head but also in the heart and blood of the writer.'

Any form of intellectual art, whether 'civic' or 'pure', whether 'social-minded' or 'aesthetic', was equally senseless and repugnant to Belinsky. An artist, worthy of the name, stands like a force of nature in the very centre of life, and cannot help standing there. That tiresome, hackneyed and fundamentally senseless controversy about 'art for art's sake', 'the ivory tower', etc., simply did not exist for him. He could not take seriously the barren intellectual aestheticism which first invented such a silly theory, and then restricted art to some dry 'pure' intellectual activity with a totally non-imaginative function, like the pursuit of higher mathematics.

For Belinsky the main duty of a literary critic was simply to discover and promote artistic talent in literature, and thus to act as an intermediary between society and the talented imaginative artist, who could not help being in advance of society. This involved a parallel obligation to pour cold water on all artistic pretensions devoid of talent. A critic who encourages counterfeit art is worse than a bad critic; he is a social criminal; for he helps swindlers to make money or gain credit through debauching people's minds. Belinsky practised what he preached. He was the first to demonstrate the genius of Pushkin, Lermontov and Gogol, and to expound their immense and lasting value. His discerning eye also detected Turgenev, Goncharov and Dostoevsky as rising stars, though he only lived long enough to read their earliest works, and though he expressed bitter (but quite unwarranted) disappointment in Dostoevsky's failure to live up to the radical standard of *Poor People*. He foretold a remarkable future for Herzen. Indeed his judgement of his contemporaries merits a study on its own.

We are apt to forget that the most mature and profound creations of Pushkin were at first coldly received by the Russian reading public, and offensively reviewed by the leading critics. Belinsky was not forcing an open door when he fought for Pushkin's fame against 'absurd and pitiful fools' who obstinately adhered to poetry as an art of squeezing conventional sentiments into correct compact rhymes or edifying parables.

'Without anger, I say to our literary Old Believers, no Russian has ever had such an indisputable right to educate our youth, our adult readers and even our old men, if the spark of beauty and human sympathy has not died in them, because we know no more moral poet with such tremendous talent.' In other words, Pushkin does not follow any ethical aims, but he is ethical solely by virtue of his brilliant expressive gifts. Consistently enough, Belinsky revolted with equal force against all moral maxims or principles applied to human conduct unless they were upheld by powerful moral emotions. He poured contempt on the 'calculating moral philosophy' of Kant, and in one of his letters to Bakunin he bursts out: 'I despise and hate the benefactor without love, and would rather decide to throw myself headlong into the abyss of vice and egoism than to be a Quaker, a vulgar rationalist, a Puritan, a Sectarian, good through calculation, honest through self-love, not to steal from others only in order not to give them any right to steal from me . . . Better to be a fallen angel, a devil, than an innocent, sinless but cold and slimy frog.' (16 August 1837.)

In the same letter he discovered that North Americans had become the living incarnation of that moral philistinism which goaded him to fury. Though this impression had no more solid basis than a rapid perusal of Fenimore Cooper's novels, it was enough to provoke the following violent and rather comic diatribe: 'Living in Pyatigorsk, I read a lot of novels, including some of Fenimore Cooper's, from which I gained a complete understanding of the character of North-American society. My sluggish but not yet frozen blood boiled with indignation at the picture of that disgustingly benevolent and honest society of traders, of those new Jews, renouncing the Gospel, but recognizing the Old Testament. No, better Turkey than America! Better to wallow for ever in mire and filth than to dress tidily, brush one's hair and to think the whole of human perfection consists in that!'[1]

Belinsky's battle in defence of Pushkin's genius and its value to Russian society was easy and straightforward compared with the next campaign which he undertook, an uphill fight to vindicate Lermontov. The tepid or cold reception accorded to Pushkin's works was nothing to the storm of indignation and outraged pride which assailed Lermontov's *A Hero of Our*

[1] *Sochineniya*, vol. 4, p. 993.

Times. Belinsky did not belong to the band of quixotic persecuted ntellectuals who leap impulsively to the defence of every lost or unpopular cause, provided it has become unpopular enough. He championed Lermontov on positive grounds, because he immediately and instinctively understood the originality of Lermontov's hero, Pechorin. He found in this figure, not just another variation of the obvious and already trite Byronic hero, the cold, self-centred, melancholy but handsome and cultured brigand; he discovered instead a living image of his own uncompromising protest against a vulgar Philistine society. Of course he revered and admired Pechorin as an imaginative creation, but he could have gone that far, as others did, even if Pechorin had been a moral monstrosity. But Belinsky felt a far stronger attraction to him as a moral type of human being, as a tragic symbol of spiritual striving corrupted and defeated by smug and vulgar surroundings. Who were those puny Russians who dared to condemn Lermontov for glorifying Pechorin's perverse and wicked cynicism? 'In that man is spiritual strength, will-power, which you have not; through his worst vices flash hints of greatness, like lightning through black clouds. He is noble, rich in imagination, even at those moments when normal human feeling deserts him. He has another destiny, another path than yours. His passions are storms, purifying the air of the soul, his crimes, however terrible, are acute illnesses in a young body, but hardening it for a long and healthy life. These are fevers, sharp attacks, but they are not gout, rheumatism or haemorrhoids, all those sluggish diseases from which you, poor creatures, suffer so unprofitably.'

Pechorin is embittered because he is unloved, but Belinsky can justify his bitterness, because those whose love he fails to win are futile paltry people whose approval is worth nothing. They cry out against him as a vicious monster, but that is only what they pretend; in truth they hate him because he towers above them in his moral grandeur. Belinsky quotes approvingly Pechorin's own confession: 'I was ready to love the whole world; no one understood me; so I learned to hate. For fear of being mocked, I buried my best feelings in the depths of my heart, where they died. When I spoke the truth, no one believed me, so I began to master the arts of of deception.' But Pechorin's unrequited love, driven underground, re-emerged in the shape of a more sinister twisted passion, in thirst for power, in a craving

E

for the satisfaction of bending other people to his will. His own experience of suffering taught him the pleasure of inflicting torment on others. Evil bred evil, and revenge was sweet. In defending Pechorin's vices, Belinsky makes a less convincing case than he did in gauging Pechorin as a Russian portent. He falls back on rather lame extenuating comparisons with commoner and meaner vices; Pechorin is no cold egoist like the self-satisfied Philistine; nor is he bored and indifferent like Pushkin's Evgeny Onegin, who never suffered so intensely as he does.

Undoubtedly the figure of Pechorin, immensely popularized by Belinsky's famous interpretation, entered deeply into the texture of Russian society. It often imprinted a misleading image on minds only too ready to be carried away by any fresh whirlwind of excitement. Crude attempts by self-intoxicated men to emulate the excesses of this hero are visible in the careers of those romantic revolutionary assassins and sadistic tyrants in the governing class, for both of which the history of modern Russia is famous. Nor was the spell of Lermontov ephemeral. Today throughout the Soviet Union every schoolchild can read his poetry and prose in excellent illustrated editions, and I was astonished to learn on good authority in 1945 that, of all the Russian classical authors, he was the favourite reading of young Red Army officers.

It would be far-fetched to conclude, from his hero-worship of Lermontov, that Belinsky should himself be numbered among those romantic revolutionaries who glorified men possessed by strong emotions uninformed by thought, and devoid of conscious concern for the social consequences of their actions. It is true that he ranked emotion higher than intelligence, but only until he discovered that they were inseparable elements of a single psychological process. Indeed in the same article on Lermontov he defines passion as the first stage of thought, and draws a rather neat analogy between the passionate stormy beginnings of Lermontov's hero and the purifying initiation rites of a long and healthy development for the Russian nation. 'Passions are nothing else than the first stage of a developing idea; they belong to a young heart, and only a fool can admire them for a lifetime; many calm rivers begin in noisy waterfalls, but not a single one roars and foams all the way down to the sea. Fulness and depth of feeling do not permit wild transports.'

VII

Belinsky's name is linked with Gogol even more closely than with Pushkin or Lermontov, for Gogol provided the maximum amount of ammunition for the busy social critic. He first established the struggling poverty-stricken commoner as a fashionable literary theme; he first lit up the sordid lives of Russian provincial landowners and officials in that type of sweeping social satire, which lent itself most readily to controversial commentary. Apart from this, Belinsky thought he had found in Gogol a vindication of what he had hitherto sought in vain, the triumphal forward march of Russian history. Gogol's famous passage about the symbolic *troika*, racing wildly onwards, made an indelible impression on his mind. It caused him abruptly to abandon his opinion that Russian society was stagnant, and to jump to the opposite conclusion that it was exceptionally dynamic. 'In Russia everything moves, not in years but in hours —five years for Russia is almost a century', he announced. 'The age of Catherine is already so far away that it seems to be a mythical perspective, not merely old, but almost ancient history.' (Letter to Kavelin, 22 November 1847.)

In one respect Belinsky remained unshaken throughout his perpetual see-saw of conversions; he never stopped denouncing the monstrosity of moral preaching. He revered Gogol (until he wrote *Correspondence with Friends*) as a perfect example of the true artist who never preached. Only works of art, Belinsky tirelessly repeated, and not merely the 'great exemplary ones', are the key to the moral world. Only a society educated on such works could acquire an unconquerable and instinctive aversion to ugliness of every kind. 'Nothing can have a stronger or more beneficial effect on morals than the novels of Gogol . . . The moral motive in an artistic composition consists in a complete absence of any attempt on the part of the author to aim at either a moral or an immoral purpose. Facts speak louder than words, and a faithful picture of a moral horror is far more powerful than any attacks on it. But such inspiration is only accessible to rare talent. Only talent can be moral in its works of art.'

Belinsky's personal taste was sound, and less insensitive to style than his own diffuse hurriedly-written essays would lead one to believe. He sensibly recognized that works of genius, in literature as in other spheres, are supremely rare events, and fully intelligible only to a few discerning minds. Therefore, with a healthy flair for satisfying wider educational demands, he assigned a function to vigorous belles-lettres and lively criticism, as legitimate secondary forms of literature, provided that they nourished and sustained people during the long intervals which must elapse between the creation of masterpieces. Without such constant exercise and stimulus of critical judgement, he argued, human desires and tastes would grow stereotyped, their spiritual standards would fall; nothing else could save society from sinking into a deadly monotonous routine, punctuated by outbursts of coarse and trivial relaxation.

The publication of Gogol's *Correspondence with Friends* profoundly shocked and horrified Belinsky, because it seemed to be a categorical renunciation of all that he had formerly loved and praised in Gogol's work. How could the genial author of *Dead Souls* relapse into a preacher of sermons—(Belinsky's *bête noire*)—a champion of the Orthodox Church and of that degrading servility and mental darkness which the Church upheld?

Belinsky's famous letter to Gogol on this occasion became a landmark in Russian social thought, familiar to every educated Russian—and so much taken for granted that later generations never troubled to read Gogol's book, against which this diatribe had been directed. That is a cogent reason why we ought to have at least a nodding acquaintance with the book before considering Belinsky's letter.

Strange as it may seem, every page of Gogol's *Correspondence with Friends* is bursting with ideals of social service. Belinsky's attack on it is animated by identical motives. The force of both is marred by strident notes. Both show streaks of religious fanaticism, but neither are conventionally Christian in content. Gogol proclaimed that he could in no way justify his literary work unless it was a service to his country, a determined effort 'to guide society, even one generation, towards the realization of beauty'. His acute sense of personal responsibility, his feverish concern for Russia's civilizing future, speak from every line. He diagnosed the same disease as Belinsky, but he prescribed a different remedy. 'You should cut down the evil at its roots, not from its branches.' Without the prior awakening of the individuals constituting society, reforms of social institutions were worse than useless.

He accepted the Orthodox Church, but more as a flexible organic part of Russia than as a sacrosanct religious phenomenon. His own heart was set on earthly happiness and not on dreams of immortality, and he described his worship of Christ in almost secular terms, setting the wise refined and penetrating human psychologist far higher than his claims to divine stature. Since the key to every outward improvement must be a radical upheaval in the human soul, Gogol recommended the firmest institutional conservatism compatible with a pure personal conscience. A landowner should remain a landowner, and a serf a serf. Each should perform the duty attached to the position he already occupied, instead of disintegrating society by yielding to his private greed, malicious envy or vicious idleness.

For Gogol social therapy lay chiefly in the art of exercising personal influence. The more privileged and enlightened people are, the bigger is their responsibility for exerting the appropriate kind of influence. The Governor's wife, for instance, should set an example to lesser women by shunning useless extravagance and ostentation. She could do this by dressing with dignified modesty and by wearing one and the same dress at all the receptions and balls which duty demands she should attend. Russians would be well advised to think more about curing their personal defects and those of their family circle and to speculate less about the brilliant future of their country in the world. 'The slumbering helmsman, instead of scrutinizing attentively and with clear-sighted eyes the banks, the islands and the land past which he is floating, still fixes a tired and senseless gaze on some dim mirage in the misty distance, although he has long ago lost any faith in that deceptive horizon.' The artist speaks in Gogol to the last, and like Belinsky, he reiterates that preaching is futile, if only because it is the least effective method of persuasion.

Belinsky hardly seems to have appreciated that *Correspondence with Friends* was little more than a bald schematic summary of Gogol's latest ideas, which he intended to incorporate in the purely imaginative setting designed for the second part of 'Dead Souls'. Unfortunately the artistic execution fell too far short of Gogol's hopes, for this was the manuscript which he later threw into the fire in a fit of despair.

We must admit that some of Gogol's social arguments are logically weak; others would have more relevance in a non-Christian type of society than in the Christian theocracy he

advocates. A Christian landowner, for instance, after long brooding and mental self-torture, would be almost certain to conclude
that it is sinful for him to own serfs. He would next want to
liberate them, and he thereby proves that Gogol's institutional
conservatism must inevitably be broken down by a consistent
Christian conscience. But a civilized pagan would not be worried
by such scruples provided that his slaves were justly treated.
Gogol loved Rome and wrote with enthusiasm about the warm
human relations, uniting landowners, farmers and workmen,
which he had observed in Italy—relations which, he claimed,
'could heal the sore of class enmity from which Western Europe
suffers'. Perhaps a pagan strain in Gogol's own mixed Ukrainian
blood, a half-conscious sympathy for the Graeco-Roman tradition of which Rome showed him so many splendid relics,
prompted his argument in favour of maintaining the Russian
status quo, if it could only be ennobled by a regenerated race of
wiser and more self-disciplined human beings. He spoke thus
to Annenkov in a conversation about the perfected Russian
landowners whom he had conceived to animate the second part
of *Dead Souls*, characters who combined Greek enterprise and
inventiveness with solid Russian common sense and Russian
readiness to obey commands from their superiors.

However that may be, Belinsky saw nothing in Gogol's book
except what he wanted to see, a plea for quietist political conservatism linked with the barren ritual of the Orthodox Church.
For him these were red rags to a bull, symbols of a return to
that intolerable stagnation and darkness against which he had
struggled all his life. Annenkov, who was staying with Belinsky
in a German watering-place at the time, relates how Belinsky's
face turned white after reading part of Gogol's book, and how,
without saying a word, he retired to his room. There, on the
spur of the moment, he composed his furious letter. Since it was
written outside Russia, Belinsky could afford to let himself go,
and he made the utmost of his opportunity. The article on
Gogol's book, which he published in *The Contemporary*, is tame
and tepid in comparison.

Starting with an exposé of his own sectarian individualistic
version of Christian ethics, rather similar to Tolstoy's final
phase, Belinsky's letter introduced a striking argument to prove
the natural atheism of the Russian people.

'Christian doctrine saved people only before it was organized

into a church and founded on Orthodoxy. The true sense of
Christ's words emerged again in the philosophic movement of
the last century. That is why a Voltaire, extinguishing by ridicule the European bonfires of fanaticism and ignorance, was
more a son of Christ, part of his flesh and blood, than any of
your priests, metropolitans and patriarchs, Eastern or Western.
Can it be that you do not realize this? And how could you, the
author of *Dead Souls* and *The Inspector*, sincerely sing a hymn to
the Russian clergy, setting it immeasurably higher than the
Catholic Church? . . . Do you not realize that our clergy is
universally despised by Russian society and by the common
people? . . . According to you, Russians are the most religious
people in the world; what a lie! Religion is based on piety,
obedience and fear of God, but a Russian pronounces God's
name while he scratches himself. . . . Examine them more
intently and you will discover the contrary, that they are by
nature a deeply atheistic people. True, they are extremely
superstitious, but without a trace of religion. There is no
mystical exaltation in their nature; they have too much common sense and clarity of mind for that, and thence may spring
the immensity of their historic destiny. A religious state of mind
has not even developed in the clergy . . . the majority of
whom are more remarkable for their fat bellies, scholastic
pedantry and barbaric ignorance. They are models of indifference in matters of faith. Only the sectarians are religious phenomena, and they are so contrary in spirit to the mass of the
people and so insignificant in numbers. . . .

'I will not enlarge on your dithyramb about the loving links
uniting the Russian people to its rulers. . . . But I make one
comment. When a European, especially a Catholic, is seized by
the religious impulse, he becomes an unmasker of tyranny, like
the Jewish prophets, accusing the strong ones of injustice. With
us, on the contrary, if a man (even a decent one) is afflicted by
the disease, known to psychiatrists as religious mania, he at
once pays more tributes to earthly gods than to the heavenly
one, oversteps all limits so that the earthly God may wish to
reward his servile zeal, and thereby compromises himself in the
eyes of society. . . . In literature alone, despite our Tartar
censorship, is there life and a forward movement. That is why
we esteem so highly the profession of letters, why literary
success comes so quickly even to slight talent. . . . And our

public is right in this respect. They see in Russian writers their
leaders, protectors and saviours from Russian autocracy,
orthodoxy, and national character. That is why they are ready
to forgive a writer for an inferior book, but they will never
forgive him a harmful one.' (Letter to Gogol, 15 July 1847.)

Perhaps the most remarkable feature of this letter, arising
from his diagnosis of Russian atheism, is the priestly rôle which
Belinsky insists on handing over to the Russian intelligentsia.
They will be the new moral leaders of society, so long as they fulfil
the confidence reposed in them as guides, philosophers and
friends. Belinsky accused Gogol of betraying the Russian people
by preaching submission to Church and State. Gogol, with equal
sincerity, claimed, in so doing, to be the champion of their
essential spiritual interests. In fact Belinsky approved only one
side of Gogol, and he could not conceal his sense of personal
outrage, when the unsuspected reverse side rose to the surface.
Gogol's crime was not that he had betrayed Russia, but that he
had betrayed Belinsky's own ideal version of Gogol as he
wanted him to be, a permanent social rebel, a consistent
satirist and atheist.

VIII

Whatever wider meaning he attached to the diffusion of
culture and scientific knowledge, as driving forces of human
civilization, Belinsky clung to his faith in the spiritual domination of exceptional personalities, and explicitly rejected the
mystic belief in the common people which he at one time shared
with the radical Slavophils and Socialists. At every stage he
reverted to Peter the Great as the model ruler for Russia. Cosmopolitan culture he found blank, featureless and repugnant;
international solidarity he never even considered in any concrete sense. But the sordid facts of Christianity in Russia, after
nearly a thousand years of Tsars and Metropolitans, led him to
question the viability of Christian ethics as a whole, as well as
to reject its supernatural side. Thus, in becoming a social
psychologist, Belinsky moved a step in the direction of the
English Utilitarians, but without succumbing to their facile
rationalization of human motives. Why, he asked, this perpetual
call to altruism, self-denial, self-sacrifice, if instead of harmonizing the impulsive and complicated Russian nature, it
makes demands which cramp and exasperate unalterable

human egoism? Is there no other way of turning egoism, the source of all evil, into the source of every good? If coarse animal self-assertion separates and antagonizes people, can it not be transformed into its opposite, into a force which unites and draws people together? 'Is egoism less capable of being transformed than other equally strong natural instincts, which are at one with it—personal ambition or sexual passion? Surely love, sympathy and respect are also manifestations of egoism, not a suppressed and mutilated egoism, but one which has been vigorously trained and adjusted to recognized moral needs?' And must this achievement remain confined to a few spiritual athletes? 'In spite of centuries of commands to love one's neighbour as oneself, have we so much as five people who would feel upset by blows which do not fall on their own backs?' It looked as if the impossible and monstrously artificial command to practise universal love—prolonged and harped on beyond human endurance—had slid over by degrees into cold indifference or smouldering hatred, ready to burst out at any opportunity into violent destructive storms of rage.

If only government and society would face the stubborn fact that most human beings are by nature ingrained but not intractable egoists, they would be less inclined to underestimate or shirk their own big educational responsibilities. Ramming a a code of social principles down their throats was a time-honoured method of goading recalcitrant Russian citizens into a course of action. But by intensifying the resentful cynicism of its victims, that method progressively handicapped its own efficiency. Therefore Belinsky started to contend that the most effective civic training could never come from church or state, but only from human beings without a civic axe to grind, and most effectively from the guiding hands of men of genius, like Pushkin or Gogol, reinforced by a devoted intellectual priest-hood, consisting of people like himself.

In its alluring but extravagant expectations this argument bears some resemblance to the claims of Communist intellectual aristocrats today. But attempts to identify Belinsky and the Communist élite in other respects are not at all convincing. In the first place, he resolutely opposed pushing intellectuals or artists into any organized political rôle; they could work best when left in peace. Of course, if they lacked the minimum pre-requisites for any fruitful work, they would first have to fight for them; and if all the healthy instincts of a free society capitulated to overwhelming force or anarchy, a self-respecting intelligentsia would endeavour to hold the last line of defence before it perished. But struggles about conditions of work derived their sense from its need for quality. Moreover Belinsky conceived the function of an 'educator', important though it was, to be an auxiliary and modest one. He never played with the idea of regimenting intellectuals as a crusading army, or as the permanent police force goading on the victims of a comprehensive and codified national programme. Unless they remained self-effacing, humble and above all a-political, they could never be whole-hearted devotees of science and art. They could not, to use a Christian analogy, serve God and Mammon, or a God-Caesar. The moment they enrolled under a political banner, they would forfeit their principal *raison d'être*. Therefore the comforting cocksureness of the obedient Communist could never be theirs.

Ultimately the kind of intelligentsia conceived by Belinsky could only be recruited from people with enough moral courage to face invincible unpopularity. Not many talents would long live up to such exacting standards. Apart from this intrinsic hardship, common to most ideals, Belinsky's argument suffers from an insurmountable weakness in lending itself to adaptation for ulterior motives. It played too easily into the hands of any ambitious autocrat or popular dictator, who needed a fresh pretext to mask the exercise of spiritual tyranny over the multitude for whose benefit he claimed to govern.

Belinsky never faced this issue squarely. It shattered his happy dream that a gifted minority, without any political or economic axe to grind, should guide a well-intentioned government and trustful people in climbing further up the tortuous path of civilized virtue. At times Belinsky seems to have inclined towards a drastically simplified faith in human perfectibility, seeing as a better world one in which healthy boisterous Russians would play a leading part, from which effete Persians and corrupt Chinese had been finally eliminated. For, he asserted, 'education cannot possibly improve people in whom there is no longer a germ of vital growth'. Applied to Persians or Chinese it would, he said, 'only make their innate vices more refined, calculating and perverse.' We should recall that he described Peter as 'a divinity, rousing us to life.'

This messianic *motif* in favour of the Russian elect hardly does justice to Belinsky in his more balanced phases. It sprang from the extremely flimsy notion that Russians possessed a special quality of universal virtue denied to other Europeans or Asiatics. Yet many of the more patriotic Russian intellectuals were tinged with this half-conscious obsession. Belinsky had tentatively suggested that Russia would move forward when her aristocracy was transformed into a bourgeoisie. Pisarev, liking the theme of innate Russian virtue thwarted by cruel circumstances, went a stage further, and rejoiced in advance about the immediately ennobling effect of western education on Russian businessmen. The large-minded Russian man of affairs, he urged, unlike the more acquisitive European, would quickly learn to see the folly and dangerous example of unscrupulous private greed; he would start to identify his own long-term interests with the personal welfare of his employees!

Undoubtedly Belinsky's fury for rational clarity never managed to dispel a diffuse mysticism about the future of his native land. Such fantasies were for him a legitimate sport or perhaps an indispensable drug. Yet he guarded himself, though he could not guard his followers, from jumping to wild unwarranted conclusions. It remains to Belinsky's credit that his intellectual honesty preserved a tinge of healthy scepticism even when he allowed his imagination to run riot; and when he could forget for a moment about the Russian enigma he could become as sane as the most scientific positivist, without being half as dull and narrow-minded. This is evident from a letter which he wrote to Botkin in February 1847, less than a year before his death. In it he indicated that he had outgrown French philosophy in the same way as previously he had embraced and finally discarded the more formidable German metaphysicians. Both, having taught him their purely disciplinary lesson, had outlived their usefulness. 'Let metaphysics go to the devil', he now proclaims; '. . . To liberate science from the ghosts of transcendentalism and theology, to demarcate the boundaries of the human mind, those within which its activity is fruitful; to cut it off once and for all from operating in the spheres of fantasy and mysticism—that is what the founder of a new philosophy should do, but that is what Auguste Comte cannot do, though together with many other remarkable minds he, makes it easier for the right person to succeed. . . . For

Comte annihilates metaphysics, not as a science of transcendental absurdities, but as a science of the laws of the mind. For him the ultimate science, the science of sciences, is physiology. He thereby shows that both philosophy and history are equally alien to his nature, that the only sphere of knowledge open to him is mathematics and natural science.'

It may seem odd that such an impassioned rationalist as Belinsky should finally emerge as the first modern Russian to state a firmly reasoned case for the liquidation of all system-building philosophy. But that is the upshot of what he did, confirming thereby the sceptical vigilance of Hume, and forestalling the vision of Tolstoy in his more lucid moments. He concluded that scientific thought derives its value as much from setting boundaries to intellectual knowledge as from enlarging its small sphere of certainty. And in so doing, he pointed to the unfettered possibilities of the unknown sphere, where a liberated imagination is entitled to reign supreme. We should be sanguine enough to hope that in the long run, Belinsky's present motivated popularity in the Soviet Union may lead to more appreciation of his far-ranging perspicacity, which the politically-guided approach to him has tended to obscure.

NICOLAS GOGOL

From a portrait by A. Ivanov

CHAPTER III

THE ORIGINAL SLAVOPHILS

I

SOVIET LINKS WITH THE SLAVOPHILS

Most Russian publicists, unless they were Slavophils themselves, have habitually underestimated or misrepresented the Slavophil movement. The more 'scientific' European historian has been puzzled or irritated by its enigmatic character, by its stubborn evasion of any precise definition formulated in normal historical terms. Its champions, even more than its enemies, have done their best to pin it down to formulae, though to contradictory ones. Yet it was born, and still remains, a motive mercurial faith, a fluctuating Protean impulse, which slips out of every attempt to crystallize it in any single intelligible doctrine or any consistent programme of action. Herzen's words about the darker side of its emotional origin apply to its whole stormy course: 'Slavophilism, not as a theory or a teaching, but as an indignant national feeling, as a dark memory and mass instinct, as a reaction against overwhelming foreign influence, already existed at the time when Peter the Great shaved off the first Boyar's beard.' Those nominalists who would neatly confine the Slavophil phenomenon to a short-lived esoteric fashion, set by a few patriotic aristocrats after the Napoleonic Wars, would do well to consider its previous incarnations and even more its later reappearance in unexpected historical shapes. The heretic martyr, Avvakum, was a remote progenitor of Khomyakov. The fierce but essentially conservative tenacity of the Sectarians and Old Believers, all fundamentally Slavophil by temperament (if not in conscious thought) continues to echo in those eruptions of nostalgia and in that more calculating xenophobia, which complicate the progress of the Soviet Union, the only major country in the world which prevents its citizens by law from marrying any foreigner.[1]

The Soviet approach to the Slavophils, especially to their pan-Orthodox extremes, has been more gingerly in theory than it has been in practice. That is why it can best be demonstrated

[1] Decree of Supreme Soviet, February, 1947.

by reference to recent historical events. The discerning literary historian, D. S. Mirsky, observed in the early twenties that Moscow had never been so *national* as since she became the seat of the International. He might have added—and perhaps he meant—that Russian nationalism, through its Byzantine legacy, had often exerted an international appeal, but never with such marked effect as since it switched from Orthodox Christianity to a more universal Orthodox Communism, which appeals most to those who know it least, and therefore finds devoted champions throughout the world.

In order to make the horrors of the Revolution seem worth while, it was imperative to wipe out the past, to start the new era with a clean blank sheet. Thus Bolshevik policy demanded at the start that the new nationalism should appear to have condemned the old beyond recall and severed every link with it. These calculations were upset when international revolution failed to spread. Bolshevik leaders then perforce fell back on building a strong 'Socialist Fatherland' within the reduced borders of the Soviet Union. An atavistic return to ancient policies and habits, if called by various new and suggestive names, may for a time create the comforting impression that one is moving forwards rather than backwards. By designedly industrializing their country at break-neck speed, the Bolsheviks were of course moving forward technically, but in their policy they reverted to methods which Peter the Great had used two centuries before—with one important difference. Whereas Peter had aimed at Europeanizing Russia, the Bolsheviks aimed at converting Europe—and the whole world—to their own Soviet Orthodoxy, a creed which, despite its novel European slogans and *furor technicus*, reverted in Bolshevik hands to more distant features of the Russian past. The crusading ferocity, heresy-hunting, the fanatical zeal, counterbalanced by love of torture and casuistry, which distinguished medieval Christianity, and reached its most Russian phase in the reign of Ivan the Terrible, seemed to come to life again in the twentieth century.

Indeed the underlying political continuity between Russian history before and after the Revolution, between the Moscow, Petersburg and Soviet periods, became so striking—and as a disciplinary drill so advantageous to the government—that it soon became respectable to talk about it in suitable up-to-date language. The moral heritage of the Revolution had been quickly transformed. Keen Bolshevik idealists turned into astute business-managers and place-hunters. This was a partial reconciliation with the familiar past, which needed to be camouflaged as another great step forward. Judicious Soviet intellectuals were encouraged to draw more overtly on the rich spiritual capital of their nineteenth-century ancestors. Of course the radical Westernizers took pride of place, carefully interpreted as forerunners of world-brotherhood between a Westernized Russia and a revolutionary West. But Tsars were praised as well as rebels. Ivan the Terrible and Peter were both revived as heroic figures, though each had merely to fulfil a transitory historic task in building up the Russian state. The more complex Slavophils could not be fitted in so categorically, but they were no longer dismissed as before in a few scornful phrases. We find a solid academic confirmation of this revised Soviet attitude in N. L. Rubinstein's *Russian Historiography* (1941). Here the Slavophils come in for the usual, now rather perfunctory, reproach about their 'unscientific' brand of nationalism. But they are allowed to atone for this by virtue of having drawn attention to the hidden treasures of Russian folk-lore and the sturdy force of Russian national character.

Unfortunately the revival of these amiable Slavophil qualities has been quite overshadowed by the more pan-Orthodox elements of Soviet nationalism, and by a deliberate but scarcely noticed absorption of the Orthodox Church into the framework of Soviet organizations. Everyone knows that the Bolsheviks started off by persecuting Christians of every denomination, especially the Orthodox clergy, as Tsarist counter-revolutionaries and 'enemies of the people', *i.e.* of the Soviet régime. But after a long period of trial and error the clumsy anti-God campaigns still failed to exterminate Russian Christians, and ended in a tacit admission of error by the Soviet Government. This admission became effective when the Party reversed its tactics on the 'religious front'. The 1936 Constitution of the U.S.S.R. formally conceded 'freedom of religious worship and freedom of anti-religious propaganda' (Article 24). In 1939 *Bezbojnik*, the monthly organ of the Militant Atheists' League,[1] published a noteworthy interview with the Orthodox Patriarch of Georgia, in which this eminent divine expressed his opinion

[1] *Bezbojnik*, No. 21, 1939.

that a powerful religious revival was at hand, but one which would fuse with Communism, since Communist ideals did not contradict Christian doctrine. Moreover, since 1934 Pokrovsky's text-books, with their strictly Marxia nclass-war interpretation of Russian history, were banned from the Soviet educational curriculum, and a new group of adaptable scholars was set to re-write history. One reason given for Pokrovsky's disgrace was that he had neglected to point out 'the progressive quality of Christianity as compared with the heathen barbarism of ancient Russia'.[1] Such incidents showed how far the Soviet rulers were prepared to go in order to mobilize Christians, especially Christian leaders, on their side, after having vainly done their utmost to liquidate them by administrative measures. Undoubtedly the new policy succeeded much better than its predecessor. During the last world war the major Christian communities in Russia, including the Baptists, appear to have loyally supported the Soviet state in the hope that it would prove to be a lesser evil for them than Hitlerite Germany.

In the winter of 1942, when the German armies were near to Moscow, and Russia's fate was hanging in the balance, there suddenly appeared under the imprint of the Moscow Patriarchate a sumptuous publication entitled *The Truth about Religion in Russia*. It consisted of a symposium written by various highly-placed members of the Orthodox clergy, with a preface by the Acting Patriarch, Sergei. The first part bore the title 'The Russian Church is loyal to its Motherland'; the second part contained lurid illustrated accounts of how Russian churches and monasteries had been violated by the 'German Fascist crusaders'. Though much of the book was skilfully designed and timed to enlist the sympathy of foreign Christians in favour of Soviet Russia, it also marked a more advanced stage in the reintegration of the Orthodox Church into the larger national Orthodoxy of the Soviet Union. Significantly enough, the book made no mention of the 'Living Church', or any of the Christian sects, formerly preferred by the Bolsheviks for their intensely anti-governmental spirit. It looked as if the Soviet Government had fallen back on the old Imperial tradition of Orthodoxy as a pillar of the State. Of course the content of both had changed, but 'la forme entraîne toujours le fond avec elle'. Soviet citizens, if they insisted on remaining Christians, would be least

[1] *Malaya Sovyetskaya Entsiklopediya*, vol. 8, p. 386.

dangerous, if not positively useful to the state, as members of a single national Church. To make sure of this, the reconstituted Holy Synod was linked with the central government by the creation of a new Council for Orthodox Church Affairs under the U.S.S.R. Council of Peoples' Commissars (October 1942).

These skilful steps reinforced the efforts made by well-meaning foreign clergymen, like the notorious Dean of Canterbury, to propagate Communism as the latest fulfilment of Christianity, rather than as the reign of anti-Christ. To the Communists either interpretation was equally good so long as it roped in more minds to support current Soviet policy. Meanwhile the Soviet rulers made no pretence that they were themselves erring sheep returned to the Orthodox fold. Even the editors of *The Truth about Religion in Russia* managed to give vent to the following inconspicuous plaint: 'It is well known that the Communist Party's ideology is anti-religious, and of course the Orthodox Church is grieved by this circumstance.'[1]

The Red Army (now re-styled the Soviet Army) pursued a more direct line of nationalist evolution. Gradually all the old officer ranks, including those of General and Marshal, were re-introduced, purged of the odium attached to them in revolutionary days. Military smartness and the old Prussian discipline rose to a premium. A decree of 1943 ordered Soviet officers to wear gold-braided epaulettes similar to those worn on the former Imperial uniforms. Occasionally the Army was perfunctorily reminded that Soviet patriotism had nothing to do with nationalism, but was the best safeguard against it, because the national aims of the peoples of the Soviet Union coincided with the international aims of humanity.[2] But the international note sounded somewhat ritualistic. Moreover, that stirring old dirge the *Internationale* had recently been scrapped as a state anthem, and replaced by the pompous *Hymn of the Soviet Union*. In any case, humanity outside the Soviet Union was not, so to speak, consulted about its own aims. When Stalin announced to the Red Army at the height of the German advance: 'May the virile image of your great ancestors inspire you in this war', and Prince Alexander Nevsky, together with the Tsarist generals Suvorov and Kutuzov (who fought against the French Revolution and Napoleon), took their places in the Soviet

---

[1] *Pravda o Religii v Rossii*, p. 26, Moscow, 1942.
[2] Broadcast Talk by A. Fadeyev (25 July 1943).

pantheon, it seemed that the Imperial Russian Renaissance would go full steam ahead.

But that was not to be. The Party in distress had pulled the patriotic string, but the cult of vanished splendour which it unleashed had gone too far. It may have helped to win the War, but it must not help to obliterate Communist prestige. What the Party required from the more glowing pages of Russian history and what many of their Soviet subjects found and valued there proved to be as incompatible as fire and water. Since the War ended, those who 'leapt back into the past too willingly' have had to pay the penalty for their 'political blindness'. Silence has descended on the virtues of the Orthodox Church, we hear little more about the historic traditions of the Army, but we are given an endless recital of dazzling and heroic feats performed by the 'great and wise' Communist Party. 'Ideological workers' on every front are instructed to re-arm themselves with Marxist-Leninist philosophy, and thus to drive out the 'obsolete things of yesterday'. Writers are persuaded to treat the real present as though it did not exist, and the ideal future (seen through Bolshevik eyes) as though it had already arrived.

II

Whether applied to past or present tendencies the epithet Slavophil is a convenient label which has stuck, but it can often mislead through being a partial misnomer. Understood literally, it should denote a preferential love for Slavs, rising into a conviction that they were racially the Chosen People, and betraying symptoms of a recurrent spiritual disease familiar to many students of history. In fact the original nineteenth-century Slavophils showed few of these distressing symptoms, which became most prominent among the later pan-Slavs. On the whole the early Slavophils opposed both racial and national megalomania, and they recoiled from the flat insipid taste of universal benevolence even among their Slav blood-brothers. Though impelled by some intuition of Russian singularity, hatred or distrust of foreigners proved in the long run to be far more powerful and precise emotions among them than love of Slavs. But most Slavophils understood foreigners in a peculiar sense. They signified, not strangers, or people of an alien race and language—hundreds of alien races lived side by side within the Russian Empire—but people who adhered to alien religions. Even then, it was not enough to be a fellow-Christian, for Christianity remained suspect unless it was the Russian kind of Christianity. Roman Catholics as rivals, and Moslems as hereditary enemies, were almost equally anathema to Orthodoxy. Therefore the Slavophils showed scant sympathy for their racial cousins the Poles, because the Poles were Catholics instead of Orthodox, and Danilevsky,[1] the first systematic pan-Slav, went so far as to assert that the racially unrelated Greeks should rightfully belong to the Russian Empire, since they professed the Orthodox faith.

Some ingenious historians have suggested that centuries of Tartar rule, of humiliating forced compromise with Tartar brutality and cunning, instilled in advance into Russian minds an ineradicable suspicion and dread of all other foreign countries with whom they subsequently entered into contact. Considering how many foreigners (other than Tartars) first marched into Russia with invading armies, such a natural Russian response to them should occasion no surprise. It is more surprising that well-founded dislike and fear of foreigners wrestled for mastery in Russian minds with admiration and wonder, with a craving to emulate that outside world which treated them so roughly. This later Russian attitude to Western nations, especially towards the French and Germans, turned into an ambivalent tension of explosively mixed feelings.

Eighteenth-century noblemen, who followed the lead of their Empress in worshipping at the shrine of French culture in its heyday, managed to ape and occasionally surpass the French in a wide range of refinements, varying from political theory to table-manners. Their admiration was sincere, and often mingled with weary contempt for their own country. Nor were they unique in this respect. Germany, where Frederick the Great had set the fashion, already swarmed with outwardly polished Francophils, and numerous miniature Versailles set a new tone of elegance among the beer-taverns of the Teutonic

---

[1] N. Y. Danilevsky (1822–1885), as a young man a member of the Petrashevsky group, later an authority on Darwinism and on the habits of fish, is best remembered for his book *Rossiya i Evropa* (St. Petersburg, 1871). Though it added little to the existing stock of Slavophil ideas, it set them down for the first time in 'scientific' terminology.

grand-duchies. But these Gallic arts and graces rarely penetrated beyond the court and aristocracy in either country. In
Russia the people as a whole were scarcely aware that the French
existed, until Napoleon invaded their country. And by that time
France had fallen to a low ebb in the esteem of cultured Russians, for she had changed abruptly from a fairy princess into
a man-eating ogre. Bloody revolution had been followed by
Napoleon's insatiable orgy of invasion and military conquest,
and that ended in the retreat from Moscow.

Germans, unlike the French, were never loved in Russia.
Yet their impact on the Russian people was broader and more
insidious, because it did not start as a stream of enlightenment
from an outside source, but imposed itself from within, through
the grip of Peter's imported German officialdom. At most the
Germans were coldly and rather enviously admired by professional Russian bureaucrats and generals, who trusted that an
industrious imitation of German methods would yield to them
the precious secrets of administrative and military efficiency.
While many educated Russians paid tribute to superior German
skill, they were rarely prepared to pay the German price in
order to acquire it for themselves. Meanwhile the masses went
on quietly loathing German officials and bailiffs, who bullied
and squeezed them in the name of the Russian government or
landowner. Their callous rigidity and meticulous thoroughness,
spreading through the Empire under the guise of Western
discipline and up-to-date organization, could hardly fail to
recall dark memories of the Tartar tyranny, and undoubtedly
intensified the average Russian's instinctive suspicion of all that
personified the State. Nor should we forget that, since 1762, all
the Romanov rulers were descended from Catherine II, a pure
German, and from her husband Peter III, German on his
father's side, and Russian only through his mother, a daughter
of Peter the Great. It was hard for such a thoroughly Germanized dynasty and court to sustain their part as Byzantium's
Russian heirs.

Gogol, who unintentionally turned into a moral leader of the
Slavophil movement, expressed this more than national hatred
in no measured terms. He summed up Germany as 'nothing but
a stinking belch of the coarsest tobacco and the most disgusting
beer'. Less violently abusive of France, he none the less deplored
contemporary France, because she had given birth to 'the

plague of revolution', and to that frivolous contempt for traditional beauty and grandeur, that cynical destructive abuse of
freedom which was degrading modern Europeans.

In preferring traditional Europe, birthplace of bold scientific
thought and vital art, to the more recent Europe of political
phobias and social disintegration, the Slavophils showed that in
a fundamental sense they were not Slavophils at all, but in
their aspirations belonged to the most cultured and discriminating group of Westernizers. They wanted to pick up the delicate
threads at the point where Europe had broken them off, and to
weave them into the primeval Russian pattern. But first they
needed to re-discover that pattern in all its freshness by forming
a revised picture of the Russian past. Most Slavophils agreed
with the Westernizer Chaadayev that Russia's present was
intolerable. Only they indignantly dissented from his next
sweeping dictum that her past was a blank sheet of paper.
They preferred to build upon the past foundation an attractive
legend based on a few pleasant facts about pre-Petrine Russia.
'The Slavophils had their ears attuned to the Liberty Bell of
Novgorod the Great, their eyes fixed on the parliament of Kiev,
on independent Communes, and the free assembly of the
Zaporozhian Cossacks writing their furious letters of challenge
to the Sultan of Turkey.'[1]

In giving rein to their nostalgic impulse, the Slavophils
showed scant concern for historical accuracy, but, to do them
justice, they rarely pretended to be scientific historians. The
facts which they selected were not often false, but they were
fragments of the whole; enough to help the Slavophils to build
the only kind of history they ever wanted, namely a powerful
legend in a continuing process of creation. Thus they deliberately endowed the Russian past with all the vivid colour and
charm of a saga, an interrupted drama ready to be resumed in
the approaching act by keen compatriots, eager to play a part
worthy of their illustrious ancestors' approval. To a large extent
the Slavophils succeeded in this endeavour. They created a
historical myth, which to this very day exerts a curious fascina-
tion over responsive minds.

From the outset the Slavophils' flattering interpretation of the
Russian past excited and pleased the majority of so-called
Russian patriots. Also it fed their growing appetite for a quick

[1] Sir J. Maynard: *Russia in Flux*, p. 162.

realization of Russia's still more fabulous future. 'The vanity
of Russians blinds them to the monstrous cruelty of their
government', de Custine observed in 1839. 'A nation in such a
hurry to play a part in the world theatre, that she would rather
be nothing and act at once, than slowly prepare herself in
fruitful obscurity to become something which could act later.'
A few of the gifted Westernizers saw the immense political
blunders to which this self-indulgent fantasy could lead.
Chaadayev and Chernyshevsky both contested it vigorously.
Herzen deprecated the Slavophils' 'childish devotion to a
childish period of our history', but after 1848 he himself turned
his back on Europe and followed the guiding star of Slavophil
aspirations, though he remained a sworn enemy of the Orthodox
Church and state.

Not only was the Slavophil legend at variance with important
historical facts, passed over by Slavophil bias, but undiscrimina-
ting aspirants, who found the legend fascinating, failed to
observe that the clumsy official attempt to realize it in political
action was leading to wholly unexpected and deplorable
results. If the Orthodox Slav peoples were, as Slavophils
claimed, so markedly distinguished from other Europeans
through their uncontaminated Christian humility and their
warm sense of brotherly love, why were contemporary Russians
turning so quickly into a mass of boastful sabre-rattling patriots,
breathing fire and slaughter against godless and degenerate
foreign infidels?

Moreover that gentle dove-like picture of the Russian
people could least of all survive the test of honest historical
scrutiny. Intelligent Slavophils struggled to correct these
demagogic diversions of their faith, and started to use the
weapon of ridicule in self-defence. Herzen preserved an anec-
dote about a patriotic banquet in St. Petersburg, towards the
end of which an excited Slavophil poet jumped to his feet and
improvised bombastic verses, reaching their climax in a
solemn vow that he would drink the blood of Germans and
Magyars. A humorous guest seized the occasion to pick up his
silver fruit-knife and announce: 'Excuse me, gentlemen, but I
have just remembered that my piano-tuner is a German. I
must go and slit his throat, but I'll be back in time for the
walnuts.'[1]

[1] Sir J. Maynard: *Russia in Flux*, p. 163.

III

Russian officialdom, in league with a few 'right-wing' Slavo-phils, managed to systematically pervert original Slavophil teaching. The most persistent misconceptions which this perversion bred are threefold:

(1) that the Slavophils were indistinguishable from ultra-nationalist die-hards, or what is now dubbed 'reactionaries'.

(2) that they themselves created a major political movement with clear-cut political aims;

(3) that they were Chauvinists who hated Europe, without really knowing her, and desired above all else to isolate Russia from any extension of European influence.

All three are equally untrue. Neither the Kireyevsky brothers nor the Aksakovs, neither Khomyakov nor Samarin, could possibly be called conservatives, *i.e.* loyal supporters of the prevailing social and political order in Russia. They were all opponents of Nicolas I's autocracy; they all wanted serfdom to end (for practical considerations of economic advantage as well as through moral conviction). The journals in which Ivan Kireyevsky published his writings were one after another suppressed by the Government. Khomyakov was obliged to write many of his articles in French, and published them abroad in order to evade the nervous and stereotyped ecclesiastical censorship. Both the Aksakovs were constantly at loggerheads with the censors, the Ministry of Foreign Affairs, and the notorious 'Third Section' (Secret Police). In 1848 they underwent a harsh cross-examination about the Slavophils' alleged connections with Western liberalism, communism, and Western pan-Slavs. Koshelëv noted that the Governor-General of Moscow, Count Zakrevsky, 'could not abide us Slavophils, called us "reds" and even "communists" (after 1848). Even the careful civil servant, Yury Samarin, was astonished to find that Petersburg circles cherished the most fantastic suspicions about the subversive political aims of the Moscow group.

Far more than domestic issues were at stake in the Slavophils' essentially anti-conservative outlook. The dynastic principles of the Holy Alliance, to which Nicolas I remained unswervingly loyal, demanded Russian support of the Austrian Empire, which contained large and varied Slav minorities, including Czechs, Slovaks and Ruthenians. To spread ideas of racial and

religious union between all Slavs was tantamount to inciting
many of them to rebel against their legitimate rulers. This was
plainly sacrilege against the Holy Alliance, even if it proved to
be a gain to the Russian Empire. An exception was made for the
liberation of Slav subjects within the Turkish Empire, only
because the Turks were Mahometans; and flaming hatred of
Turks, stimulated by more or less perpetual propaganda and
sporadic wars against the Turkish infidel, formed an old-estab-
lished element in the Russian Empire's Christian tradition.
We can trace an analogy with today in that a ring of willy-nilly
Communist states has replaced the voluntary Holy Alliance,
while denunciation of the infidel has widened to cover any non-
socialist or heretically socialist state, which may be powerful or
bold enough to resist the progress of 'Orthodox' socialism under
the sheltering wing of the Soviet Empire.

Not only were the early Slavophils anti-conservative, but they
strenuously shunned all political entanglements, in order to
launch their broader human appeal. Arguing that history
moves forwards, not backwards, they pictured Russia as having
temporarily lost her way, because she had taken a wrong
turning on the road. She needed only to profit from her error,
return to the right road, and then continue straight ahead.
I. Kireyevsky explicitly stated that 'to restore the weak and dying
forms of Russian life would be absurd where it was not harmful'.
Strictly speaking, it was a deliberate part of Slavophil policy to
be without a political programme; it was enough for them to
face piecemeal the political implications of their social faith.
First and foremost they were men of the widest European culture, who struggled to free the embryonic Russian civilization
from the strait-jacket of the Russian bureaucratic state, from
the stranglehold of dense officials who choked her spiritual
vitality. Nearly all the leading Slavophils had travelled and
studied outside Russia. They respected and loved Europe for
her splendid civilization, though the latest political instability of Europe filled them with legitimate misgivings. Need
Russia follow the same unhappy and uncertain course?—they
asked. Could she not avoid shipwreck by steering her own
separate course, guided by a sense of her unique historical
constellation?

Although most Slavophils were, at least nominally, Orthodox
Christians and Khomyakov a brilliant lay theologian and

religious reformer, they showed far less concern for the niceties of Christian doctrine than for the unique spiritual qualities which, they claimed, could lift Russians above the Catholics and Protestants of Europe. Hence the Orthodox quality of faith seemed far more important to them than the Orthodox Church as an institution. One is tempted to say that the value of Orthodoxy in their eyes turned rather into a sacred manifestation of emergent Russian national character than into an organized form of Christianity. Unfortunately they defined Russian national character in such nebulous terms that they played into the hands of the mentally poverty-stricken group of pan-Slavs, who exploited them for blatantly Chauvinist aims.

Alarmed by the new spectacle of Russian political power after 1815, misinformed by biased Westernized Russians, foreign observers were far too prone from the start to identify all Slavophils with their nationalist exploiters, or to accept as true the ridicule and abuse showered on them by their allegedly more liberal up-to-date Westernizer opponents. Since Napoleon's wars had changed the face of Europe, a number of intelligent Europeans had thrown themselves into the study of international affairs and, among other things, 'discovered' Russia. A talented French writer, the Marquis de Custine, created a wide sensation by his book *La Russie en 1839*. He mentioned there a long discussion which he held in the English Club in Moscow with a certain 'philosophic Russian' (probably Chaadayev), but he does not appear to have met a single Slavophil.

His main practical conclusion was to urge vehemently that France should put no trust in any agreements with Russia, and to suggest that his country's national security would be much better safeguarded by a long-term alliance with Germany. 'If the Russians ever managed to conquer the West,' he wrote, 'they would hurry to leave their own frozen plains. One needs to have lived in that solitude without rest, that prison without a moment's leisure, in order to appreciate the liberty which one enjoys in the other countries of Europe. Whoever has seen this country at close quarters will be content to live anywhere else.' One-sided though he may have been in underestimating the strength and sincerity of the Slavophil internal opposition, he showed amazing insight into the policy of governmental

Russia and into Nicolas I's dangerously skilful handling of the national psychosis which contributed to the Crimean War. 'I fear nothing more than inflexible logic applied to politics. If France has known rather more material happiness in the last ten years, it is because the apparent absurdity presiding over her affairs is the result of a certain practical wisdom. . . . But Russian despotism is a false order, even as our republicanism is a false liberty. . . .' 'Une ambition désordonnée, immense, une de ces ambitions qui ne peuvent germer que dans l'âme des opprimés, et se nourrir que du malheur d'une nation entière, fermente au coeur du peuple russe. Cette nation, essentiellement conquérante, avide à force de privations, expie d'avance chez elle, par une soumission avilissante, l'espoir d'exercer la tyrannie chez les autres. La gloire, la richesse qu'elle attend, la distrait de la honte qu'elle subit, et pour se laver du sacrifice impie de toute liberté publique et personelle, l'esclave à genoux rêve la domination du monde. La Russia voit dans l'Europe une proie qui lui sera livrée tôt ou tard par nos dissensions; elle fomente chez nous l'anarchie dans l'espoir de profiter d'une corruption favorisée par elle, parce qu'elle est favorable a ses vues.'[1]

It is the early Slavophils' misfortune that, while foreigners often chose to see them as budding Russian Bismarcks, their compatriots in the Government suspected them, on the contrary, of pursuing the most sinister revolutionary plans. Their spiritual ancestry owed much to a European strain, but it derived from a more complex native blend than the plain reforming zeal of the politico-economic Westernizers. Of recent individual contributions to it, Schelling's was the most potent,

---

[1] Marquis de Custine: *La Russie en 1839*, vol. iv, pp. 466-7:

'An immense disorderly ambition ferments in the heart of the Russian people, one of those ambitions which can arise only in the feelings of oppressed people, and must be nourished by the misery of a whole nation. This nation, essentially militant, greedy as the result of privation, expiates in advance, by her own degrading submission, the hope of exercising tyranny over others. The glory, the wealth, which she expects, distract her from the shame which she endures; and in order to cleanse herself from the impious sacrifice of every liberty, public and personal, the prostrated slave dreams about conquering the world. Russia sees in Europe a prey which will sooner or later be handed over to her by our dissensions. She stirs up anarchy among us in the hope of profiting by a corruption which she favours, because it furthers her aims.'

but the romantic historian Karamzin as well as Gogol and Sergei Aksakov, came earlier and proved to be more lasting sources of inspiration.

Schelling, so unlike his compatriot Hegel, felt unaccountably attracted by the spacious lure of Russia. And his system of thought appeared to rescue religion from the ravages of philosophy, or rather, to find a method of running them in double harness. Such a congenial preoccupation endeared him to the hearts of many like-minded Russian intellectuals. His reputation among them reached its zenith during the skilful Schellingian propaganda of Prince Odoevsky (Chaadayev's Slavophil counterpart in the Moscow salons). Odoevsky asserted that, if Schelling had been bold enough to put his philosophy into practice, he would have joined the Orthodox Church. He encouraged a calm confidence in his country's future as a still youthful monarchical state, which had no cause to envy the over-complicated and precarious political structure of the modern West, and ran little risk of falling a victim to the vulgar obsessions of European economic expansion. Nevertheless, in a moment of honest doubt, he proposed that lazy unmethodical Russian landowners should be compelled to undergo stricter training and to pass a test for fitness to fulfil their administrative and agricultural duties. Otherwise he seems to have indulged in rather facile and self-satisfied speculation about 'brave new worlds' of civilization, which Russia alone would prove fit to conquer. The following is a reasonably exhilarating specimen. 'Europeans sense the approach of the Russian mind like sleepwalkers feel the lure of a magnetic force from which they recoil when they are awake. Europeans see this approach in the clumsy shape of a material conquest. There will be a Russian conquest of Europe, but it will be a spiritual one; for only Russia will be able to unite and give integrity to the chaos of European knowledge, to cast off the accumulated dust of every kind of dead authority which till now has stifled European intelligence . . . but in order to do all that, Russia must first learn to surpass all these authorities.'

Odoevsky gave rein to his lively imagination in composing a number of stories, pointing sometimes contradictory morals. In one of these a Russian Anglomaniac, who became a Benthamite, is shown to have improved his estate and increased his income tenfold. In another, a fantasy about the forty-fourth century (not the twentieth), he pictures the English nation going bankrupt, and selling their islands in a public auction, where they are bought by triumphant Russia. During this period, a rejuvenated China stands in the same heir-presumptive relation to Russia as nineteenth-century Russia did to Europe. Horses are as obsolete as railways. The problems of transport are solved. Everyone either flies or is painlessly propelled through tunnels by electric power. Odoevsky (like Khomyakov with his patent steam-engine) demonstrated that a Slavophil could be just as keen a champion of applied science as any Westernizer.

Odoevsky, whatever his merits as a popularizer of Schelling, was hardly more than an engaging but minor figure in the native sources of the Slavophil tradition. S. T. Aksakov, even more than Gogol, was a tower of strength to it. His half-imaginary memoirs have preserved a limpid classical picture of the vigorous patriarchal mode of life. No jarring notes of latent social discord or uneasy conscience mar the self-confident and self-contained life led by this small rural community of equally industrious masters and serfs. It is appropriate that two sons of this robust and devoted family became the leading publicists of the Slavophil movement in its later phases.

S. T. Aksakov had been a life-long friend and helper of Gogol. His son Konstantin grandiloquently compared Gogol to Homer, and praised *Dead Souls* as the only truly epic sequel to the Iliad and the Odyssey in modern European literature. Such a blatantly nationalist exaggeration infuriated Belinsky. Gogol himself complained bitterly to Annenkov that the satirical and destructive side of his work had always been glorified by Belinsky and the Westernizers, at the expense of his constructive Russian faith. True, he had revealed Russians to themselves, and that was anything but a pleasant process. But he intended the second part of *Dead Souls* to correct the brooding self-depreciation induced by a too literal reading of the first part, and to unfold his intense patriotic morality in all its glorious colours. In this he failed, but an observant reader can detect unmistakable signs of the same intention already in the first part of *Dead Souls*, especially in the famous invocation at the end: 'And you my Russia, are you not also speeding along like a *troika* which none can overtake? Is not the road smoking beneath your wheels, the bridges thundering as you cross them, and everything else being left behind; and the spectators, struck

by the portent, stopping to wonder whether you are not a
thunderbolt launched from heaven? What does that awe-inspiring progress of yours foretell? What unknown force lies hidden
in your mysterious steeds? Surely the winds themselves must
live in their manes, and every vein in their bodies be an ear
stretched to catch the heavenly message which bids them, with
iron-girt breasts and hoofs barely touching the earth as they
gallop, fly forward on a mission of God? Whither then are you
speeding, oh my Russia? Whither? Answer me. But no answer
comes. Only the strange sound of your collar-bells. Rent into a
thousand shreds, the air roars past you, for you are overtaking
the whole world, and one day you will force all nations, all
empires, to stand aside and give you way!'

Herzen observed that the Slavophils were apt to call *Dead
Souls* an apotheosis of Russia and to overpraise it as a national
epic, whereas their opponents, even when they admired it,
treated it as an anathema, a denunciation of Russian life.
'Great is the quality of a work of art which can survive un-
touched by every partisan interpretation. To regard it as an
apothesis is absurd—to see it merely as an anathema is unjust.
It contains words of reconciliation, premonitions and hopes . . .
but that does not prevent it from reflecting the present in all its
repulsive reality.'[1]

IV

Turning from the spiritual ancestors of the Slavophil movement
to its more conscious intellectual founders, the first though not
the most important place belongs to the brothers Ivan and Peter
Kireyevsky. Like the Aksakovs, members of an ancient line of
landowners, adhering to a strict tradition of public service, they
provided human channels for the flow of underground streams
which bore the accumulated urge of centuries of Russian social
experience; only at intervals and in a few open clearings did
their waters rise visibly to the surface. Even so, the Kireyevsky's
scanty and scattered writings revealed no more than glimpses of
the invisible source from which sprung their intricate conception of Russian civilization.

The father of Ivan and Peter Kireyevsky calls to mind the
more energetic and cultured type of landed aristocracy which
flourished in eighteenth-century England. An Anglophil

[1] A. Herzen : *Polnoe Sobraniye*, vol. 3, p. 34.

himself, without being an Anglomaniac, he yet remained so
devoutly Orthodox that he hunted through the Moscow book-
shops buying up copies of Voltaire's wicked works, solely in
order to throw them on a blazing bonfire. This zealously discriminate burning of books did not prevent him from collecting
an excellent international European library (he spoke five
languages) or from teaching half his male house serfs to read
and write. He strictly forbade the infliction of any corporal
punishment throughout his estates, and even reproached himself in his diary for having on one occasion lost his temper with
a servant. If his serfs needed to be punished, they were obliged
to undergo the chastening exercise of bowing to the ground
in front of ikons up to forty times or more. In his later years the
old Kireyevsky started a chemical laboratory in his country-
house, and on his deathbed he advised his sons to devote themselves to the study of chemistry, which he called a 'divine
science'. As might be expected, they never followed this last
piece of paternal advice, but they inherited their father's
strong moral sense and some of his eccentric habits; they
showed the same vigorous enquiring intelligence, more widely
if diffusely applied, and they retained throughout life an
unswerving loyalty to each other.

Ivan Kireyevsky (1806–1856) is often called the father of
the Slavophil movement, because most of the later Slavophils enlarged on some of the various lines of thought first
adumbrated by him. It is a mistake to shelve him as a stuffy
religious philosopher with whom none but Orthodox theologians can ever feel at home, though naturally his upbringing
coloured his mind in favour of Christianity in its Greek Orthodox expression. This prejudice often clouded his thought, and it
has in turn caused non-Christian thinkers to misjudge him as a
sort of freak Byzantine obscurantist. But much of Kireyevsky's
thought is original enough to stand on its own legs without the
support of any theological props. Moreover, he absorbed like a
sponge the latest flow of secular European ideas, and the
breadth of knowledge and culture which he assimilated would
have put many educated Europeans to shame. He was far more
at home in French and German affairs than the Westernizer,
Belinsky, who knew no German.

In 1830 he followed up his youthful infatuation with Hegel
by spending a year of study in Germany. This journey

resembled a pilgrimage to the sacred soil of European culture. Kireyevsky had nothing in common with those blasé young Russians who paraded their melancholy or boisterous ennui at the card-tables of German watering-places. 'Every minute of my life', he wrote to his sister from Berlin, 'I regard as if it were someone else's property, confided to me on my honour, a trust which I cannot lightly throw to the winds. Perhaps this attitude of mind will save me from futile behaviour and make me worthy of my noble and strong-minded brother.'[1]

He sent home to his sister notes of the more interesting lectures he attended, and expressed his delight with the Professor of Geography in Berlin. But Hegel at close quarters proved to be a bitter disappointment. 'He speaks abominably, coughs over almost every word, swallows half his sentences, and indistinctly mumbles the other half in a trembling plaintive voice.'[2] From Berlin he travelled eagerly to Dresden in order to hear Schelling's lectures, but this early Slavophil idol also turned out to have feet of clay. 'You won't receive my notes of Schelling's lectures', he wrote to his sister, 'because the mountain has given birth to a mouse.'

He tried to console himself with the stimulating reflection that he was at last surrounded by the leading minds of Europe. Nevertheless this sobering encounter with German philosophers in flesh and blood extended to all he saw of German public taste. Their theatre audiences especially appalled him. 'If you could only see what Germans admire,' he wrote, 'and with such ridiculous excitement. In spite of their more advanced education they are in the mass just as soulless and crude as the crowd which fills our theatres in Moscow. During a tragedy, every shout (most of all if uttered in the wrong place) immediately evokes applause. Every genuine direct appeal escapes their attention. In the main, the more the actors grow excited, the more bombastic their lines become, the more loudly they are applauded. The jokes the Germans like are monotonous and heavy. Nothing could be more stupid than a laughing German.' After his brother had joined him in the latter part of his stay, he wrote home, 'We are fed up to the neck with Germany . . . And to think that our compatriots, who are perhaps the only ones in Europe still capable of devoted enthusiasm, are called

[1] *Letters from Germany* (February 1830) : *Russkii Arkhiv*, No. 1, 1907.
[2] *Ibid.*

uncultured people.' In the tone of this invidious comparison, with its crescendo of national self-confidence, we can discern Kireyevsky's whole future in embryo.

On his return to Russia he ardently pushed forward his ambitious project to found a new journal called *The European*, for which he managed to secure support from such distinguished contributors as Baratynsky, Yazukov, Zhukovsky and Khomyakov. 'I gave it this title,' he told Pushkin modestly, 'not because I can already hope to make it European in its merits, but because I propose to fill it with articles more concerned with Europe than with Russia.' The first number duly appeared in 1832, but it was banned by the government after the second issue. Nicolas I himself had carefully read Kireyevsky's own article, 'The Nineteenth Century'. He commented in the margin that, although the article purported to deal with literature, it thinly disguised some dangerously subversive suggestions about high politics. Kireyevsky was thereupon forbidden to publish any further writings. He remained silent for eleven years.

Whatever his other limitations, Nicolas I had an unerring flair for maintaining political discipline, and from that point of view it is idle to dispute that he interpreted Kireyevsky's article correctly. Even in its brusque literary judgements the article defied conventional Russian taste; but its political implications plainly verged on treason.

Kireyevsky started by complaining that Russian literature was marred by a number of glaring defects, notably by 'a thirst for strong sensations and shocks, without any discrimination about their effect on the mind', a tendency to harp on 'actual realistic facts in all their nakedness', and on the whole by a prevalence of noisy enthusiasm over sensitive feeling. For us who know Russian literature best, not through coarse bestsellers, but by the well-sifted surviving classics, this complaint may seem at first sight puzzling and unjust, and in some respects more applicable to the cheap twentieth-century crime fiction of the West. But we should recall that at this time (January 1832) none of the subsequently world-famous Russian novels and stories had yet been written. Kireyevsky follows up this criticism by his daring announcement (and here he *outwesternizes* Belinsky) that the most characteristically national element in Russia represents nothing worth striving for, but rather the reverse: 'While it was victorious in Europe, Christianity suffered defeat in Russia. Russia, after proving herself incapable of spiritual cohesion, was obliged to go ahead with the formation of a crassly material unity.' She had to construct an enormous unwieldy Empire for the sole purpose of re-conquering her independence from the Tartars. 'Our unification sprang less from any expression of unanimous desire than from plain physical conjunction, brought together by brute force, and not alleviated by any redeeming touch of culture. . . . Our material hypertrophy has stultified a corresponding spiritual growth. That explains many things, including the reasons for the geographical immensity of Russia.'[1]

Consequently it was absurd for Russians to concentrate their minds on what is exclusively national. That meant in reality 'to persist in the absence of civilization, by forfeiting the advantage of European improvements. For whence can we acquire our culture except from Europe?' Nevertheless, so long as Western civilization had remained primarily religious and Catholic, it had been difficult for Russia to participate in it, because her roots lay elsewhere. This situation changed when the secular civilization of the eighteenth century rebelled against the organic development of its own past. It was true that the destructive movement had in its turn aroused in many European minds a renewed desire for harmony and continuity. 'But both the preceding phase of disruption and the latest tendency towards re-integration by force are equally hostile to the spirit of the centuries that went before.' The old culture of Europe had been inextricably bound up with an enduring system of gradual change. In order to take part in it, Russia would first have to live through the whole past life of Europe. But the new European doctrines were hostile to her old culture, and could exist without it. Therefore a people just beginning to learn, like the Russians, can promptly borrow such doctrines in their entirety, and graft them on to its existing state of affairs, without needing to prepare the ground in advance.

Kireyevsky's argument is a patchwork of ill-matched fragments from Chaadayev and German sources, relieved by some flashes of polemical brilliance. On the face of it, he is pouring cold water on Russian official nationalism by showing that the desire to be *national* has a valid *raison d'être* only when it does not

[1] I. Kireyevsky: *Sochineniya*, vol. i, p. 79, Moscow, 1861.

destroy culture, as in Russia it obviously does. Such a heretical statement was alone enough to damn him in the eyes of Nicolas I, and that does him credit. But in a more fundamental sense the article was a specious exercise of Hegelian dialectic applied to Russia's future advantage. Since Europe has become, both nationally and socially, a house divided against itself, the time is ripe for Russia to step in. The phase of antithesis (negation) for Europe is taken over as a positive thesis by Russia, who thereupon concocts a grand future synthesis of universal Russian-European civilization.

We in our later more prosaic age have witnessed the ghastly pitfalls to which these teutonic *jeux d'esprit* lead their devotees, if they play them too seriously. With Kireyevsky the wish was father to the thought when, in his previous article, 'Russian Literature in 1829', he had emphasized that Europe, apart from growing more chaotic, presented a scene of psychological paralysis. 'Political and moral progress have come to an end— Europe is like a dammed-up river which turns a once flourishing countryside into a stagnant marsh.' Yet none of the European countries can continue to live either in isolation or in suicidal conflict. 'The unity of Europe needs an undisputed centre, a single nation which will dominate the others by its political and intellectual superiority. Only two countries in the civilized world do not share in the prevailing state of paralysis; two young and fresh peoples breathe with hope. They are the United States of America and our country. But distance, and still more the one-sided character of America's Anglo-Saxon culture, make Europe pin all her hopes on Russia. The action of the most important European states on us has determined and formed our character, has made it truly European, and has thereby given us the means of reacting in our turn on the whole of Europe. . . . The supple and adaptable character of our people leads towards the same goal, so do our political interests and our geographical situation. The future of each European country depends on its conjunction with all the others—the future of Russia depends on herself alone. But Russia's destiny depends on the quality of her civilization; that is the condition and source of all advantages. When these benefits become fully ours, we shall share them with the rest of Europe and repay to Europeans a hundred times more than we owe them.'[1]

[1] *Sochineniya*, vol. i, p. 46., Moscow, 1861.

Undoubtedly *The Nineteenth Century* is a consistent sequel to this earlier article. When Kireyevsky started off, he had been as thoroughgoing a rationalistic Westernizer as Chaadayev had been a religious one. To the horror of the more orthodox Slavophil, he even defended Peter's reforms with conviction. For, whereas in Europe education emerged as a natural consequence and expression of national character, 'With us the national element is crude and brutal; to cultivate our national character by ceasing to borrow from Europe would be to drive out education altogether.' Where, except in Europe, could Russia find these intellectual riches which she lacked? At this stage Kireyevsky came so close to Chaadayev that it it was reasonable for the latter to take up the cudgels on behalf of *The European*, when officialdom stepped in to strangle it.

Kireyevsky did not begin to turn into a full-blown Slavophil until he took over the editorship of the *Moskvityanin* in 1845. Nevertheless the transfer of editorship immensely improved the policy and scope of that influential journal. The former editors, Pogodin and Shevyrev, who fawned on the favour of Nicolas I, had damaged the Slavophils in public esteem by identifying them with Uvarov's discredited school of 'official nationalism'. Hence arose the legend that the *Moskvityanin* articles so flatly and monotonously contrasting the decay of the West with Russian national virility reflected the honest convictions of all the leading Slavophils. (How strangely contemporary this century-old cliché sounds!) But actually the *Moskvityanin* was disliked and shunned by the Aksakovs and Kireyevskys, and prior to 1845 Khomyakov only contributed to it occasionally and then *faute de mieux*, because no other journal was open to him at the time.

As soon as Kireyevsky and Khomyakov took over the editorship, they demonstrated that the main tradition of European culture was still dearer to the true Slavophils than it was to the Westernizers, though clearly less for the sake of the European present than for its more impressive past, and therefore not as a ready-made model to copy, but as an auxiliary to stimulate specifically Russian improvement. When Kireyevsky published his first authentically Slavophil article ('Review of Modern Literature') in this journal, he protested against the German-inspired autocracy of bare intellect, in order to argue the superiority of Russian rational faith to the European and

American type of rational knowledge. 'Faith is not a dim concept which only belongs to an inferior stage of mental evolution, insufficiently developed by intellect, and which needs to be raised by intellectual effort to the dignity of exact knowledge. Nor is faith an absolute external authority before which reasoning should be dumb. It is, on the contrary, the highest form of rationality, a power, at once internal and external, which is the vital source of the intellect itself.' That fresh element which Kireyevsky claimed to find in the Orthodox Slav world appeared to be the sole surviving active faith which could both assimilate and fertilize Western scientific knowledge.

Kireyevsky realized acutely that the many current misinterpretations and abuses of Slavophil thought were partly due to incorrigible loose thinking and scholastic verbal squabbles among the Slavophil leaders. 'We start to call ourselves Slavs, but everyone understands that word in a different sense. Some people see in Slavism nothing but language and unity of race, others conceive it as a necessary attitude of hostility to Europeanism. A third person takes it as a striving to achieve 'national character'—a fourth—as a striving to achieve Orthodoxy. Each sticks to his own interpretation as the only legitimate one. We have not yet explained either what these contradictory conceptions really are, or what they have in common.

The essence of 'national character' is still wholly undefined. Some mean nothing but the so-called common people, some, the unique characteristics of the common people as expressed in our national history, others mean the product of our peculiar type of religious discipline. So long as our ideas are so confused, our sympathies will be barren in result, and we cannot move a single step forward.'[1]

Unluckily the purged *Moskvityanin*, though infused with honest vigour, fared little better than *The European*. After a few issues had appeared the government pounced on it and suppressed it. Stranded again, the long-suffering Kireyevsky went back to his country estate. His next opportunity did not occur till several years later when the irrepressible Slavophils launched yet another journal, the *Moskovskii Sbornik* (1852). For the first issue of this he wrote his most notorious article, 'About the Character of European Education and its Bearing on Education in Russia'.

[1] Unpublished letter to A. Koshelëv: *Russkii Arkhiv*, No. 8, 1904, p. 495.

Chernyshevsky described it as substantially misleading, but by far the best single summary of Slavophil thought, revealing for the first time what all the Slavophils held in common. A mature and chastened Kireyevsky, already seeking in Orthodox mysticism a refuge from the harsh blows of fate, observes without regret how quickly the cordial post-1815 relations between Russia and her war-time allies have cooled down. But he interprets the latest signs of the times to Russia's immense advantage. The European educated man had reached the point of believing that by the power of his perfected intellect alone he could rapidly build up a more prosperous and rational social organization, which would be the prelude to a human paradise on earth. Centuries of bloody but futile political experiments had failed to teach wisdom to this 'educated man'. Though the laws of nature continued to wreck his shallow plans, nothing could cure him of the boundless intellectual conceit which deified his puny ego, while it continued to drag him slowly but surely downwards. Confronted with this horrifying example, what lessons could Russia learn, what course of action should she pursue?

'Thirty years ago,' wrote Kireyevsky, 'one could hardly meet a single thinking person who would have admitted the possibility of any kind of Russian education other than to learn from Western Europe. Public opinion was such that the distinction between education in Europe and education in Russia existed only in the different amount achieved by each, but not in any difference of spirit or basic principles. We (they said then) were formerly barbarians; our culture only began when we started to borrow from Europe.'

But between now and then a change had taken place. European education had reached that fullness of development where its own particular basis had been worked out to reach the utmost clarity. This complete clarity and conclusiveness resulted in a widespread feeling of disappointment. Not because Western sciences had lost their vitality; on the contrary, exact sciences flourish, material needs are better satisfied. But life has been deprived of inner meaning; no longer penetrated by any strong uniting convictions, it cannot be ennobled and warmed by ideal hopes or stirring sympathy. Centuries of cold intellectual analysis undermined those foundations on which European civilization had been built up. Simultaneously this analysis, through its logical activity and abstract reasoning, reached the point where it recognized its own narrow one-sidedness. It became aware that the highest intellectual truth of fundamental conviction lies outside the abstract circle of its dialectical process. This conclusion had been admitted by some leading thinkers of the West.

As a result of this process the Western individual either acquires an animal indifference to everything higher than selfish material interests—but that is unnatural and humiliating—or he reverts to those rejected convictions which inspired the West before the latest wave of abstract reasoning overcame it—but those convictions are already shattered. Therefore almost everyone, in order to escape from a sense of tormenting futility, begins to dream about discovering fresh principles of existence and truth for the whole world, muddling old and new, possible and impossible, contradicting each other, but each expecting to be believed by all the others.

In Russia most people who have studied the latest phenomena of European life have reasonably concluded that this phase of European education fails to satisfy them. Consequently they start to pay attention to those special characteristics of civilization by which Russia lived before, and which are still noticeable, in spite of being overlaid by a veneer of European features. 'These native foundations, which we previously ignored on account of our blind partiality for Western civilization, our reckless neglect of our own past history (regarding it as barbarous), are quite distinct from those elements which compose the civilization of West European peoples. . . .' Nobody, said Kireyevsky, appreciated more than he did the comforts of social and private life which are based on intelligent organization. He thought, however, that in its morbid restlessness the rational criterion ultimately shows itself up to be one-sided, illusory and treacherous. The best minds of Europe complain about the present state of moral apathy, lack of belief and universal egoism; they call for a new spiritual force in addition to reason, a new incentive apart from the pursuit of money.

This outspoken article created in Russian society a stir comparable to Chaadayev's *First Philosophic Letter*. But, unlike the latter, the consensus of intelligent opinion was unfavourable to it. The Westernizers, especially the radical Chernyshevsky, considered that the hard judgement it pronounced on Europe was superficial, not borne out by a thorough study of what was happening there, nor even by a correct diagnosis of what the most self-critical Western thinkers had observed. Official circles, with their heresy-hunting obsession, habitually detected camouflaged treason in every line the Slavophils wrote. The *Moskovsky Sbornik* lasted no longer than two issues. After its suppression, the patient Kireyevsky retired once more to his country estate, where he was placed under police supervision.

At last the death of Nicolas I (1855) enabled the Slavophils to found a new journal (1856) under his more tolerant successor Alexander II. The first number of this journal, the *Russkaya Besyeda*, contained Kireyevsky's pathetic final article 'About the Necessity and Possibility of New Foundations for Philosophy', but the same issue published his obituary notice. He had died of cholera in Moscow.

For many years Kireyevsky had lived in close touch with a number of Orthodox monasteries, and he translated some works of the Greek theologians into Russian. From these activities he appears to have derived his stronger emphasis on the orthodox mode of reconciling the human intellect with functions of the will and the emotions. 'In their pursuit of truth, the Eastern thinkers pay most attention to the rightful inward condition of the thinking mind, whereas Western philosophers care much more about the external relations of ideas. The former seek an inner unity of mind, a focus of mental forces, where all separate activities of the soul are fused into a complete living unity. The latter, on the contrary, believe that a full understanding can only be reached by still further differentiation of mental faculties. With one faculty they grasp moral, with another artistic phenomena; a special organ exists for the "useful" and truth is found by abstract reasoning. Not one of these faculties knows what the other is doing until the action is completed.'

In his last article Kireyevsky summed up the stages he had found in the disintegration of Western moral integrity through the cumulative splintering effect of rational thought. From Aristotle arose 'the scholastic philosophy *within* the Christian faith, next came the reformation in faith, and finally the philosophy *without* faith'. Thus Aristotle culminated in Hegel, and imagination died together with religion. 'Industry' and 'science' reigned in their stead. But—wonder of wonders— Kireyevsky finds the new foundations for philosophy in a return to the old Orthodox Church. The wish was father to this musty defeatist thought, for though he devoted much time to studying the lives and reflections of the ascetic Orthodox saints, we have no reason to believe that the results of his search encouraged him. On the contrary, he complained to Koshelëv shortly before his death that his immersion in the Christian East had intensified in him that barren mental conflict and split personality 'which rightly-directed intellectual activity aims to break down!'

Later Russian protagonists of Orthodox Christian revival, Berdyaev, Bulgakov and others, seem to have strangely ignored Kireyevsky's cogent negative evidence. Herzen thought that Kireyevsky admired the Orthodox church only against his better judgement, because he saw how greatly it helped poor ignorant people who knew no better comfort. This pragmatic view, which many Slavophils shared without a trace of cynicism, is borne out by an account from Kireyevsky's own experience : 'Once in a chapel I was gazing at the miraculous ikon of God's Mother, and pondering over the childish faith of the people who prayed to it; women, sick people and old men bowed to the ground and crossed themselves before it. No, I thought, clearly this cannot be an ordinary piece of wood, with an image painted on its surface. For centuries it has received such outpourings of confidence, witnessed these prayers of unhappy suffering people. All these must have filled it with a certain power which now streams out from it, and is reflected back to those believers. Thinking thus, I looked again at the old men and women and then at the sacred ikon. At that moment I myself suddenly saw the features of the Virgin Mother come to life, and light up with a look of mercy and love for these simple people. . . . And I fell on my knees and humbly prayed to her.'[1]

How deeply, almost enviously, Kireyevsky must have wondered at the miracle of faith in ignorant people, to make him pine to share their superstitions. But ignorance is like a delicate exotic fruit; touch it and the bloom is gone. It was no way out—and no help to them—for the learned critic of Schelling and Hegel to abase himself before the illiterate peasants, striving to worship their idols. Indeed he knew better than to mistake a momentary mood of sympathy for the straight and narrow path into a peasant Nirvana.

[1] V. Astrov: *Ne Nashli Puti*, p. 71, St. Petersburg, 1914.

Even if the voice of the heart (for the few who heard it identically) became Kireyevsky's social religion, it was never, like Rousseau's, the wild appetite, impervious to reason, of a lone nomad without any need of his fellows. Accepting the indispensability of logical thought, he merely denied its primacy, because logic, being ethically neutral, exacted as the price of perfect intellectual clarity a corresponding impotence to move the heart and will. Such an icy metaphysical Olympus could never rule human beings who were linked by bonds of mutual sympathy. Therefore, in making reason the industrious servant of faith, Kireyevsky was thinking of the world (expecially the Russian world) as he knew it; he fought to save his compatriots from resigning themselves to the plague of intellectual locusts which was already starting to devour the fresh green shoots of Russian spiritual life. He wanted them to make their thought more fertile by making it subsidiary. 'So long as we live within the confines of our intellect, we live in a ground-plan instead of in a house. Having done nothing but draw the ground-plan, we imagine we have already built the house. And when we perceive our mistake, we act too late, for it is terribly hard to fetch and carry stones instead of flourishing a pencil. That is why, in our time, only ignorant or spiritually educated people retain their will-power and ability to act.'[1]

Unluckily, Kireyevsky's laudable distrust of logic out of bounds broke down at the crucial test. It failed to save him from that glaring *non-sequitur* which, through a logical abuse of faith, identified the native institutions of pre-Petrine Russia (though not the modern Russian state) with the most promising future instruments of moral advance for mankind. It needed a naïve and self-intoxicated national mysticism to invent and pursue such a fantastic inference. A logical deduction from a mystical premise is neither sound logic nor sound religion. And only an unbalanced underestimation of the West (not to mention a withering contempt for the more ancient East), ignoring the inner substance and subterranean currents of other civilizations, narrowing Europe down to some shadowy new-fangled cult of absolute logic, could lead to such a wildly exaggerated estimate of primitive Russia as the world's last hope.

[1] Letter to Khomyakov (July 1840), pub. *Russkii Arkhiv*, No. 1, 1907, p. 256.

Of course the opponents of the Slavophils seized on and ridiculed these far-fetched arguments, which were pushed into the foreground by the more politically minded Slavophil publicists. Their strident exploitation of the maddest national pretensions came as a boon to the supercilious Westernizers, who readily concluded that all Slavophils were equally absurd. In the heat of these partisan battles, both sides overlooked the validity of Kireyevsky's soberer social perceptions. They hardly paused to fathom what he meant when he argued about the need to keep intact the Russian type of moral integrity, or why he found in this the touchstone of practical judgement, and the only unfailing source of that inherent strength of character which had formerly rescued Russians on the verge of calamity.

The Westernizers impatiently equated this attitude with an old-fashioned desire to be left undisturbed by the outside world, with a lazy reluctance to brace slovenly Slav minds for the effort of making desirable changes. They ignored the peculiar possibility that the more intelligent Slavophils might show an ancient Asiatic wisdom in the selective way they strove to bring European culture to fruition within Russia. Some Westernizers, like Chernyshevsky, thought that modern Europe had degenerated on top, but not below. Yet none of them shared the extreme Slavophil view that European society had degenerated as a whole, from top to bottom, that her moral disease was spreading like an epidemic, and threatened to kill the last healthy shoots of native civilization in every country falling under European sway. If the Slavophils were right, then Russian 'backwardness' contained a blessing in disguise—among the common people unique devotion and Asiatic endurance, among their educated leaders a clear perception, which modern Europeans had lost, of the most valuable and realizable European ideals.

That Europe, and her more vigorous extension in America, still fostered hidden reserves of strength, which might enable them to conquer their own disease, while weaker outsiders, infected by them, succumbed to it, was a more remote alternative, and one less flattering to Russian dreams. It did not occur to Kireyevsky or to any of the original Slavophils, but Konstantin Leontiev thought it possible. Kireyevsky's Russian future might be a glorious vision for his unhappy compatriots, but its fulfilment demanded a steady process of European senile decay, which he somewhat naïvely took for granted. Gershenzon, writing half a century later, hit the mark when he observed that Kireyevsky's paradoxical prophecies afflicted Russian political thinkers with a certain high-flown indifference to nice distinctions between wishful speculation, strict truth and downright falsehood. Often the glamorous legend proved more attractive to them than scientific honesty. But the legend itself could be scientifically dressed. Lies with a system and a driving purpose exerted greater persuasive influence than unpalatable truths. That is how well-intentioned Russian patriots fell easier victims to the Chauvinist spell, at a time when the more experienced Western European minds were starting to recognize that it led to mass insanity.

V

The rock-like Peter Kireyevsky (1808–1856) presents a striking contrast to his unstable and tormented brother Ivan. A harmonious embodiment of the most active Slavophil qualities, he spent an inconspicuous but industrious life-time working out the improvement of his own estate, collecting hitherto unwritten folk-songs, and helping his peasants in all the ways open to a conscientious but impecunious landowner. Herzen, while he respected Ivan, called Peter Kireyevsky a personality who stood out head and shoulders above all the other Slavophils.

He wrote little, but on various issues he expressed himself more cogently and unequivocally than his brother. He opposed autocracy on principle, he condemned Peter the Great for having torn the aristocracy from their Russian roots, and broken their links with the common people; but he upset his fellow Slavophils because he also deplored their fashionable but pedantic cult of pre-Petrine Russia, which, he said, resembled a stale Chinese ritual, weighing its adherents down under a burden of customs, useless because they were deprived of any living sense.

For him the much-vaunted Russian national character was nothing but a shapeless and misleading abstraction, unless it expressed spontaneous personal desires. 'What is called common to all mankind means looking like everyone else, a vulgar trivial physiognomy. Whatever is alive, is original, with an expressive face of its own.' In the latter case the Russian character, in order to be worth preserving, must be closely linked with the Orthodox faith, for only that faith distinguished amorphous Russians from the more definite West and East, and had saved them from the worldly vices of Western Christianity. If it allowed the faith which nourished it to die, whatever was best in the national character would surely deteriorate and disappear. The dreary dictatorship of Nicolas I was crushing the spontaneous core of religion, while the stupid alternative of lax and leaderless liberalism was frittering away the spiritual treasures of the West. True Orthodoxy alone revealed a wiser course, an orthodoxy which sprang, not from the priests, but from the congregation of the church.

The following passage states a plain-spoken indictment of Nicolas I, as the natural consequence of Kireyevsky's religious convictions:

'Papists believe in the infallibility of the Pope, Protestants in the infallibility of human reason, Orthodox Christians—in the infallibility of the elected apostolic church. . . . Nominal equality of many beliefs means in fact nothing but the oppression of all beliefs for the benefit of one utterly heathen faith—faith in the state. . . .

'We have innumerable examples to show how little a single human being can rely on his own strength. Yet there are people who think it the height of political wisdom to entrust the fate of a nation, and even of the church, to the unimpeded passions and caprice of a single man. They say no people can exist without a single autocratic ruler, even as a herd cannot survive without a shepherd. But the shepherd who leads the flock is a man, by nature higher than the flock, and therefore their rightful leader. It would be mad to rely on the safety of the herd, if a herd of oxen were led by an ox, or a flock of sheep by a sheep. Clearly the comparison is false, and who, except God, is as much higher than man by his nature as man is higher than a sheep? For a single man to lead men he must either rise to God, or his people will be lowered to the level of a herd of cattle.'[1] A strong argument against autocracy, but equally one which might be turned in favour of a religious-minded oligarchy.

His views about serfdom were still more precise, and they could be stated without theological backing. Though he disapproved of serfdom as un-Christian, he did not therefore commend sentimental landowners who generously freed their serfs and then left the helpless creatures to fend for themselves. For it

[1] Dmitriyev-Mamonov: *Slavyanofili, Russkii Arkhiv*, No. 11, 1873, p. 2492.

was no moral solution to transfer the peasant's welfare from the power of one good landowner to that of a horde of petty and corrupt government officials. 'The best intentions of the government are perverted by going through the hundred thousand hands of officialdom', he remarked, while trying to be scrupulously just. A responsible and conscientious landowner could help and protect his serfs much more effectively if they were *not* freed, until such time as local officials and law courts improved beyond recognition. Though Peter Kireyevsky deliberately kept his serfs under his own benevolent command, he favoured sweeping agrarian reform by law. In fact, he put forward proposals which demanded a far heavier financial sacrifice from the landowners than did the measures eventually adopted by the government in 1861. He recommended that half the landowners' estates should be freely handed over to their liberated peasants, without any liability from the latter for redemption dues.[1]

Many of Kireyevsky's outspoken writings were only discovered among his private papers after he died. He shunned any kind of notoriety, and never went out of his way to win a single convert. The imposing example of his consistent life first attracted attention to his mode of thought. Multitudes of ancient and beautiful folk-songs, handed down orally from one generation of peasants to another, were brought together and written down by him for the first time. As a landlord he appears to have been efficient as well as benevolent. In the 1840 famine he distributed freely the large quantity of grain stored in his barns, giving it not only to his own peasants, but also to the many destitute wanderers who had migrated from other villages in search of food.

By devoting much energy to promoting the healthier local traditions in which he so firmly believed, he sought to limit the damage done to the roots of national life by the advancing flood of administrative centralization. His view of the state as a necessary evil, but an evil which could be mitigated and kept within bounds, was as typically Slavophil as it was untypical of the increasingly self-inflated Russian bureaucrats. His innate and rare sense of flexible organizational compromise emerges with particular cogency in his view about the future of the *mir*. Wherever the *mir* still functions through its assembly as a going

[1] Letter to Koshelëv: *Russkii Arkhiv*, No. 8, 1873.

concern, he said, it should be carefully preserved by the good landowner, but where it has already become inoperative through abuse of the landowner's power, it is useless to think that it can be revived effectively by piecemeal local experiments. Here the state should step in to restore and reconstruct it by means of a statutory and firmly enforced law.[1]

Europeans find it hard to appreciate the burning controversy which raged throughout nineteenth-century Russia over the relation of the *mir* [2] to the organs of central government. Far more was at stake than the proper allocation of administrative functions as between old local and newer central bodies, for the *mir* embodied a host of complex traditions, a whole way of thousand-year-old social life. The Kireyevsky brothers defended the way of life rather than the institution, and not out of stubborn conservative pride, but because they were convinced that, change as it must, it was adaptable, and offered brighter prospects of healthy growth if it could avoid being swamped by an avalanche of unrelated modern Western institutions.

[1] Letter to Koshelëv: *Russkii Arkhiv*, No. 8, 1873.

[2] The village assembly (*mir*) was an ancient institution of peasant self-government, which existed centuries before serfdom. It was strengthened, rather than changed, by the Emancipation laws (1861). The *mir's* main function was to organize the periodical redistribution of strips of land among individual households, and to regulate agricultural work on land, such as pastures, which served the whole commune. Until Stolypin cancelled all remaining redemption dues in 1906, the peasants were harassed by legal disputes about the ownership of their newly-acquired land, between 1861 and the final discharge of their dues.

A. S. KHOMYAKOV

From an engraving by I. Pojalostin

CHAPTER IV

A. S. KHOMYAKOV

I

AMONG the original Slavophils A. S. Khomyakov (1804–1860) stands out as their most powerful single personality. Since the study of his work became a virtual monopoly of theologians, his religious opinions have emerged into a dry and restricted limelight. Unfortunately this persistent theological slant has obscured from laymen and non-Christians the fact that Khomyakov was an exceptionally versatile, eloquent and prolific writer. Thus, while his modern compatriots have relegated him to their historical scrap-heap, the outside world, if it knows him at all, sees him almost entirely as a Christian pundit. Both have been hindered from recognizing how much of what he wrote is modern, and enters deeply into the tangled skein of European-Russian relations, even though it rarely touches the more popular economic strands.

Khomyakov was descended from an ancient land-owning family. He received the broad and lavishly cosmopolitan education customary among the higher Russian nobility since the eighteenth century. Then, after instructive travels in France, Italy and Switzerland, he entered the Imperial army, where he served creditably in one of the many campaigns against Turkey (1828). His mother, a strong-minded and efficient woman, took over the management of the family estates from her easy-going and feckless husband just in time to prevent them from being ruined. She made her two sons take a vow (which they appear to have kept) that they would remain chaste until they married. At an early age Stepan directed his superfluous energy into omnivorous reading. He records that in a single year he spent ten thousand roubles on buying books from abroad. What is still more unusual, he evidently remembered what he read, for he amazed and often defeated his antagonists in argument by the aptness and exactitude of the many quotations at his command.

After marriage Khomyakov settled down on his main estate, which he started to farm energetically. Like other enterprising landowners, he branched off from agriculture into industry, successfully organized a local sugar-factory employing serf-labour, and introduced mechanical improvements. He himself invented and patented a rotatory steam-engine, which he patriotically called *The Moskovka*, and in 1845 he started a Press campaign in the *Moskvityanin* advocating the construction of a railroad network throughout Russia. Thoroughly disgusted by the gross incompetence and apathy of country doctors, he also plunged into the study and practice of medicine, treating with newly discovered remedies victims of cholera in his villages—although, as he sardonically observed, 'the regulations do not permit me, without a diploma, either to kill or to cure a person'. When the Crimean War broke out, he was already too old to take an active part in it. But he pronounced his own sure judgement that Russia's defeat was God's punishment for years of criminal national arrogance and false pride. 'Strengthening the army, increasing our wealth, frightening other people, widening our territories—such was our obsession. To respect justice, to protect the weak and unsheltered, to lift up the spirit of our own people, seemed to us useless activities. We showed no sense of real spiritual improvement. In our blindness we had turned into slaves more than twenty million of our own brothers. Such were the fruits of our pride. God punished us by defeat in the Crimean War.' (*Message to the Serbs*, 1859.)

In 1859 Khomyakov's literary achievement received a seal of public recognition; he was elected President of the Society of Friends of Literature. After systematically setting free the majority of his own serfs, he spent the last years of his life assiduously promoting local measures preparatory to the Emancipation Edict of 1861. 'I wish success to any measure adopted', he wrote, adding characteristically, 'provided it does not confer liberty without land or an empty unattached individual liberty.'

II

We shall pay a harmless tribute to convention if we start by considering Khomyakov's religious opinions, though only where they bear clearly on his social thought. When Peter the Great abolished the autonomous patriarchate, and substituted for it the state-appointed Holy Synod, he put the finishing touch to the totalitarian shape of Eastern Orthodoxy. While accepting Peter's career as 'a horrible but beneficial thunderstorm',

Khomyakov contended that the Tsar's new position as administrative Head of the Church, though it enabled him to turn priests into civil servants, gave him no authority to define or modify religious doctrine. Nothing short of an Oecumenical Council of Eastern Churches could take decisions within that sphere. Furthermore, Khomyakov claimed that the Orthodox Church retained its inward freedom even if weak ecclesiastics allowed it to fall into dependence on the state. Outward slavery did not preclude inward emancipation. The body of a church, *i.e.* all its members, lay and clerical, gathered together in humility, could still preserve the purity of faith. Personal conscience could thus achieve collective validity in the light of faith— though not in any other way.

Recognizing that the shadow of a free conscience was a meagre consolation, which did not get one very far without the substance of free expression and activity, Khomyakov consistently attacked censorship—not in principle (censorship must ban vulgarity and maintain high moral standards) but specifically in its muzzling of politics and religion. When sincere thought on such vitally important subjects is stifled by the dead weight of lies or flattery, he asserted, then all honest people will keep silent; intellectual life dries up at the source, and there gradually spreads throughout society 'that personal indifference to truth and moral values which is enough to poison a whole generation and to spoil many generations to come.'

As Khomyakov interpreted the course of European history, the Catholic Church had inherited from the Roman Empire the ambitious misapplication of a codified legal system. That system had distorted and commercialized the natural Christian relation of man to God, by reducing it to the mean character of a moral bank-account, in which every man's good and bad deeds, specified as such, were entered with meticulous accuracy in the credit and debit columns. Protestants had rebelled against this degrading bondage. The Orthodox Church, on the contrary, had never followed either Catholic or Protestant examples. It refused to degenerate into a stereotyped ethical book-keeping transaction; it always attached more importance to the motive underlying an action than to the action itself. By rejecting formal stipulations and legal guarantees, it proved that it could still rely on healthy direct Christian relationships which had been mutilated or crushed in the more materialistic West.

H

Here we find the basis of Khomyakov's firm argument that Orthodoxy is superior (in moral value) to all Western brands of Christianity. 'Romanism is an unnatural tyranny, Protestantism an unprincipled revolt. Neither of them is acceptable. But where is unity without tyranny, where is freedom without revolt? Both can be found in the ancient continuous unadulterated tradition of the Orthodox Church. There a unity can be found more authoritative than the despotism of the Vatican, for it is based on the strength of mutual love. There a liberty can be found freer than the licence of Protestantism, for it is regulated by the humility of mutual love. There is the Rock and the Refuge!'[1]

We are not told whether this is meant to be a statement of fact or merely a pious hope, a description of the Orthodox Church as a going concern, or as it used to be before the Schism, or as Khomyakov fondly imagined it ought to become. The latter seems most probable, for one can hardly attach more than the vaguest subjective aspiration to the term 'mutual love' on which the force of this argument hinges. But even that interpretation fails to reveal a sufficiently exclusive trait of Orthodoxy, since similar sentiments fall only too glibly from the lips of innumerable Christian congregations, however rarely they may rise from a single heart.

Indeed the reader will discover that Khomyakov has a perplexing habit of confusing doubtful potentialities with accomplished facts, and that he sometimes speaks of the Orthodox Faith as if it were a synonym for the Orthodox Church, even though elsewhere he clearly and rightly distinguishes them. In one significant passage he puts his finger on the most sensitive spot by exclaiming that, for Russians, faith must be a thing apart, divinely unattached to any external bonds or obligations, 'that faith which, thank God, and owing to an instinctive sense of truth, *no one has yet called religion* . . . faith with its enlivening constructive vigour, freely moving thought and tolerant love.'[2] But people must live according to this truth before they can start to understand it.

He not only separates the institutional Church from personal faith, he discerns the battle-ground where they are bound to interlock and clash. The essence of the Russian Orthodox

---

[1] W. Birkbeck: *Russia and the English Church*, p. 102.
[2] A. S. Khomyakov: *Sochineniya*, vol. 1, p. 256, Moscow, 1911.

Church, most notably since Peter made it Erastian, was total self-denying conformity of mind, body and soul. Often its demands from the Faithful were more exacting in minor ritual observances than in vital matters of personal conduct, but none the less the Church reserved more drastic powers; it could hardly be called lukewarm or lax, whenever a major government policy was at stake. The desperate struggle for survival of the schismatic sects provides the most sombre illustration of the awful gulf dividing Church from Faith. Whole communities of 'Self-Burners', men, women and children, would set fire to their homes and throw themselves into the flames, preferring to commit suicide rather than submit to the emissaries of forced conversion. Passive resistance, carried to that pitch, was more impressive than armed rebellion. But the authorities had inexhaustible theocratic arguments to justify their persecution of disobedient citizens. Such were the methods which the horrified de Custine called 'that monstrous combination of Byzantine minutiae with the ferocity of the Tartar Horde'.

Khomyakov evades these troublesome entanglements by speaking of the Church *as if* it still embodied that pure primitive Orthodoxy, which the Old Believers had fought to preserve when they first disobeyed the Patriarch Nikon in the seventeenth century. Or rather, he hints that the Church could do no good until it recovered that degree of independence. 'Christianity does not constitute a state. It has been artificially mixed with the idea of the state. As for wars of religion, or wars under a religious pretext, they degrade religion to the level of the state. A conquering Christianity cannot be anything but repulsive.'[1] Meanwhile he proves his mental honesty by firmly shifting the centre of gravity away from the state-tainted official hierarchy, and placing it indisputably in the purer hands of small voluntary congregations. Only thus can he remain sincerely Orthodox and yet assert, in full sympathy with the dissenting sects, 'In matters of religion, forced unity is a lie and compulsory obedience is death.'

We may profitably ask, without straining the analogy, how Khomyakov, had he lived today, would have reacted to the depressing degree of total personal allegiance exacted by the Communist Party Church. Would he have accepted it as a regrettable but necessary transformation of Eastern Orthodoxy

[1] *Sochineniya*, vol. 8, pp. 303–4.

in the task of moulding primitive men to modern economic needs? The liquidation of all the supernatural Christian elements might hardly have worried the scientific Khomyakov, who put his trust in the efficient operation of faith and conscience, and heartily approved of steam-engines. He might even have supported the attempt to preserve a semblance of organized faith, if it were the only alternative to abandoning human society to bestial cynicism. On the other hand, he would certainly have found that the Soviet brand of 'forced unity' bore too marked a family resemblance to its disreputable ancestors. He could only have revolted against its crafty lip-service to democratic institutions, 'spontaneous' popular demonstrations etc. And while he might have approved the genuine desire of Soviet rulers to substitute persuasion for coercion, whenever possible, he could never have condoned camouflaged violence. It would seem that most of what Khomyakov said in favour of Orthodoxy, whether as a Faith or as an organized Church, conflicts with the realities of Soviet Orthodoxy. And that is probably why most Soviet scholars have carefully steered clear of him. Admittedly, he believed that the Russian people still needed autocratic rulers. But he spoke of an open, personally responsible autocracy, not of a power which could mask its responsibility by manipulating a maze of elected committees. And while administrative severity imposed a heavy burden on the people, at least the sense of its inevitability made it more tolerable. There was no such excuse for adding to this the torture of despotism over their minds and feelings. Having surrendered almost every personal right to society and the state, the people guarded their remnants of spiritual liberty as an inviolable treasure.

Khomyakov is haunted by this line of thought, to which he frequently returns. One aspect of it comes out clearly in a parallel he drew between the Russian and Byzantine Empires, defending the latter's underestimated service to civilization, but also elucidating the good citizen's mode of resistance to the insufferable demands of that nominally religious state. For centuries, he wrote, Byzantium resisted barbarian attacks of a severity which no other kingdom in the world could have withstood. In the long run the perpetual conflict between heathen and Christian motives wore it down and left it morally exhausted. Finally no outlet remained for people of spirit and thought except escape from a society to which they refused to submit, but which they were powerless to overcome. Therefore they took refuge in monasteries, abandoning to corruption and greed a state already in the grip of incurable decay. 'Only in the sanctuary of deserts and monasteries could the true purity and integrity of moral life be preserved to the end. And these proved their value when they became the salvation of our future Russia.'[1]

III

Quite apart from his notoriety as a lay theologian (and even in this capacity his theological polemics now count for little beyond the social judgements which they support) Khomyakov ranks very highly as a patriotic poet and prophet, who despised conventional patriotism, and as an original civic teacher. He elaborated a Russian mission to the world, a mission, which, far from being another Empire-building march of conquest, imposed a national duty more morally exacting and universal in scope than Kipling's *White Man's Burden* (borne too exclusively on the shoulders of the muscular Anglo-Saxon race). Moreover, in the midst of this Messianic feeling for his country's destiny, Khomyakov remains surprisingly tentative and modest.

He can hardly mention Russian affairs without immediately switching over to a comparison with Europe, usually unfavourable to the former and always searchingly candid. He is renowned for the self-critical *bon mot*, popularized by Turgenev, 'all our mental brilliance has so far been unable to invent so much as a decent mouse-trap'. But he is candid too in revealing the extent to which Europe bristles with conceited or ignorant prejudice against Russia. In his article, 'Foreigners' Opinions about Russia' (*Moskvityanin*, 1845) he stated the deplorable fact that Russia, in spite of all her sincere strivings, had so far evoked from Europe only one response—namely, mockery or curses, a mixture of fear and contempt. 'The European, eternally praising himself for his "humanity", falls painfully short of this sentiment when he extends to remote and savage tribes a sympathy which he completely witholds from Russians, related to him by race and culture. . . . Our physical strength excites jealousy in Western peoples, and our admission of spiritual or mental impotence deprives us of their respect.'

[1] *Sochineniya*, vol. 1, p. 219.

His companion article, 'Russian Opinion about Foreigners' (1845) points warningly to the widening rift between Russia's traditional mode of living and her imported education. The plague of a Westernized intellectual proletariat, cut off from the roots of Russian life, seemed to him far more dangerous to his country's future social health than the more easily curable native plague of village poverty. 'There are no limits to the damage which clever men, devoid of conscience, can inflict on society, when they use the pretext of useful and legal action. Once you surrender yourself into the hands of a bad doctor he will kill you so imperceptibly that you will never be aware of it.' Thus unscrupulous men, under a respectable mask of learning can the more easily disseminate ideas which poison society. These self-styled social benefactors know how to injure people with impunity when it serves their own advantage. Always the 'subtle' men pervert the 'simple' and the 'weak'. At the same time their pale language and sickly thoughts—though hardly more than a veneer over a thoughtless savagery—betray the foreign origin of a grafted growth. 'Our own character peeped out timidly from underneath these foreign shapes, without recognizing its own face, sometimes merely ashamed of itself. However that may be, its natural claims to life belong to the future, not to the past.'

It should be observed that the Slavophils' call to the future animated all their social thought. Their unimaginative opponents never understood this call, or contemptuously ignored it, while cheaply ridiculing their cult of the *Kaftan*, of decorative ancient Russian dress and the more pleasant patriarchal customs. Khomyakov was innocent of antiquarian pedantry. He explored the Russian past solely for the sake of shaping her future out of the best available ingredients, and these included European ones. We see this double quest most vividly in his political poems. In his *Ode on the Polish Revolt* (1831), after cursing the Polish rebels for having yielded to 'the senseless shame of family strife', he foretold the proud day when the 'Slav eagles' would fly freely over the whole world, but would still bow their heads obediently to their Elder, the 'Northern Eagle'. His poem *The Island* (1836) pays a warm tribute to England's civilized glory, but pictures it withering away under the blight of her cold self-satisfied pride; he concludes with the prophetic words:

God then to a land more humble,
Marked with Faith and signs of fear,
Shall the Empire and Earth's Thunder,
And the word of Heaven transfer.

By this humble land he meant of course his own, humble, he fondly believed, behind her arrogant façade. The future would belong to her, if only she could prove that she deserved it. Could Holy Russia out of the tiny spark she had preserved, re-kindle the pure creative flame of the older Europe, which the new Europe had so wantonly extinguished in her shallow commercial society? If the most promising form of Russian future lay in a fulfilment of the older European aspirations, how could it ever materialize without breaking free from the corrupting tutelage of the modern West? How could Russia demonstrate her superior culture by assimilating modern European science without being simultaneously tainted by Western commercial vulgarity, spiritual decadence or revolutionary madness?

In paying such devoted and discriminating homage to the still unfulfilled promise of the European past, Khomyakov only proved his loyalty to one of the most vital and least recognized Slavophil motives. He loved the ideals which ancient Europe stood for, partly for their own sake, but still more because they foreshadowed his own country's ripening civilization, which from the beginning had transcended national boundaries. This vision reached the height of eloquence in his poem *The Dream* (1834) which ends in a solemn invocation to Russia and to the whole of Asia.

Dark shadows spread throughout the distant West,
Over the land of sacred wonders; now
The former stars turn pale as they die out.
How beautiful it was, that glorious West;
For ages the whole earth on bended knees,
Miraculously glowing from her spendour,
Bowed down to her in humble silent awe!

There wisdom's sun first rose before our eyes,
And calmly, like the moon, love shone in blameless joy.
In brilliant rainbows inspiration rose,
The fires of living faith spread floods of light. . . .

Alas, that age has died; now funeral palls
Fall on the Western World. There blackest night will reign.
Hark to the call of fate, rise to the new dawn,
Awake, slumbering East!

Khomyakov pictures his country as one of the bereaved rela-
tives taking part in the funeral procession of the West. The
funeral is taken for granted, but the Russian cousin is not shedding crocodile tears over his loss, still less is he shouting for joy
over the prospect of a rich inheritance. His love and grief are
genuine, the more so because he is haunted by the conviction of
Russia's spiritual backwardness, her more than technical incapacity to shoulder the immense responsibilities of carrying on
the interrupted work begun by European civilization. His notorious poem *To Russia* (1854), published at the beginning of the
Crimean War, confirmed this wise diffidence with a courage and
sincerity for which the Slavophils are rarely credited. Of course
so-called patriots howled it down as a treacherous insult to the
sacred fatherland. It roused such a successful uproar of protest
from the ever-influential Russian 'Blimps' that the government
promptly muzzled Khomyakov by issuing an order to ban any
further publications of his writings. The following are the most
relevant lines of this dangerously thoughtful poem:

But remember, to serve as God's weapon
Is hard for any earthly being.
Sternly he will judge his followers,
But as for you—alas! how many
Terrible crimes weigh on your head.

Blackened by the dark injustice of the law-courts,
And branded with the mark of slavery,
Riddled with godless flattery, foul lies,
With deadly apathy and every kind of vice,
You, unworthy of your mission, are none the less the Chosen
    One.

Since Khomyakov so openly deplored the sinister and squalid
realities of Russian life, we may wonder what made him so
tenaciously Slavophil, what hidden lure he found within his
country, which checked him from recoiling against her in hopeless indignant disgust, as many of his educated compatriots did.
If Russia was already so abominable, could she sink any lower
by joining up with the materialist and nearly socialist West? To

this leading question Khomyakov gave a firm unequivocal answer. Vile as the Russian state and officialdom undoubtedly were in many of their institutional aspects, the Russian people of all classes, so long as they remained traditional (in the supernational aspiring Russian sense) preserved redeeming qualities. Moreover, if Russia ever became completely Westernized in contemporary Western spirit and technique, she would be transformed, not into a superior copy of her model, but into a new monstrosity, a thousand times more horrible than the modern West.

Western vice, worldly cunning and ambition, cold calculating greed, coarse indifference to pure religious feeling, all these, said Khomyakov, Russians picked up with relish from abroad and then proceeded to exaggerate, unaware that they were grafting on themselves only 'diseased shoots from the Western tree'. 'It makes no difference whether we foster ambitions to become in our turn the most powerful people in the world, the richest or the most thoroughly educated. . . . We shall not achieve those aims. And why? Because no such mean task will be admitted by the conscience of our whole people, or can attract their innate sympathy. Russia must either become the most moral, the most Christian of all human societies, or be wholly insignificant—and it is easier for us to cease to exist than to be insignificant.'[1]

> Of all that strength and glory be not proud!
> Every proud mind is sterile,
> Gold deceives and steel is brittle,
> The luminous world of sanctity alone is solid ground,
> The strongest hand is the hand raised in prayer.[2]

We are told emphatically that the Russian government and Russian governing class (to Khomyakov at once her heaviest encumbrance and her most recent Western acquisition) provided no key to that invaluable unknown quantity, the underlying Russian character. Even Peter the Great's Westernizing frenzy had been partial and motivated. According to Khomyakov, his ultimate aim was not to turn Russia into a better replica of the modern Western state, but to shake off the slumber of centuries, to awaken sleeping Russian minds by means of a

[1] *Sochineniya*, vol. 3, p. 337.
[2] *Ibid.*, vol. 4, p. 56.

wholesome blood-transfusion and a painful shock. But the result fell a long way short of Peter's aim. The most solid legacy he left was a centralized bureaucratic state, a thoroughly Westernized machinery of Government, though magnified to the Russian scale. The clever bureaucrats who ran it, like Turgenev's Panshin, learned how to play skilfully with every important political or economic problem like jugglers who keep several balls or knives revolving simultaneously through the air. The most efficient ones never stopped trying to prove how skilful, smart and up-to-date they were, and believed that their quick and shallow reasoning entitled them to push aside all national traditions and customs as if they were outmoded relics. Meanwhile they had forgotten how many of these had a social character quite apart from their secondary economic utility, and were held sacred by the Russian common people. For the Westernizers had sold their Russian souls for a lot of imported theories and bright new toys. On that account they condemned themselves to sterile work, even in that limited field of social reform, where they capriciously fancied themselves to be pioneers on virgin soil. 'One cannot live in St. Petersburg without serving it, but to serve St. Petersburg is to betray Russia.'[1]

When Khomyakov insisted that politics left him cold, he explained himself by adding that only social questions were important, and they were important for still unrecognized reasons: 'Social life (*obshchenie*) consists not in mere exchange of ideas, not in the cold and egoistic exchange of services, not in dry respect for an alien law, always reserving its own rights—but in the living interchange both of ideas and feelings, in sharing not only grief (sympathy is all too common a feeling) but also the joys of existence. Only this kind of social life can guide us out of a maze of barren abstractions devoid of any national character, and lead us towards a full participation in the qualities of our people. . . . Our half-baked schoolboy knowledge would then turn into science and would promote science, by contributing to it those vital hitherto untapped sources which distinguish our people from the Western world with its Latin-Protestant one-sidedness and historical dualism.'[2]

Unfortunately the official preachers of Russian 'national

[1] *Sochineniya*, vol. 12, p. 322.
[2] *Ibid.*, vol. 1, pp. 98–99.

character' doped themselves with high-flown ambiguous talk. In their self-intoxicating discovery of Russian 'originality', they failed to realize that they had in fact advanced no further than transposing to their native land the stale themes of second-rate European intellectuals, especially the romantic nationalism of Schelling and the ultramontane royalism of J. de Maistre. With all their strident claims to be so fresh and young, they were really the last people who could save Russian thought from degenerating into a large dried-up branch sticking out from the main tree of European rationalism. Having hastily borrowed a few of the more nonsensical intellectual fashions from Europe, they were determined to show that they had nothing more to learn from her. As one of their critics caustically observed: 'Our nationalists too often obliged us to walk on all fours, in order that we should not appear to be imitators of bipeds!'

Moreover the Schellingian version of national character had manifestly reached a climax of self-expression in the materially powerful, spiritually self-satisfied, and mutually jealous sovereign states of Western Europe. The sensible Russian, even if he could visualize no better alternative, felt far from keen on turning his disorderly fatherland into yet another embodiment of the same self-absorbed and aggressive social organism. Khomyakov was one of the first to recognize this ideal for what it turned out to be in fact, a treacherous decoy leading each nation in turn to war and ruin.

Therefore he turned instead to all that was furthest from the cult of Russian patriotic virtue, to rare qualities of character undefiled by the official world, pure imaginative visions which made the grandiose national dreams of Westernized intellectuals look lurid, feverish and futile. Nor did he crudely idealize the common people. The following lines from *The Spring* (1835) express his most intimate vision better than any of his political or theological essays:

> Hid in the wilds, in forest glades,
> Favourite of muses and quiet thoughts,
> O living fountain, nameless spring,
> How dear to me your gentle murmur sounds. . . .
>
> On sultry days you still flow fresh and clear,
> Far from the trampling hoofs of thirsty herds;

The roaming peasant leaves you undisturbed.
You are not hardened by the frost,
Nor parched and dry from summer heat.
Alone you shed your silver tears,
In inexhaustible cascades.

Within your breast, oh Russia mine,
Flows such a quiet and limpid spring.
Its living waters also rise,
Hidden from sight, unknown but strong.

No mortal passion can disturb
Its clear crystallic depths, nor can
The frost of alien power congeal
Or stem its ever-flowing waves. . . .

But look, how widely now the waters
Have spread all over the green fields,
How foreign peoples, parched with inward thirst,
Gather together round its banks. . . .

Khomyakov felt fortified because he found in this faith the
same uncompromising quality which he valued in outstanding
Russians of every class. Vague and exasperating as his attitude
might seem to outsiders unable to share it, it was obviously
irreconcilable with uncritical loyalty to any system of political
leadership, whether this took the shape of Nicolas I's régime, or
whether it turned into an institutional assertion of social desiderata like *The Rights of Man*. Moreover, such a firm but eminently
personal faith was bound to come into mortal conflict with the
new credulity, miscalled faith, which believed that the mechanism of legally reformed institutions would automatically produce the miraculous benefits which the reformers so loudly
advertised. It seemed therefore indisputable to Khomyakov
that Russian society, though still inchoate, instinctively recognized an intangible moral basis, which was the exact reverse
of that 'scientific' institutional principle on the ascendant in
modern Western society.

IV

The Declaration of the Rights of Man (1793) had torn the modern
Western state from the rock of religious sanctity and transferred
it to the shifty foundation of positive law, shaken by the fitful

winds of every representative assembly. This change of position
might have been less fraught with peril, if the state had simultaneously dwindled in importance (as it had done in England
since 1688), if it had begun to content itself with the minor and
prosaic rôle of a moderately respectable limited liability company, no more than *primus inter pares*, a rôle which it might
suitably have played in the industrialized society of nineteenth-
century Europe. But in fact the continental secular state clung
to a spurious legend of sanctity, and it hastily exalted the haphazard will of so-called representatives of the people into the
highest criterion of right and wrong. Thus it became responsible
for that mortal conflict waged between the still-living voice
of personal conscience and the crushing requirements of a
legal machine, manipulated by time-serving and ambitious
demagogues.

Khomyakov was one among many Russians who, after intently studying this process in France, concluded that the far-
reaching tyranny of all-powerful popular assemblies concealed
a more insidious menace to civilization than the familiar perversions of monarchical rule. Whereas the latter, if we may
borrow a Jewish metaphor, killed some fish outright, the
former, at its most favourable, slowly drained the water out
of the whole pond. Khomyakov could not conceive a life worth
living unless it gave scope for the exercise of a dissentient conscience. Without enlarging on the desperate dullness of a world
in which everyone agreed, he implied that mutual agreement
took a multitude of shapes, including pacts between bandit
gangs to divide the fruits of their plunder, and that legislation
by majority agreement was grossly deceptive without reference
to its underlying motive. 'A gathering of political representatives cannot possibly have any personal conscience,' he declared. 'Conscience can only be collective in the light of faith.'

Worst of all, the powers of formerly absolute monarchies
(except for a time in England) were hardly shorn at all by the
new Western *Rechtstaat*; in many ways they were extended.
Sheltering behind the legend of national sovereignty and the
popular cliché of reform, the peoples' representatives revelled in
a spate of new laws and regulations. Hence there spread an ever-
widening breach between the inward sense of justice and the
nominal legal justice derived from squabbling over the ambiguous clauses of unwieldy statute-books. The increase of appeals

from lower to higher courts was one symptom of the gross discrepancy between legal justice and equity. Enforcement of the most elaborate criminal codes had only proved that laws were powerless to diminish crime, let alone to cure the causes of crime. The imposing accumulation of new civil laws had not ensured, and never could ensure, that justice would be better carried out.

In any case the tightening legal network provoked bolder defensive measures to evade the law. And all the time, whether or not they successfully circumvented the laws, the minds of more and more dissatisfied men were burning with a vague desire for primitive vengeance, 'an eye for an eye and a tooth for a tooth'. This concealed civil war between rulers and subjects had been intensified by the false promises of the French Revolution, and was still fostered by its inept political legacy which confused the life of a state with its institutional forms. In the long run, Khomyakov estimated, internal moral decay, leading to mental enfeeblement, would ruin the West.

Did Russia as a state present a less gloomy picture of spiritual dry rot than the steady decline of Western standards during the impressive advance of Western economic prosperity? In fact, she hardly did, and Khomyakov honesty admitted that unpalatable truth. But in so far as Russians, while conscious of its evils, still preferred their own enlightened autocracy (a personal state conscience overriding the mechanical tyranny of state law) their country had not yet forfeited her eventual chance of giving birth to a more civilized society. 'All the benefits of social autonomy, a free Press, independent science, security of individuals from arbitrary violence, all these will lead to nothing, if at the head of the state there does not stand an unrestricted living integrity of conscience, feeling its own responsibility to God and to History, unswayed by human prejudices and temptations.' For instance, the Emperor reserved an overriding right (outside the law) to expropriate private property, if his sense of justice demanded such drastic intervention. Khomyakov commended that right. In spite of his disgust for Western socialism, he readily maintained that there is no such thing as inviolable private property; all property confers an obligation that it should be rightly 'utilized'; the holder must be prepared to justify his ownership. But Khomyakov refused to jump to any legal conclusions about what constitutes abuse of property.

Each case should be judged on its own merits. 'Let conscience also play its part in civil law.'

Khomyakov's defence of Russian autocracy on grounds of moral unassailability is full of fairly obvious pitfalls. It may happen that an able sovereign, confident that he incorporates God's will, can fruitfully set at naught the more exasperating man-made laws. But these autocratic actions, even if semi-divine, rarely further the cause of justice, as most human beings conceive it. So far as we can see, God is completely unconcerned with human justice, and what we call 'acts of God' are much more inscrutable than Acts of Parliament. The universe does not exist in order to please or displease a few human beings inhabiting a minor planet. Moreover, assuming, like Confucius, that monarchs could really stand above all factions, and are therefore bound to promote the rule of wise and virtuous men, Khomyakov draws a veil over the frightful mess that can be made by feeble, foolish, or merely lazy autocrats.

Indeed he senses the untenability of his position, and half retreats from it, or finds more *terre à terre* reasons to condone it, He is appalled by the grossly exaggerated importance which modern minds attach to political institutions. Seen in their proper light as mere concessions to human weakness, they deserved a less conspicuous place. In any case a religious-minded autocrat might minimize the idolatry extended to political machinery, and prove to be at least no worse than his self-seeking competitors for power. Better the devil you know than the devil you don't know. 'We already have an autocratic government', Khomyakov observes; 'be that as it may—but let us beware of producing a despotic society—that would be fatal. If society is to prove fertile, it must on no account become embroiled in politics. . . . The Government can and must protect, but only society creates.'[1]

In other words, the life-blood of a nation, far from circulating in its government, may flow sluggishly even through its social organism, unless society is protected, stimulated and granted discriminate freedom in order to create. Such a task demanded exceptional powers of insight and forbearance from the ruling minority. 'Social organization when it changes, ought to apply the inner life of peoples to their outward life. But is our inner life ready for any such change? Is our culture mature? Only a

[1] *Sochineniya*, vol. 8, pp. 391 *et seq.*

process which develops slowly and imperceptibly can be fruitful and viable; whatever changes too quickly and abruptly must be unhealthy and subject to disease.'

The prospect for Russia is promising in that it opens a fresh vista which the West can no longer provide. But it will prove to be a deceptive mirage, unless Russians make up their own minds in time, and learn to distinguish the latest European follies from the more solid European achievements. That was Khomyakov's principal, though still very tentative, recommendation to his puzzled compatriots. The new Russian intelligentsia, on whom so many future decisions depend, must start by shaking themselves free from that arid foreign scholasticism 'which embraces everything and everywhere brings death. Some people vainly imagine that their scholasticism is still alive, because it is dying to the latest tune in a different hemisphere.' Ivan Kireyevsky had voiced the same thought more mildly: 'I think German learning can serve us as a most useful method of passing over from borrowed systems to an autonomous mode of thought which will correspond to the vital needs of ancient Russian culture. . . .'[1]

V

Khomyakov lived long enough to witness the havoc wrought on impressionable Russian minds, too easily carried away by the stream of seductive Western sophistries. He himself admired Hegel sufficiently to understand him, but not enough to be misled. 'The Phenomenology of Hegel will remain the immortal monument of an inexorably severe and consistent dialectic. . . . It is none the less surprising that no one has observed till now that this immortal work is simultaneously a decisive condemnation of all rationalism. . . . The passage of thought into the world of finite phenomena is in no way an act of logical necessity, but it is an act of moral liberty.'[2] Indeed he praised Hegel's philosophy most of all for its *negative* achievement, for its unconsciously solemn liquidation of all the old towering claims of systematic rational thought. While he urged that 'the fight against Hegel should teach us mental discipline', he warned his compatriots emphatically against the snare of taking Hegel too seriously or literally. 'Severe though one-sided in its

[1] I. Kireyevsky: *Sochineniya*, vol. 1, p. 263.
[2] *Sochineniya*, vol. 12, pp. 187–8.

analysis, utterly null in its synthesis, the failure of Hegelianism
revealed the depth of the spiritual abyss over which German
philosophy had hovered for so long, without being aware of it.
Thereby Hegel incontestably rendered us a great service. For
after him all further efforts to formulate pure philosophic
thought are proved to be utterly impossible. In the same way,
all attempts to build systems, like the already old-fashioned
Owenism, or the new socialism, will fail and lead to nothing.'[1]

Take heed from the German lesson, Khomyakov warned. For
a few years Hegel reigned as Germany's intellectual idol, an
article of German faith. And though that phase was over, he
had established himself as a German habit of mind. 'Pure
rationalism and modern materialism are merely two sides of one
and the same system, for which I can find no better name than
predestined denial of liberty'; and in more concrete terms:
'Between Hegel's philosophy and French communism there is
a close and legitimate bond, though no one has yet defined it.'[2]
Khomyakov found the nearest religious counterpart to Hegel in
Buddhism, yet Buddhism, he said, 'is as much superior to it as
any faith is bound to be superior to any philosophy'.

Many Russian intellectuals, after their first flush of enthusiasm had waned, were apt to find that their German or French
idols had feet of clay. But while their naïve sense of history
taught them that the latest European fashions were the best, it
also encouraged them to infer that they themselves might herald
the most startling and brilliant of all the new phenomena. So
their next step was to fall back on the worship of mother Russia,
arrayed in the visionary and borrowed plumes of German or
French speculation. Hence emerged the successive waves of
Russian Schellingians, Fichteans, Hegelians, Fourierists, Positi-
vists and Marxians, each rising to an aggressively self-conscious
crest of Russian foam. But Khomyakov refused to swim with
that tide. Like Turgenev in *Smoke*, he abandoned hope in the
politically minded Russian European. Strange as it may seem
today, he pointed instead to England, for he found in England
not only an encouraging exception to the normal course of
European history, but also a living though limited example of
the type of society which Russians were struggling to achieve.
Apart from any soothing gratification which they may give to

[1] *Sochineniya*, vol. 1, p. 150.
[2] *Ibid.*, vol. 12, p. 178.

the universally vilified inhabitants of the British Isles, Khomyakov's views on England are instructive and almost unique; for, though there have been Russian Anglomaniacs as well as the more familiar Russian Anglophobes, intelligent and well-informed Russian Anglophils are few and far between.

To start with, England appealed to Khomyakov as the only country in Europe still governed—and proud of being governed —more by custom and healthy instinct than by Roman administration and law. 'Thought moving in harmony with life is a great thing. It is sad when the two are separated. That lesson can be learned from England, from the people which best represents in Europe a civilization other than the Roman one. England is faithful to the past. Therein lies her intellectual strength. But one could hardly accuse her of remaining stationary, of turning her face away from new things. Only she does not cut down century-old trees in order to plant in their place feeble year-old seedlings. Therefore she will bequeath no deserts to coming generations. Strange land! It somehow guessed that only by preserving could it move forward, that the only true progress consists in what never repudiates its own origins. But other countries of Europe have not acted thus. They have cut off the roots of everything alive, so that their society disperses like sand, scattered by the gusts of every storm. History will show to what extent destiny or human folly are chiefly responsible for this work of destruction. But whatever opinions we may hold about the causes, the effects are manifest.'[1]

In England the hidden springs of life flowed strongly because her free society, while firmly regulated by tradition, had escaped being paralysed by a rigid network of laws. The state was strong, and not at the mercy of ignorant unstable crowds; but it was strictly limited in its range of power; it kept within reasonable bounds and wisely minded its own business. In a letter to the *Moskvityanin*, published there in 1848, Khomyakov drew the Russian public's attention to the secret of England's social stability and prosperity. 'In reality every Englishman is a Tory at heart. Exceptions are rare, and then as a rule they are people who have been enslaved by some system of thought, beaten down by poverty or corrupted by the way of life in large towns. . . . The history of England is to an Englishman much more than a mere thing of the past. It lives in all his present customs,

[1] *Sochineniya*, vol. 1, pp. 187–8.

in every detail of his daily life. The Englishman enjoys to see
the broad-shouldered beefeaters guarding the Tower of London
dressed in their strange medieval costume. . . . He is happy
that the boys in Christ's Hospital school still wear the long blue
coats which they wore in the reign of Edward VI. He walks
through the long aisles of Westminster Abbey, not with the
puffed-up vanity of a Frenchman, nor with the antiquarian
pedantry of the German, but with a deep sincere ennobling
affection. These graves belong to his family, and a great family
it is. I do not speak of the peer and the professional man, but
of mechanics and cab-drivers—for Toryism is just as strong
among the common people as it is in the upper ranks of society.
Luckily every Whig is also something of a Tory, merely because
he is English. Liberalism may provide his daily bread, but
Toryism is all his joy and charm in life.' 'England is a country
in which Tories fight with Whigs'; Khomyakov observed; and
pointedly added: 'To the intelligent observer, and certainly to
the impartial Russian, the paralysing aridity of Liberalism in
its efforts to destroy the past, and its deadly lack of feeling when
it attempts to construct, are plainly evident.' His own sympathies did not blind him to unpleasant probabilities, and
he feared that the Whigs might prevail. 'The blows of the
Protestant axe resound ever louder and more regularly. They
cut away the thousand-year-old roots, and the mighty tree is
groaning.'

While he delighted in the cultured conservatism of England,
coinciding so surprisingly with her technical and industrial
revolution, he also saw the ugly side of English arrogance and
insular self-satisfaction. Indeed he prophesied that these corrod-
ing vices, if they spread unchecked, would hasten England's
downfall. Nevertheless, his benevolent eye discerned redeeming
qualities hidden beneath the surface. 'Every foreign country
regards England as the product of convention, strict formality,
cold calculation and a soul-destroying struggle for material gain
—all joined up with national and personal vanity, only modified
by some half-sincere, half-hearted charity. Such is England in
her foreign policy, in everything of which she seems to be proud,
and which makes her the envy of other nations. Yet inward
England is not like that; she is full of spiritual life and strength,
of wisdom and love. This England, in many ways so different to
the other Western countries, remains incomprehensible to them,

and often to English people themselves.' In the English character, he observed, there was one affinity with the Russian people, 'an instinctive and altogether sound distrust of the human intellect'.

Some of our neo-Christians have jumped to the conclusion that Khomyakov wished to commend exclusively the virtues of energetic English Protestants. This seems unlikely, especially if we consider his scathing comments on the Anglican Church. 'Neither a tradition nor a doctrine,' he called it, 'but a mere establishment', and therefore a moribund thing. . . . 'Like a narrow isthmus of sand, beaten by the powerful waves of two enemy oceans, the Anglican Church crumbles on both sides into Romanism and Dissent. In principle it belongs to Orthodoxy, but is kept outside by its petty historical provinciality.'

He expressed greater enthusiasm about the law-courts, and he singled out the English jury system as an institution which embodied the most profound moral intuition, notably because it insisted on a unanimous verdict in all civil and criminal cases. Having visited London and Oxford, Khomyakov had acquired some chastening experience of English peculiarities. He conducted a lengthy correspondence with Mr. William Palmer, a Fellow of Magdalen College, Oxford, who, dissatisfied with Anglican insipidity, was toying with the idea of becoming a convert to the Orthodox Church. In spite of Khomyakov's eloquent encouragement, Mr. Palmer resisted the charms of Orthodoxy, and after an exhilarating sojourn in Rome he entered the safer Roman fold. 'Poor Palmer', was Khomyakov's comment; he pitied him as another victim of Catholic wiles.

Writing in the palmy days of the mid-nineteenth century, Khomyakov undoubtedly admired England for qualities which have not noticeably survived, but among these the English brand of Christianity occupied a minor place. Chiefly, and so unlike his radical contemporaries, he respected the tenacity of traditional culture which went hand in hand with such a dazzling and adventurous industrial progress. Therefore he considered that during the parallel age of transformation which had clearly started for Russian culture, Russia could learn more solid social lessons from England than from any other Western tutor. He qualified this advice by adding a strong word of warning: 'God preserve us from self-satisfied people and from national self-satisfaction.' For he regretfully observed these same

English national vices taking shape among his own compatriots, and without the compensating English sense of compromise and philosophic scepticism. He feared that the newly-educated Russian's attitude towards his country's primitive millions was growing too self-important, patronizing or priggishly doctrinaire. 'Perhaps a love for Russia really exists in us, but it is dangerously like the love for Hottentots, negroes and Indians, cherished by the virtuous Englishman in company with the conviction that he is their moral and intellectual superior, and with his self-gratifying desire to play the part of a benefactor, either present or future.'

The Jesuit convert, Prince Gagarin, in his book *La Russie sera-t-elle Catholique?* had wounded many Slavophil susceptibilities when he warned people that 'Orthodoxy, Autocracy and National Character' represented in truth nothing other than the oriental Russian formula of the nineteenth-century revolutionary Idea. Khomyakov, though he deplored Gagarin's renegade example, came closer to him than he realized when he voiced his own horror of Russian national pride, 'a crazy and false patriotism expressed in deeds of violence and anger'. If this was the miserable Russian alternative to the dry rot of Western rationalism, then surely both were sterile. Surely there must be a more authentic Russian advantage over the West.

For Khomyakov the canker of modern Western civilization lay in its one-sided faith in the triumph of cumulative rational knowledge. Having first smothered personal conscience, this knowledge had next, through gradual disillusion with its own results, led to a nervous repudiation of logical analysis as a valid method. The devouring analysis of science, because it was pursued without a sure guiding sense of value or suitable application, had fostered a hopeless cynicism in the conduct of human affairs. Therefore some Western intellectuals, terrified out of their wits, were rushing to the opposite extreme, denouncing science as a suicidal weapon and preaching a return to noble savagery. Only a virgin Russia, partly inspired and partly warned by European experience, could soberly take stock of the whole Western impasse, and thus avoid falling in her turn a prey to either of these devastating errors. She could safely borrow and apply European science in all its ramifications, provided she remembered 'l'esprit qu'on veut avoir gâte souvent celui q'on a', provided she knew how to test each experiment by her native powers of judgement, and so long as she maintained intact her ancient striving for moral integrity. Such was Khomyakov's picture of Russian potentialities, and of the indispensable provisos attached to their fulfilment.

VI

In his few but pointed remarks about the function of education, Khomyakov failed to elaborate the means by which incipient Russian education could steer a successful middle course between Western extremes. But he had no vestige of doubt that the parents of every child, his home and the society around him, provided the absolute essentials of education, and that school teaching could at best contribute a minor and technical part. He deplored the ill-considered modern spread of useless University chairs and senseless petty specializations, which, he said, far from helping true learning, gradually undermine its severe discipline and forfeit the respect of its pupils. At the same time he felt strongly that a truly civilized state must be ready to bear some moral responsibility for keeping society up to the mark. But what might be a virtue for the enlightened Russian state would easily become a vice if applied to over-democratic America! 'No doubt a state, which claims to be no more than an accumulation of business people in defence of their material interests, like for instance, the North American state, has almost no right to interfere in matters of education. . . . But what in America appears to be a doubtful right, becomes not only a right but a direct obligation in our land of Russia, with its duty to bring forth a human society founded on laws of the highest morality and Christian truth.'[1]

Khomyakov also favoured the inculcation of that uncomfortable and peculiarly Russian conception of collective guilt, arguing that the whole of society must bear the blame for every crime or error committed by any of its members. He hardly paused to investigate the intolerable demands which this principle, if taken seriously, would make on honest people who wanted to enjoy life, although they knew that numerous fellow-citizens swindled, stole or murdered. Nor did he face the hitherto insoluble problems which it created by turning punishment into a colossal branch of corrective education, obliged to treat

[1] *Sochineniya*, vol. 1, p. 348.

crime with sentimental tenderness like an interesting illness, rather than as an evil to be stamped out. Unfortunately his writings on education form the most scattered and untidy section of Khomyakov's social thought. We should bear in mind how much of it had to appear in veiled forms in order to pacify the nervous censors. For the same reason, most of his theological writings first saw the light of day in French.

His *Message to the Serbs* (1859), first published abroad (Leipzig, 1860), embodied a frank and full summary of his final social recommendations, and he himself attached importance to it as a comprehensive statement. All the survivors among the leading Slavophils approved it. Pogodin, Koshelëv, Elyagin, Yury Samarin, and the brothers Aksakov, agreed to append their names as co-signatories. The message thus assumed the character of a joint Slavophil manifesto, apart from being Khomyakov's spiritual last will and testament, and his final bequest to the Slavophil cause. He died of cholera in the following year.

Though addressed to the Serbs, it is clearly intended to apply to all Orthodox peoples, especially to Russians, who stood most in need of its exhortations. It throws a revealing light on Russian relations with Poland and with the Slav minorities within the Austrian Empire. More than any other of Khomyakov's writings, it expounds Orthodoxy as an active personal and social faith rather than as a politico-religious creed or organized church, and it firmly sets this kind of Orthodoxy higher than any racial or state ties as the most sacred source of human union and the final criterion of social behaviour. No doubt the Communist creed, in so far as it still manages to keep a religious grip over frustrated human emotions, owes a lot to its skilful exploitation of this inherited Orthodox frame of mind.

'Only the Orthodox believer, preserving his whole personal freedom, but meekly acknowledging all his weakness, submits to the unanimous conscience of the whole commune. That is why the rural commune cannot preserve its basic rights outside Orthodox lands; that is why a Slav cannot be wholly Slav without Orthodoxy. Even our blood-brothers, corrupted by Western lies, whether Catholic or Protestant, admit that ruefully.

'Therefore the heretic should be for you like a guest, protected by you from injustice, and enjoying all your privileges in personal matters, but he should not be a citizen with full powers or a son of the great Serbian house . . . It is bitter to think that not all Slavs are Orthodox. We believe that in course of time the truth will enlighten them. . . .

'You are happier than all other peoples, in that every Serb treats another as his brother; you have no higher and lower, except the service of society, which defines people of different ranks according to the needs of the government. Keep that equality. Value that great treasure! Refuse to accept any laws, any Government measures or interference with your customs, which might destroy your natural brotherhood. All other countries follow an evil principle; in them pride of so-called higher class, anger and envy of so-called lower class, lead to internecine conflict and social decay. . . .

'Do not be infected by the example of the Poles, your blood-brothers. There a few thousand called themselves the nation, and the nation as a whole was treated like a herd of cattle, hardly worthy of a human name. And so in spite of her military prowess, her courage and glory, the Polish state fell. Do not forget such a lesson! Let the courts judge, let the ruler rule, let the prince reign, as society needs—but outside the sphere of his specific duties each Serb, now as ever, remains on equal terms with his neighbour. . . .

'You must learn a lot, brothers, from those peoples to whom God granted long ago freedom from political bondage, and who have therefore taken that opportunity to devote their thought and time to perfecting science and art. You see for yourselves, and there is no need to prove to you, what powers science gives to men, and how it enables them to harness nature to their service. You need to acquire much good and useful knowledge from other nations (whether they are Germans or not) in order to rise to the level of mental development to which you are entitled. Knowledge is an increase of mental enrichment, but true enlightenment transcends knowledge by including moral and spiritual elements. Many people who, owing to adverse circumstances, lack scientific knowledge, but are penetrated by moral conviction, come nearer to full enlightenment than those who know many things but lack the power of spiritual life. . . .

'It is better to inflict a severe punishment which impresses the criminal than one which appears to be light, or can unjustly be transferred to his family. Above all, preserve every kind of

communal institution and court. . . . The meeting of the *mir* is
for the people a school much more useful than any book education. The strong spirit and reason of the Russian peasant were
preserved by the *mir* meetings in spite of the slavery to which
they were bound by an unjust law. It is desirable that meetings
should settle issues by unanimous agreement. Such was the
ancient Slavonic custom. The custom of counting voices came
to the Slavs from Germans, as if wisdom and truth resided in the
majority of voices, whereas in fact the voting is often fortuitous.
Consider also that where a matter is decided by a majority vote,
the desire of people to convince their neighbours vanishes, or
is weakened; consequently the striving for agreement in conscience and reason is also weakened. . . .

'Many people think it is possible to reach a good end by employing an evil means. . . . Such a hope is deceptive. Evil means
generate a ferment in the good end, and cause the expected
good to turn into an unexpected evil. . . .

'You cannot surpass the Jesuit or the Austrian in cunning, but
you can easily conquer their cunning by your straightforward
frankness. In that you are strong. . . .

'Do not dwell a lot on the law and on your rights; but listen
to those who talk to you about your obligations. Respect your
spiritual pastors. They bear a heavy responsibility to God, and
it is right that they should enjoy our esteem. But do not
allow them to exalt themselves above you, as if the Church were
a thing apart and superior to the people. Guard your honour
jealously in this, for you are all members of God's Church.'

CHAPTER V

FIVE POLITICAL SLAVOPHILS

I

FYODOR TYUTCHEV (1803–1873) is less familiar to students of social thought than he is to that dwindling international group which still prizes thoughtful and intelligible poets. His intense and militant Slavophil actvity has long been eclipsed by his more lasting and sensitive evocation of 'magic thoughts that hide away from the noise and glare of day'. At first sight, especially for those who are determined to equate Slavophils with pan-Slav politicians, these twin aspirations of Tyutchev seem strangely discordant. But closer scrutiny reveals that his Slavophil ideal of human culture flows as a natural consequence from his poetic imagination, through a struggle to find for his vision a more coherent and immediate shape. At the same time his work is tinged with a haunting sense of failure to achieve this fusion. His poem *The Spoken Thought Becomes a Lie* is an ominous reflection on that conflict within him.

Tyutchev spent most of his early adult years in Europe, served his country as a diplomat in Munich and Turin, married two Bavarian wives in succession, and he both spoke and wrote most naturally in flawless French. Not till 1844 did he return to his native St. Petersburg, where he was appointed a Court Chamberlain and served at various posts in the Ministry of Foreign Affairs. There his intellectual eminence alone excused his eccentric behaviour. At court functions he is known to have disguised himself as a footman in order to observe more freely what was going on. On one occasion he became so absorbed in argument with a friend that he halted the procession of the Grand Duchess whose train he had to hold. Count Sologub found Tyutchev's principal charm in his vivid flow of conversation, in which all his remarks *coulaient de source*. Awkward and shy until he warmed up, he shone in his element at Petersburg evening receptions under the soft glitter of chandeliers, when the gay rustle of ladies' silk dresses mingled with rippling laughter and brilliant repartee.

KONSTANTIN AKSAKOV
After a photograph

Most people expected that twenty-two formative years of cosmopolitan life in European cities would have turned Tyutchev not only into a polished worldly European, cultured to the finger-tips, but thence into a Westernizer as thoroughgoing as Turgenev in his painful conviction of boorish Russian backwardness. In fact the reverse took place. The longer Tyutchev lived in Europe, the less he liked it, and the more incurably Russian he felt at heart. Though he much preferred French to Germans, he called the French 'that charming and absurd people, who inspire you with every kind of sentiment except respect'. It is true he made scathing remarks about Russia as 'the realm of official ranks and the knout', and sometimes pined to escape from the tedious Petersburg society which later lionized him. Nor did peasant Russia offer him the ideal haven of refuge which some of this contemporaries found in it. The soothing but bare and poverty-stricken countryside depressed his spirits. Nevertheless some inscrutable awakening of mind impelled him to give voice in his native tongue to an intimate vision of his motherland, a vision first seen in focus when he contrasted it with his prolonged but bitterly disappointing experience of Europe.

These poor villages, this niggardly nature,
Land of long endurance, land of the Russian people,
The proud stranger fails to see or value
What shines secretly and modestly through your meek nakedness;

You, my native land, the King of Heaven trod
In the guise of a serf, bowed down by the weight of his cross,
And blessed you in passing.
(1855)

Even as Tyutchev's mature lyrics penetrate far beyond the fleeting personal moment, so do his political poems and essays transcend the topical political issues which first provoked them; they build up step by step an increasingly articulate and emphatic plan of human action pieced together out of his mystic intuitions and ingrained Slavophil beliefs. Major historical events, impinging on the growth of his personal experience, clearly decided the shaping of this plan. As early as 1830 the Russian Government's suppression of the Polish revolt impelled him to write:

Even as Agamemnon sacrificed his own daughter to the gods,
So we in unhappy Warsaw
Struck our fateful blow,
Redeeming at the cost of blood
Russia's integrity and peace.

Cast away that infamous wreath
Woven by a slavish hand!
Not for the Koran of Autocracy
Did rivers of Russian blood flow;

Another thought, another faith, fired Russian hearts.
By the threat of a saving example,
To gather under a single Russian banner
The scattered family of Slavs,
And lead them, like an army with one mind,
Forward to feats of human culture!

His poem *The Alps* (1831) pictured the Slav countries as a range of frozen mountains lit up by the dawn, but significantly the lesser peaks shone with a rosy light *reflected* from the highest one, the Russian mountain, and the first to catch the rays of the rising sun.

The astonishing poem *Russian Geography* (1829) indulges in a more sinister piece of distinctly spatial megalomania;

Seven inland seas and seven mighty rivers,
From the Nile to the Neva, from the Elbe to China,
From the Volga to the Euphrates, from the Ganges to the
    Danube,
That is the Russian Empire.

By bringing this dream-Empire one step nearer to waking life, there would arise a new Eastern Europe, welded into a solid phalanx of states inspired and led by Russia. For Russia was neither a part of Asia, nor a world of its own detached from Asia and Europe, but a legitimate sister of Western Europe engaged in a heroic reconstruction of the Christian Eastern Empire, more European in essence, in uncorrupted Christian civilization, than Western Europe had been since 1789. Tyutchev clearly envisaged that immense Eastern bloc as the only rightful counterbalance to a Western Europe dominated by the German race (at that time represented by the Austrian Empire and Prussia).

Moreover, he conceived the Slav struggle with Germany not merely as a fight for political and economic supremacy in Europe, but as an indispensable prelude to the next step of world-wide unification on an Orthodox religious basis. 'Will Eastern Europe, this genuine Eastern Empire, already three-quarters formed, for which the first Empire of the Byzantine Cesars, and the second of the Orthodox Tsars, were only a feeble preliminary sketch—will this Empire ripen naturally into its final completion, or will it be obliged to win its rights by force of arms, by subjecting the whole world to the direst miseries?' (*Russia and Germany*, 1844.) 'There exists only one secular power, leaning on the Universal Church, which is capable of reforming the Papacy without injuring religion. No such power ever existed or could exist in the West. Nor is this power in present-day Russia. It will be in the great Graeco-Russian Orthodox Empire into which Russia must expand. . . . If the Russian Empire does not develop, it will explode.'

Tyutchev was obsessed, and rightly so, by thoughts and forebodings about the German race as the most formidable obstacle to Slav fulfilment. His essay *Russia and Germany* is objective enough to admit that there exist two conflicting Germanys—or rather two contradictory tendencies fighting for mastery there, 'On the one hand you have the sovereigns, the governments of Germany, with their reliable carefully considered policy; on the other stands that second master of our age, public opinion, which turns and twists wherever it is blown by winds and waves.' Germany owed to Russia her liberation from Napoleon. Her rulers recognized this debt, and never had relations between the German states and Russia been friendlier and more fruitful than in the last thirty years. But German public opinion, in the shape of the popular Press, was fanning the flames of a senseless hostile clamour against Russia. Its favourite slander was to say that Russian policy aimed at luring the smaller states into her orbit at the expense of 'the legitimate influence of the two great states of the Union' (Austria and Prussia). Others, with equal injustice, accused the Russian government of systematically opposing constitutional reform in Germany. This irresponsible campaign was influencing German rulers against their better judgement, and it encouraged throughout Europe the imbecile fashion of gaping with horror at Russia as 'the ogre of the nineteenth century'. Such was her bitter reward for all she had endured in raising her Western neighbours from their downfall, for her valiant efforts 'to replace Europe on her former pedestal'. 'There is no need for me to plead in defence of Russia', Tyutchev concluded in proud disdain; 'her most reliable defender is History itself. All the trials suffered by Russia in the last three centuries History has irrevocably decided in her favour!'[1]

Tyutchev's impassioned argument successfully pricks the bubble of pan-German pretensions, without convincing us that his country is therefore predestined to rule Europe more beneficially than Germany could. Rather, it looked as if the Russian government, with its German dynasty, Germanized officialdom and Prussian administrative methods, would continue to incorporate within its system a multitude of German defects. His criticisms of the Austrian Empire, which he aptly called 'an Achilles with heels everywhere', have sometimes a harsh but unadmitted relevance to his own country. 'Through her and in her, the German race feels the power to crush, exploit to its own advantage, and, even more in a moral than in a political sense, to reduce to nullity the two other great European races, the Latins in Italy, and the Slavs wherever they may be found. It seems absurd and laughable that people who for a thousand years proved so conspicuously unsuccessful in organizing their own affairs should be so possessed by the passion for dominating others.'[2] Tyutchev felt sure that Western hatred and dread of Russia would sooner or later lead to 'a second Punic War of the West'. That war would finally decide whether the most numerous of the three main European races, after having lost in the struggle against the other two for so long, was destined or not to be crushed by them, to lose its historical autonomy and to cease to be anything except 'a huge corpse with a borrowed soul'.

Tyutchev's next major political essay, *Russia and Revolution* (1848), widened the scope of *Russia and Germany*, by dividing the whole world into the two rival camps which its title indicates. In its forecast of implacable hostility between two major groups of Powers, the essay is prophetic. Only more recently the rôles seem to have been reversed. Russia (in the eyes of her new leaders) stands for the borrowed principle of revolution,

[1] F. Tyutchev: *Stikhotvoreniya*, p. 11, Moscow, 1945.
[2] *Ibid.*, p. 296.

discarded by the leaders of the West, while Europe, or Western Union, appears to have taken up the anti-revolutionary banner of Tyutchev's aspiring Empire—but on the whole without its ambiguous Christian faith, its iron discipline or far-reaching territorial ambitions. And what was for Tyutchev a spiritual duel, fought to the death for straightforward vital principles, has today cooled down and turned more visibly into a clash of power politics, of astute calculations in gaining economic advantage, thinly disguised by moral or economic slogans which fewer people take at their face value.

Tyutchev's words glow with the fire of conviction: 'Already in Europe there exist only two powers, Russia and Revolution. . . . Between them no negotiations, no treaties are possible. The existence of one of them alone is equivalent to the death of the other. On the result of that struggle now opening between them depends for many centuries to come the political and religious future of mankind.

'Russia is above all the Christian Empire. The Russian people are Christian not only in their Orthodox faith, but especially by virtue of a quality even more intimate than Faith—I mean that faculty of self-renunciation and sacrifice which is the very core of their moral nature.

'The Revolution is above all anti-Christian . . . the human ego referring to itself alone, recognising and accepting no duty beyond its own personal pleasure, the ego, in a word, substituting itself for God—that is not a new thing in history, but what is new is the absolutism of the human ego erected into a political and social right. . . . That novelty in 1789 was called the French Revolution. Since then, through all its external transformations the Revolution has remained true to its essential nature, and perhaps it has never felt so intensely anti-Christian as at the present moment, when it has adopted the Christian motto of "brotherhood". . . . Instead of a brotherhood preached and accepted in God's name, it claims to establish a brotherhood imposed by terror of the "sovereign people". . . . There is not a single human desire or need in our contemporary society, however sincere or legitimate it may be, which the Revolution does not capture and convert into a lie. . . .

'Is it surprising that the West hates Russia, is ready to start a crusade against her—a crusade which was always the cherished dream of revolution? . . . But the West is vanishing, everything will fall and perish in that widespread conflagration—the Europe of Charlemagne and the Europe of the 1815 Treaties, the Roman Papacy and all the Western Kingdoms, Catholics and Protestants, faith long ago exhausted and reason carried to a senseless extreme. Law and order will become unthinkable, freedom no longer possible, and over all these ruins prepared by her own actions, Western civilization will commit suicide. And when, over that vast shipwreck, we see that still vaster Empire floating like a sacred ark, then who will dare to doubt the Russian mission? Will we, her children, show ourselves poor in faith or paltry in spirit?' (*Russia and Revolution*, 1848.)

The 1848 revolutions inspired this *cri de coeur*. At that time the Russian Empire towered like a giant in solitary strength, and like an impregnable cliff withstood alone the waves of revolution that swept through a Europe of toppling thrones. So Tyutchev pictured her in his triumphant poem 'The Sea and the Cliff' (1848). But a few years later came the Crimean War. The granite cliff began to crumble. Only the blind could fail to see that governmental Russia had in fact lost all sense and feeling of her vaunted historic mission. Tyutchev ruefully admitted that his hopes were dashed. 'Will those dry bones come to life?' Could God's breath revive them, 'the breath of a storm?', he asked in one of his most disconsolate poems.

Yet since the Holy Alliance, and the majestic solidarity of European culture which it claimed to stand for, had collapsed before his eyes, Tyutchev believed more firmly than before that Western Europe was disintegrating. His injured patriotic pride found relief in even stronger moral condemnation of a West, victorious in arms and incontestably superior to Russia in material progress. 'Every blasphemous brain, every atheistic nation, has risen from the depths of the kingdom of darkness in the name of light and freedom', he wrote about Russia's enemies in the Crimean War. Nor had he any illusions about the kindly intentions expressed by the liberal Western politicians: 'The more liberal they sound, the baser they are; civilization is their fetish, but they have lost the key to its idea.'

Where Tyutchev saw most clearly the writing on the wall was in the latest European perversions of religion. His remarkable essay, 'The Papacy and the Roman Question' (*Revue des Deux*

Mondes, 1850) pays equal attention to the decline of genuine
religious faith and to the infectious popularity of its misleading
substitutes. He indicated that the organized brute force of
Rome, deprived of its original spiritual virtue, might conquer
in the end. 'Meanwhile Protestantism with its numerous ramifications, after having functioned for barely three centuries, is
dying of senile decrepitude in all the countries where it reigned
till now—with the solitary exception of England, and there its
few remaining signs of life aspire to rejoin Rome. . . .

'We know the fetichism of the West, which clings to all forms,
formulae and political mechanisms. *This fetichism has become the
last religion of the West.* But only those with eyes blindfolded
against evidence can suppose that the liberal or semi-liberal
institutions imposed on the Pope will, in the present state of
affairs in Europe, Italy and Rome, remain for long in the hands
of moderate, balanced, temperate opinion.' . . . Soon they would
turn into a battering-ram, not only against the temporal power
of the Pope, but against the very foundations of religion. Such a
result was inevitable, because the human ego, delivered to itself,
becomes passionately anti-Christian. 'What is the sovereignty of
the people except the human ego multiplied by numbers, *i.e.*
relying on violence? That is the great novelty which the French
Revolution brought into the world. For the first time a political
society accepted to rule over it a state divorced from any super-
human sanctions, a state which admitted it had no soul, or if
it had, a non-religious one. . . . But we know very well their
so-called neutrality in religious matters is not a sincere com-
ponent of revolutionaries. . . . If that hypocritical neutrality
were to acquire a sense, if it could grow into something better
than a lie and a trap, the modern state would consent to re-
linquish all moral authority, and resign itself to being a simple
police institution for enforcing the law, a mere material fact.
. . . But the modern state does not proscribe state religions
only because it has produced its own, and that religion is
revolution!' How can so-called liberal opinion, Tyutchev concludes, pride itself on being so eminently reasonable and be so
blind? How can liberals fail to see that institutions, once they
have been wilfully deprived of the soul which gave them life,
turn into nothing more than a dead encumbrance?

Because he ridiculed attempts to make the Papacy 'constitutional', it would be wrong to infer that Tyutchev cherished any

K

sympathy for the Catholic Church as a bulwark of religion in a chaotic world. On the contrary (and in this he forestalled Dostoevsky) he vehemently loathed Catholicism, and he seems to have sincerely believed that the ambition and crookedness of Rome were largely responsible for Europe's spiritual decline. Certainly the curbing of the Pope's temporal power and fiscal privileges since 1848 had done nothing to decrease his spiritual claims. The famous Encyclical of Pope Pius IX, condemning the free exercise of individual conscience as one of the several 'errors of the age' (November 1864), roused Tyutchev to a fury of denunciation:

> Still more terrible and merciless
> In our time—the day of God's judgement,
> Will punishment overtake the false Vicar of Christ
> In apostate Rome.
> Throughout the centuries much was forgiven him,
> Crooked reasoning, blackest crimes,
> But God's truth will not forgive
> His latest censure . . .
>
> (December, 1864.)

His increasingly cynical view of Russian political relations with the West was the consequence, not the cause, of Tyutchev's profound moral opposition to a sworn enemy. 'The only natural Russian policy towards the Western Powers—is not an alliance with one or the other, but a deliberate disruption and division of them all; divided against each other, through impotence, they may cease to be our enemies, but through conviction they never will!'[1] Even though a sullen neutrality might occasionally give place to a short-lived tactical alliance with one European country or another, he reminded people of Danilevsky's trenchant saying that *civil war in the West is Russia's best ally.*

In 1858 Tyutchev was appointed President of the Committee on Foreign Censorship, where he started to serve as a link between the Ministry of Foreign Affairs and his son-in-law, Ivan Aksakov, whose eloquent articles played such an important part in rousing Slavophil opinion and action throughout the sixties. He praised the veteran Foreign Minister, Prince Gorchakov, for bringing to bear on world affairs the spiritual power of Russia, for being the first statesman to turn this power into a potent factor in international politics. In 1870 he wrote an enthusiastic

---

[1] K. Pigarev: *Literaturnoe Naslyedstvo*, No. 19, p. 206, Moscow, 1935.

poem to celebrate Russia's unilateral repudiation of that clause in the Treaty of Paris (1856) which restricted the movements of Russian warships in the Black Sea.

In his *Letter about Censorship in Russia* (1857), deploring the baleful influence of Herzen's *Bell* on immature minds, he urged the formation of a new officially-sponsored Russian journal, which should counteract sedition by attempting to direct and guide public opinion—a duty of the state, 'which', he said, 'bears as much direct responsibility for human souls as the Church does'. In the same letter he rather inconsistently argued, 'all the efforts of the crew will be in vain, unless the rising tide of national life itself lifts up the vessel and sets it afloat'. And despite the constant activity of these later years, Tyutchev was haunted by pessimistic forebodings about his country's future. 'Our days are numbered, who can count what's lost? The living life is now left far behind;'[1] he wrote, and with an extra touch of premonition, 'Mental debauchery, distortion of words, still spread, still threaten you'. Sometimes even the threatening outlook in the West seemed to him brighter than his gloomy native land.

> Shadow has darkened half the sky, only the West is bright with
>   moving rays.
> Linger, twilight day; prolong, prolong your enchanting spell.

While he clung to minor consolations, Tyutchev saw no civilized future in a Europe which had neither restored nor superseded the guiding insight of her religious-minded monarchs and aristocrats. For European monarchy, though it precariously survived, had been adulterated, vulgarized and spoiled. One by one he caustically summed up the motives of Europe's principal rulers : the Emperor Franz Joseph, that 'Austrian Judas', Louis Philippe, 'the shopkeeper king', the last Napoleon, ambiguous heir of mighty powers, who in 1871 paid the penalty of having been no better than 'a popular actor on the throne'. Towards the end his doubts began to tarnish even the sacred Imperial halo of Holy Russia. A year before his death he wrote an enigmatic letter, appearing to welcome the maximum chaos and destruction in the outside world, if nothing but these disasters could save the Russian Empire. Some Soviet critics have taken it to mean much more than that; they seem to think that

[1] F. Tyutchev : *Sochineniya*, p. 345, St. Petersburg, 1900.

Tyutchev, having recognized his error, thereby renounced his lifelong crusade against the anti-Christ of Revolution, and now looked forward to see revolution rage through Europe and destroy her, in order that a strong *republican* Russia might rush into the resultant vacuum and start to lead the world.[1]

'In the present state of minds in Europe', he wrote, 'that government which takes the initiative in making a major transformation, opening the republican era in the European world, would enjoy a great advantage over all its neighbours. Dynastic feeling, without which monarchy cannot survive, is waning everywhere, and even if sometimes an opposite movement takes place, that merely delays the huge flood.' This rounds off what he wrote in 1854. 'If the West were united, we should probably be destroyed. But there are two, the Red West and the one which is to be swallowed by the Red. For forty years we have held back the Red from his prey. But now that we stand ourselves on the edge of an abyss, it is the turn of the Red West to save us!'

II

The most militant and temporarily influential publicists of the Slavophil movement were Konstantin and Ivan Aksakov, the two robust sons of the famous author, Sergei Aksakov. The whole of Konstantin's decidedly impulsive mode of thought revolves round the well-conducted family as the core and pattern for every larger social organization. On this basis he made some wise remarks about the need for powerful state authority which held its strength in reserve, and about methods of harmonizing the more strident discords between spontaneous moral action and coercive 'law'. He belonged to that happy breed of buoyant self-reliant individuals who are assailed neither by preliminary doubts nor subsequent disillusion. He knew no tentative testing of his solid ground, no unhappy sense of preaching in the wilderness for infinitely distant hopes. His faith was inborn, vigorous and complete. Only when he tried to transform his personal convictions into a coherent national policy, he became naïve and one-sided, a fighter for a circumscribed but intangible cause.

The Aksakovs' family background of prosperous enterprising country squires is akin to that of the Kireyevskys, but the former

[1] See L. Grossman: *Tri Sovremennika*, 11 ff., Moscow, 1922.

were more urban and widely international in their sympathies, less centred in the isolated village commune and the Church. Sergei Aksakov's wife was of aristocratic Turkish descent. The Aksakovs' Moscow home showed all the informal geniality and generous abundance of an old-fashioned Russian country-house transferred to the metropolis. It swarmed with good-natured servants and a medley of serf craftsmen. Every day the huge dining table was laid with places for at least twenty people, and streams of guests, whether invited or unexpected, were wel-comed by the hospitable family. This happy active existence came to an end when Sergei Aksakov died (1859). The devoted Konstantin was broken by his father's death, and he himself died of grief and consumption a few months later. Foreign specialists called in to treat his illness gazed in helpless amaze-ment at this handsome giant pining away under their eyes in the full flower of life.

Konstantin Aksakov was unusually bold and persistent in his expression of political heresies. This ardour earned him the nickname of 'the Slavophil Belinsky'. He regarded the state in any and every form as an evil, a necessary one within a limited sphere, but pernicious and destructive of human conscience the moment it trespassed beyond its boundaries and abused its powers. Ivan Aksakov thus summed up his brother's teaching in a private letter: 'The essence of my brother's attitude lies in this, that the Russian people are not politically minded, never rebelled to fight for political rights, but are social people con-cerned with their inward lives and their agricultural mode of existence. They aspire, not to a perfect state, but to the crea-tion of a Christian society. Consequently their ideal is higher than that of Western nations who believe in the state, in out-ward organization, who seek only material well-being, and constantly change the form of the state, forgetting that the evil lies not in its form, but in its very principle. . . . The origin of government is the beginning of force and bondage; the origin of law (according to the apostle) is sin. The origin of Christianity is liberation from law, inward freedom. . . . The Russian ideal is higher, though doubtless a thousand times harder and more im-practicable. . . . In the West, the soul degenerates; its function is usurped by the increase of government regulations, by organiz-ing public welfare through a police system; law takes the place of conscience, regulations stifle inward impulse, even charity is

turned into a perfunctory mechanical business in the West.'
(Letter to Countess Blyudov, 15 January 1862.)[1]

Those in a position to judge cannot fail to be struck by some
ominous similarity between Aksakov's picture of what the West
was becoming and the internal state of modern Russia as Westernized by her Marxist leaders. Whereas Aksakov's ideal of a
more Christian society seems still an equally remote Utopia
everywhere, his forecast about the darkening course of history in
the West has been fulfilled more completely in the semi-Asiatic
Empire which he so clearly warned against these perils, than in
those European countries which first engendered them. At
least this proves the soundness of his instinct, in so far as he
sensed the approaching danger, and told his compatriots how to
act while there was still time to fight against it.

Aksakov saw the red warning signal ahead more clearly than
he saw the road to circumvent it, and in any case his advice
was made light of or unheeded at the time. But the fact that he
could not prevent the worst from happening does not detract
from his prescience; it cannot help to explain away a hideous
calamity as if it were the only high-road to improvement. He
and the early Slavophils remained obscure and without honour
until their teaching was degraded into political propaganda
against the Turkish and Hapsburg Empires. By that time its
avowed goal, the peaceful growth of a new Russian-European
civilization, a synthesis of all the noblest living elements in both,
had been abandoned as an over-arduous task, at once too
complex and too delicate for the majority to desire or understand. Changing their tactics, the crafty politicians and eloquent
demagogues extracted from the murdered corpse of Slavophilism a set of pan-Slav pan-Orthodox slogans, and with this
highly combustible fuel they lavishly fed the rising flames of
Russian nationalism in its first Imperial phase.

K. Aksakov exemplified most conspicuously the robust refusal of one clear-thinking group to succumb to that theoretical
fever, the outcome of the universal historical fatalism with
which Hegel and his politico-economic followers hypnotized so
many unstable intellectuals, No barren die-hard conservatism
at bay drove the Slavophils to set the Russian way of life *im
Werden* against the direction being taken by the modern West.
Only because they were convinced that Russia was following,

[1] N. Brodsky: *Ranniye Slavyanofili*, p. LIV, Moscow, 1910.

and should continue to follow, a wiser alternative course, did they exert every ounce of strength to save her from drifting into the adjacent whirlpool of contemporary Western political 'progress'.

Moreover, the Slavophils propounded the Russian alternative not only as a sound and feasible line of development for their own country, but equally as one which would shower civilizing benefits on the future world at large. In order to convert this idea into a driving force fit to move a historically minded age, a fresh interpretation of the Russian past became the first indispensable factor.

To propound and convincingly publicize such an original interpretation was Aksalov's principal task. He never tried to reconstruct a factually accurate picture of ancient Russia. A mass of cumbersome incoherent detail could only dim the purport of the living message. The most glaring naïveté of his approach was to deduce the principal features of the ancient Russian state from the single historically uncertain fact that their Varangian rulers differed substantially from ordinary conquerors, because the Russian people had freely invited them to come. Thus Aksakov attributes fantastic significance to the Russian delegates' legendary appeal to Rurik: 'Our country is great and abundant, but there is no order in it; come and rule over us.'

The popular election of the first Romanov Emperor by an Assembly of the Land provides a sounder factual example to support Aksakov's argument. In any case his underlying motive hardly required a multiplication of evidence to prove its worth. He needed merely to prove its practical possibility, and that much he did. In attaching so much importance to the non-political psychology, one might say the political incapacity, of the Russian people, he brought to light its two most pregnant consequences—first their wisdom in handing over the invidious task of government to the most efficient foreigners available, but secondly their firm retention of all their native customs and institutions, of all that was *not* handed over. Aksakov was determined to recall the social value of many traditional bodies which Peter's reforms had reduced to a shadow, but which had flourished in pre-Petrine Russia—the *Vetche* (an old Slav local Assembly), the rural commune, and the Assembly of the Land.

He set his heart on bringing to fuller fruition that peculiarly

Russian relationship which seemed in those archaic times to link the monarch and the multitude, *personifying* a religious bond which rose above ordinary national ties and commanded more fervent allegiance than any law. Only because the Russian temperament is so averse to political entanglements—and hence so free from political hypocrisy and its resultant cynicism —can Russians still treat government as a sacred trust, handed over with confidence to responsible individuals. For the same reason the moment their trust is betrayed and their moral indignation stirred, they can rebel against the government furiously. The Russian peasant will always hate and distrust administrative machinery the moment it interferes with his cherished local independence. He is associational only on the level of the family and the *mir*. He continues to revere the Tsar so long as the Tsar is his Protector and retains his absolute authority to override the whole administration, should he think fit to do so. The Tsar and his appointed Ministers cannot shirk direct responsibility by delegating it to a network of committees and public representatives. Thus Autocracy, held as a sacred personal trust, far from degenerating into a 'totalitarian' state, becomes the ultimate safeguard against despotic self-important officials and inhuman laws. Indeed it would be fatal to national morale if the Tsar were either identified with the administrative machine or overpowered by it. His function must be to stand above it and apart from it, with power to intervene on appropriate occasions, like Jupiter launching a thunderbolt from heaven.

. Such is Aksakov's view of government in the best Russian style. He expressly refutes the familiar Westernizers' charge that his defence of autocracy and his passion for ancient Russian institutions revealed him to be nothing better than a reactionary renegade. 'We often hear the Slavophils accused of wanting to go backwards instead of forwards', he wrote in the journal *Molva* (1857). 'This accusation is unjust. The Slavophils believe we should go back, not to the ancient state of Russia (that would mean fossilization and stagnation) but to the rightful road along which Russia was travelling (that means movement). Where there is movement, where there is a road, that movement is forwards! The phrase "go back" is senseless.'

His almost childish idolization of the Russian past was refreshingly free from any trace of racial pride or lust for power;

as a plea to preserve organic continuity it fitted into his plan of action for the Russian future. He found the most indispensable and vital link in preserving mutual confidence between rulers and people, together with mutual respect for each other's limited functions—an ideal which flatly contradicted the latest Western trend of compulsory regimentation by the state. The latter bred a negative reliance on obedience to laws and contracts, backed by force; therefore it sapped the positive confidence and faith which ought to inspire and stabilize relations between the 'land' and the Tsar. 'Laws do not demand sincerity, cannot secure that a man's actions harmonize with his conscience. They demand only that actions should be or *not* be of a certain kind. The legal formula cannot possibly be comprehensive, and being compulsory, imposed from outside, it loses that most potent virtue, the power of inward conviction and free acknowledgement of truth. Laws also lull the human being, so prone to laziness, soothe him and rescue him from the need for personal exertion and inward moral revival. . . . That way of legal conformity, of more and more government, is the way people have followed in the West.'[1]

Aksakov had grown up on the fertile and prosperous family estate in the Orenburg province. No doubt idyllic memories of childhood in this delightful countryside implanted in him his lasting devotion to the Russian peasant at his best; hence, too, his generous but childishly optimistic view of human nature. He never faced the familiar psychological problem that conscience tells different things to different people, or of what to do with people who remain deaf to any call of conscience. That call was too self-evident for him to doubt that others heard it as insistently as he did. Or perhaps he took for granted that the spur of hunger would always prick sharply enough in Russia to prevent the human will from being paralysed by apathy.

All thinking Russians hoped, and many believed, that Alexander II would open a new and brighter era in Russian history. The Crimean War, followed by the death of Nicolas I, had spelt the collapse of a rigid régime, In 1855 K. Aksakov wrote to his successor, Alexander II, an eloquent memorandum entitled *The Inner State of Russia*. This contained a brief diagnosis, followed by the most practical advice that the Slavophils

[1] N. Brodsky: *Ranniye Slavyanofili*, p. LI, Moscow, 1910.

could offer to the new sovereign. But the government considered it too dangerously frank to be published, so that it did not see the light of day till 1881 (*Rus'*, Nos. 26, 27). The document starts by re-asserting one of the most persistent Slavophil tenets: the Russian people as a whole have never wanted or pursued the exercise of political power and ruling rights. But this is far from meaning that they are natural slaves, weaklings, or broken victims of tyranny. When Pogodin wrote in the first issue of the new *Moskvityanin* that Russians had never been fierce aggressive conquerors like Europeans, but had shown throughout their history how indifferent they were to politics, how meekly obedient to their rulers, Aksakov protested that, on the contrary, Russians had always proved to be brave and tenacious fighters, throughout the duration of the Mongol yoke and again in 1612 and 1812. Although they shunned political initiative, the people's courage constantly rose to the occasion. Their appeal to the foreign Varangians brought Rurik to rule over them, and in 1613, after rescuing Moscow from the intolerable Poles, the people, left without a ruler, freely elected a new Tsar to fill the gap.

Even when popular rebellions broke out, they never sought to win political rights or change the form of government, rather than its personnel. Pugachëv, leader of the most formidable peasant revolt (1773) demanded the abolition of serfdom, possession of the land without rent, and punishment of 'malefactor landowners and bribe-taking officials'. But he claimed to be the rightful Tsar, Peter III (who had in fact been secretly murdered). The people wanted from their rulers no more than protection of their spiritual freedom and peaceful well-being. Their deliberate political restraint, Aksakov argued, proves their instinctive wisdom, for had they aimed at political rule for themselves they would be torn and distracted from their more important personal tasks by meddling with the gunpowder of state-power.

State-power must remain unlimited and monarchical, since every other form would involve interference by the people, which for their own sake is undesirable, because participation in government would corrupt them and destroy their peace of mind. On the other hand, while government can and must preserve society, it must never meddle with the people's chosen mode of life, though it should set them a worthy example. The Russian people, for their part, recognizing their government to be well-intentioned, with a legitimate need for unlimited powers, voluntarily and consciously recognize it also as a 'power of this world', far from perfect, truly a necessary evil. Their attitude to government and the state is therefore soberly matter-of-fact, without being cynical, for it does not expect too much and is thankful for small mercies. It is the exact reverse of the political attitude prevailing in Western Europe, where people, having lost faith in themselves, either find a wretched substitute faith in the chimera of a perfect state, or are swept off their balance by the crazy ambitions and false promises of popular agitators.

Autocracy can be at least as representative as elected government, provided that it takes the best advice. Therefore Aksakov urges a revival of the *Zemskie Sobory*. 'Our wise Tsars recognized that, with a sincere and reasonable desire for the happiness and well-being of the people, it was essential to know and sometimes to ascertain its opinions. Therefore they often called together an Assembly of the Land, composed of elected representatives of all classes in Russia. Their recommendations to the Tsar always took the following form, 'This is our advice, but act as you think best.'

But Peter the Great tore asunder the ancient links between Tsar and people, already worn thin by earlier abuse. His 'revolution' was a living proof of how much harm the most gifted autocrat can do when he works without spiritual association with his people and treats them as an architect uses bricks. Peter used his titanic strength to destroy his subjects' national customs. He even forbade them to wear their traditional dress. He built a foreign capital with a German name, and filled it with foreign officials. 'In place of the former natural alliance between them, there pressed down the heavy yoke of the Tsar over his people. The Russian land became like a conquered land, and the government a rule of conquest. In this way the Russian autocrat acquired the invidious title of 'despot', and his free subject people turned into slaves tied to their land. Only then, for the first time, a striving to seize political power arose in certain classes torn away from the pattern of national life, principally among the nobility, and in the form of revolutionary conspiracies. But all this time the masses of the people were calm. 'The shaved beard and the German costume rebelled, but when did the Russian beard and the *Kaftan* rebel?

So long as the Russian people remain Russian, inward peace and security of government are guaranteed.'

The crowning distortion of formerly healthy social relations is another baleful result of Peter's handiwork. Instead of being personally respected and loved as before, the Tsar has been transformed into a remote tyrant, who is either idolized or feared. The people's honest representatives no longer have access to him. Cringing flattery surrounds the Tsar, and strives to hide from him the immense internal corruption of Russia. 'Now the people no longer trust the government, and the government does not trust the people. . . . This sinister system, if it continues, will turn men into beasts, who submit to force without thought or conviction. Their minds will grow blunted, and their feelings increasingly brutalized. Deprived of moral freedom, they will degenerate into soulless creatures, cynical and sly, stealing and swindling wherever they get the chance.'[1]

There was still time to avert the culmination of this national calamity, Aksakov concluded. The government had trespassed far beyond its rightful allotted boundaries. Fools had rushed in where angels feared to tread. There lay the root of the evil. Instead of pettily pretending to be infallible, let the government generously admit its errors and promptly start to make amends; let the new Tsar, with his virgin mind and will, uncontaminated by degrading compromises or bitter experience of rule, inspire again respect and awe in his long-suffering subjects.

III

Ivan Aksakov (1823–1886), like his brother Konstantin, drank in the Slavophil faith with his mother's milk. A man of immense energy and resourceful mind, he carried the initial impulse of Slavophilism unimpaired into the depressing reign of Alexander III. After his brother and Khomyakov both died, genuine Slavophil thought began to peter out in formal academic side-issues or puffed-up Chauvinist adaptations. Ivan Aksakov rescued it, and raising political journalism in Russia to Herzen's level, he entered into a tireless fight against the sterile obstinacy of the official conservatives, and simultaneously against the rising tide of Western revolutionary frenzy. Mystic nationalism and irresponsible economic *laissez-faire* were the two prevailing

[1] *Memorandum to Alexander II* (1855): pub. *Rus'*, Nos. 26, 27, 1881.

political tendencies of the period. As chief publicist for the liberation of the Balkan Slavs, he felt unconsciously drawn towards the former, but he warned against its pitfalls; he expounded the perils of the latter more convincingly in his attacks on liberal politicians. In an age of embittered party strife, he was one of the few Russian public men respected by his opponents.

Together with a share of his father's power of observation, and much of his brother's broad philosophic detachment, he combined a rare gift for disinterested action in public affairs. He thus developed a versatile ability which in Europe would have brought him into the front rank of statesmen. In Russia this was too much to expect. After a legal training, followed by a period of apprenticeship in government service, Aksakov found his mixed vocation as a publicist, leader-writer on social, political and international themes, director of a Moscow bank, and, in the seventies, the moving spirit of the Slav Committee.

From 1850 till his death he perseveringly edited one periodical after another, despite preposterous interference from the censors. In 1859 he wrote, rather pathetically: 'Not a single Westernizer or Russian Socialist is so terrifying to the government as a Moscow Slavophil; no one else is subjected to such persecution.'[1] His weekly *Parus* (1858) took a pioneering step. It started a separate Slavonic section, featuring special contributions from Czech, Serb and Polish correspondents. This policy roused three separate government departments to fury— the Ministries of Public Instruction and Foreign Affairs, and the Third Section. *Parus* was banned after the second issue. His daily *Moscow*, in the twenty-two months of its harassed and precarious existence, was officially rebuked nine times and banned three times. Perhaps the most successful and solidly educational of his journalistic ventures was the weekly *Den'* (1861–1865), which stoutly defended peasant interests in the many irritating problems arising out of the complicated agrarian reforms. *Rus'* (1880–1886) was Aksakov's swansong, and it contained a number of mature and powerful articles.[2]

By dint of his tenacious business-like efficiency, harnessed to

[1] Brodsky: *Ranniye Slavyanofili*, p. 129.
[2] Ivan Aksakov's scattered articles and speeches were first collected and arranged in book form in the seven-volume edition of his works published in Moscow between 1886 and 1891.

his rapid flair for detecting the most important issues of the moment, Aksakov first turned the Slavophil movement into a part of the normal working capital of Russian thought. He diligently sifted and elaborated all the viable implications of the rich but rather esoteric legacy, bequeathed by his brother and Khomyakov. Both had maintained that the Russian people are essentially social-minded but resolutely a-political—*i.e.* not wanting or needing for themselves the regular exercise of governmental power. Aksakov enlarged the logical conclusion of this premise, that the centre of gravity lay in the autonomous vitality of society, and not at all in the organization of the state. His brother had written: 'We do not need worldly success, we do not want it. Successful officials cannot represent the nation, they only represent the government; and what kind of civilization can be fabricated out of any government monopoly?' Ivan carried this basic motive a stage further, starting as usual from the burning question of Peter's reforms, that inescapable symbol of the widening rift between government, society and the common people.

He shared the view of several intelligent Slavophils that Peter's persistent blows had provoked a violent but indispensable national awakening, but these were only a crude beginning, a temporary governmental means of dragging Russians out on a broader road which led to a freer social end, 'We do not deny the redeeming effect which the Petersburg period of our history has had and still has on the internal development of Russia.'. . . 'But woe if the tree turns to bark, if the bark, while increasing the volume of the trunk, begins to absorb all the vital juices of the tree and starves the core! Peter paid attention to the bark, to the outside defences, but the strength of the tree is not there. Is the core healthy?'

Aksakov finds that 'core' in society, by which he does *not* mean either an amorphous network of functional groups, or any kind of organized public opinion, and he takes more trouble than his predecessors to define what he *does* mean by that cruelly overworked word. 'Society, in our opinion, is that medium in which is shaped the conscious mental activity of a people, arising out of its whole spiritual strength; society alone can save the people and stop the diseased overgrowth of the state. Has it any external political organization? No, and it can never have one. It is neither a class, nor a trade union, nor a corporation, nor a clique, nor any other specific institutional organization of people. The strength of society is a moral strength, expressed through 'public opinion'. But society can consist only of educated people—or rather, people belonging to all classes and occupations united to each other by that level of culture which makes social communion possible. This alone raises the common people to a knowledge of their own spiritual goal. It mediates between them and the government.

Society is none the less liable to be infected by the governmental disease which kills its spontaneity and its social character. Nothing is more dangerous and injurious to it than the political prejudices by which our publicists are so readily carried away. We do not speak of their political criticism which is a social right, but of their obsession with legal compulsion, with rigid convention and organized conformity. . . . The state must be kept apart from the life of the common people and of society; it should stay strictly within those necessary but modest limits, demanded by the spiritual activity of society itself. . . .

Classes may change or disappear. There may or may not be an aristocracy. Society need not disintegrate on that account, because its virtue does not spring from one class or another, but from the sum-total of the genuine culture penetrating all classes. The fewer the classes are, and the fewer the barriers separating one class from another, the easier it is for them to co-operate. . . .'

Without society, or when society is crushed, government sooner or later betrays a fatal instability. The people become impotent and apathetic, yet the government cannot do without popular support to justify its own actions. Macaulay said that when English history fringed on the danger of parliament turning into despotic rule, society, not parliament, saved the country by setting limits to the powers of government.

Society by virtue of its intrinsic nature is bound to be progressive, for it represents the common people in their striving to advance, though certainly not in that vulgar political sense in which the terms 'progressive' and 'conservative' have been borrowed from the West. 'For us those terms are meaningless, and when they are transplanted into Russian life they can only aggravate the confusion and ignorance from which we already suffer enough. *Conservative* means only what preserves national character (*i.e.* what really lives or is capable of life) and only what has character (and is therefore conservative) can possibly be *progressive*.'[1]

For a Slavophil to be capable of constructively criticizing both his own country and the West, he had to feel at once too basically Russian ever to turn into a cosmopolitan European and too sympathetically European to be able to renounce the best of Western civilization. It is striking that precisely the most Europeanized of Russian thinkers, like Tyutchev and Herzen, turned later into the most passionate and persuasive Slavophils. Yet their consciousness of their organic links with their own people and traditions, their manner of formulating Russian national character, the terms in which they criticized the modern West, reproaching it with one-sided rationalism, sterile and sterilizing preoccupation with machinery and abstract formulae—sometimes a just reproach—all showed how thoroughly they had assimilated Western thought. Ivan Aksakov followed a similar course. His ideal was 'to stand on the pinnacle of European civilization and yet remain Russian, faithful to my Emperor and people, without renouncing the special historical development of the Russian Empire and the difficult tasks which it imposes on us.' Difficult enough for strong-minded outstanding leaders! How much more so for average members of Russian society, hazily educated on cosmopolitan lines, still unable to disentangle the underlying virtues from the more flashy and tempting vices of the West, lacking self-confidence, and therefore alternately fawning on Europe and cursing her, and indiscriminately embracing cheap slogans and trite political generalizations as the 'last word of science' from the West.

'The despotism of theory over life is the most abominable of all despotisms,' Aksakov proclaimed. 'It becomes most bitter and horrible when the theory of freedom, armed with the axe of the state, puts on the cap of the Jacobin instead of a monarch's crown or the helmet of a feudal lord[1]. . . . We are too poor in social creativeness, but too rich in educated and well-intentioned officials. Our national life is for these people a *tabula rasa* on which they think they can write whatever their theories demand.' The most deceptive façade is that of liberalism. Respect for the people means nothing to liberals. Their eyes

---

[1] I. Aksakov: *Sochineniya*, vol. 2, pp. 46–55.
[2] *Ibid.*, vol. 2, p. 264.

are still fixed on the example and experience of the West. They fail to see that England's vital strength lies in her society and not in her more recent political organization. As for France, whether republic, Empire, or constitutional monarchy, she remains the same embodiment of statedom, centralized despotism. 'The French Republic revealed that hideous tyranny which results when "freedom" and "the people" put on the royal purple! The infatuation bred by theory, allied with bureaucratic power, and helped by the apathy of society, that is a temptation hard to resist!' Russian society would soon learn to see how under the masks of democracy and liberalism there lie concealed a lust for despotic power and an impudent contempt for the Russian people, their spirit, reason and will.

France provides an obvious example, but surely the last example to imitate. 'Her history enables us to see what can happen to a kingdom of "intelligence", naked, abandoning the historical and earthly human being, eternally carried away by the latest human theories and armed with the crippling weapons of administrative power. A kingdom of anarchy, where parties fight for power and for nothing but power, inflicting monstrous tyrannies in the name of the most liberal democratic slogans in the world, and thus holding down a mute and morally stunned people.'

Starry-eyed Russian intellectuals in their turn had swallowed the imported slogans of 'democracy', 'freedom', and 'equality', without questioning either what they could mean in a Russian context or what havoc they had already wrought in Europe. 'That word, democracy, is only comprehensible in a live sense when it is opposed to aristocracy, but in our mode of life and history there is no place for it', Aksakov boldly affirmed. In the West it means the erection of the social ideas of the lower classes into a political principle; in other words, an attempt to transfer political power to the common people, in fact to bring all classes of society down to the level of the lowest class. Such it is in theory. In practice democracy has proved to be nothing but the claim of 'democrats' to take the place of 'aristocrats'. In its essence democracy is the crudest worship of the governmental principle, of material coercive and conventional power, together with a blindly ambitious striving to inject this principle into the spiritual life of the common people.

'For us this word has no living political sense, and is nothing but a misapplied expression of sympathy with the masses. How

L

perverse to call the Russian peasant a democrat, infected with the craving to rule, when he in every way shuns political responsibilities, and struggles to preserve his free agricultural organization from the incursions of the state. If the whole people turns into a government, there is no people left, and coercive law will drive out conscience.'

'Democracy in the West emerges from a past conditioning background. It has a legal and historical sense expressing the enmity and struggle between enslaved conquered people and their aristocratic conquerors. . . . Actual equality in the West is nothing but external equality before the law, and it co-exists with a seething internal rivalry and dissension. But the equality of which Western socialists dream is a barrack-like one, a monotonous regimental drill imposed and supervised by the authorities. Russians and other Slav peoples, especially Orthodox ones (who, unfortunately, have preserved this principle better than in Russia) cannot conceive equality in this way. They know something higher than that democratic equality of which Western Utopians dream; they cherish brotherhood, that religious principle of equality which allows different professions, positions and fortunes to exist freely and legally side by side. . . .'[1]

Of course this *fraternité* business, as a political stunt, was originally more French than Russian, and Aksakov, in adopting it, was merely lagging behind Proudhon, who emphatically objected that if the whole world was his brother, then he had no brother. Since the abuse of the idea has so effectively crushed the feeling, it sounds ridiculous, or hypocritical today to talk about the sentiment of brotherhood as if it were a real motive force in social life, let alone in international relations. Phrases so hackneyed and debased have acquired an ironic sense which bans them from honest and civilized language, except as a *façon de parler*. But the rather odd, though sincere, Slavophil presumption that Russians are more brotherly by nature than Europeans, attempted to prove that they were to an ascertainable degree less class-conscious, less brutally egoistic, and therefore less at daggers drawn against each other. The Slavophils seem to have derived this self-gratifying comparison more from a gloss on Guizot's writings than from close personal observation of their compatriots. According to Guizot, the social

[1] I. Aksakov: *Sochineniya*, vol. 2, pp. 87–88.

structure of all West European states had been moulded by three main historical constituents, which they held in common —the pagan heritage of Roman law, the Roman Church (whose effective Christianity was tainted by inheriting the world-wide material ambitions of the Roman Empire), and a constrained stratification into rival social classes. The latter was the work of foreign conquerors who, having first subdued the native populations, then perpetuated a ruthless struggle for position and power between rulers and subject peoples.

This triple formula captivated many Slavophils, who hardly worried about its exact validity (though some, like Khomyakov and even K. Aksakov, admitted that Russian rulers had managed to enslave their subjects as successfully as foreign conquerors had done elsewhere). They wishfully interpreted it to mean that the three historical constituents, instead of fusing, had grown into self-destructive contradictions, from which Russia alone was mercifully absolved by Providence. It thus provided them with one of those deceptively simple historical deductions, whose gross artificiality—despite a grain of truth— soon becomes so obvious in application that a mere theoretical refutation sounds too frivolous. Indeed a short step from this inadequate formula led on to the Marxian historical analysis in terms of economic class-warfare, and thence to the Russian interpretation of it as a European class-war under Russian leadership. But it should be remembered that the Slavophils applied the Guizot formula exclusively to Western European states, and in order to demonstrate how essentially *different*, and more pacific, Russian development had been, and must continue to be.

Be that as it may, Aksakov was even less concerned with the scientific accuracy of his conception, than were his friends, the more antiquarian-minded Slavophils. He extracted from recent history what seemed to him the two most vital contemporary facts—that Russia and Europe had grown into separate and spiritually antagonistic worlds, and that Russia was moving closer to the European orbit at a moment when the European example seemed least encouraging to follow. What should his country's plan of action be? Only short-sighted people, dazzled by the onrush of material prosperity in the West, could fail to see that it was being won at the cost of an accelerating mental instability and coarseness of moral fibre. Was it not high time for Russia to stop cringing to such a brutalized unbalanced West?

In the first place, stricken by fear of Russian strength and by hatred of Russian originality, the leading European countries were themselves straining every nerve to undermine the integrity and national character of their sole surviving rival. 'Whatever services we render to the West, we are not believed, we are not respected, we are counted deceivers, hypocrites, not fellow Europeans with equal rights. We remain for them barbarians as before, unwanted guests at a stranger's feast, illegitimate children of civilization, with no share in the heritage of the cultured world—upstarts, parvenus, plebeians. Not even plebeians, but a race of outcasts, to whom the laws of justice, the demands of natural humanity cannot be extended. . . . It would be futile for us to console ourselves with the thought that Europe's attitude to us proceeds from ignorance or misunderstanding, to waste our energy and money on enlightening her by spreading a true knowledge of Russia, etc. When it is a question of Russia, Europe looks without seeing, listens without hearing. She does not want to understand or know us.'[1] In her relations with Russia she abandons every principle on which she prides herself in dealing with others.

Furthermore, Aksakov asked, what can Russia gain by continuing to borrow Western institutions and Western methods when they have so clearly degenerated in their countries of origin. 'To talk of parliamentary government as an ideal or crowning achievement for Russia is merely to be retrograde. Should one push Russia into this course just now, when even in England, the birthplace of that form of government, people begin to recognize its defects and the need to transform it, and when in continental Europe (where it was till now more or less a revolutionary product, which did not strike deep roots in national consciousness) it is changing its views, or being exploited only as a plausible instrument of party rule for masking tyranny over the people. . . .

'*Our own revolutionaries are merely such reactionaries*; their whole mind and creation has been exhaustively expressed in dynamite, and in the words, *nothing, down with it!*' According to Bismarck, the golden age of parliamentary government has passed away even in England. In America Congress has turned into a

[1] I. Aksakov : *Sochineniya*, vol. 2, p. 359.

business-men's racket, and the best people in America keep aloof from politics.

When the whole political life of a country is built on the shifting sands of ephemeral and squabbling delegates, the resultant instability of power breeds inaction and inefficiency in the administrative hierarchy. And if in addition the state swallows up all social interests and virtually the whole national life, then its helpless dependence on the fluctuation of parliamentary intrigues leads to horrible results. 'What kind of personal responsibility can one expect from the impersonal administrative machine which is derived from a majority of votes in a Western representative assembly? Only a personal supreme power can bear a heavy responsibility to God, to its own conscience, to history, to its country. . . .

'For Russia no legal order, no further acquisition of European institutions can possibly calm that hostile spirit of denial and destruction, whose emergence from the West has captured our defenceless youth and turned them into social-revolutionaries, federalists, collectivists and even anarchists. . . . *This savage phenomenon has no living roots in our historical and national soil.* If it has so forcibly taken hold of our younger generation, and manifested itself in such horrible deeds, that is solely due to the barren abstraction and rootlessness of the educational system now prevailing in Russia. . . . Yes, it is clearly savage, but it is none the less a product of civilization, in the sense that it is a fruit from the tree of culture grown in the West. . . .' What is responsible for all these bestialities, this triumph of brute force, these poisonings, burnings and murders? Is it lack of education, the ignorance of the masses? By no means. *The much-slandered masses take no part in these crimes* . . . even if some of them are used as instruments. . . .

Moreover, ideas of freedom, humanity, justice, rightful and equal distribution of material goods, are the main avowed motives of the educated criminals. . . . 'How can such exalted and moral ideas lead to such monstrously immoral deeds? Who are these new anarchists and revolutionaries? They are really a new breed of savages, armed with weapons of science and culture; they are swindlers—in the name of higher honesty and justice; they are wild beasts—for the sake of "humanity"; they are bandits for progress, demons preaching paradise. . . .

'Yes, this is what we see before our eyes today. Education,

leading only to the most sinister darkening of the mind, tyranny, masquerading as freedom; equality, turning into violation of the most sacred rights of a human personality; justice into gross denial of justice, knowledge into ignorance, intelligence into blank stupidity.'[1]

IV

Aksakov, be it observed, absolves the Russian masses from any share of blame in bringing about this ugly tragedy. Weak or foolish rulers play a dubious part in it, but a perverse intelligentsia supplies the villains of the piece. He concludes that, even though Western parliamentary institutions are wearing out, political revolutionaries will prove unable to replace them, because they lack the strength of genuine constructive desires. These embittered creatures are merely suicidal symptoms, instruments of a more deep-seated decay. Therefore they are unfit to create any new, freer, more moral institutions on the ruins of the ones which they destroy. Aksakov's final judgement sounds like a death-knell, ringing down the curtain on expiring Europe; the next scene is likely to disclose the burial of the corpse and rival heirs quarrelling over their rich inheritance. But on second thoughts we become aware that his funereal sequence is subject to two very important modifications. First, it applies to Europe only so long as she surrenders herself to revolutionary decomposition, but not if she recovers her constructive self-confidence; secondly, it applies with equal force, not to indigenous Russia, guided by a blend of wise tradition and strong benevolent rulers, but only to a Russia which imports the disintegrating virus of Revolution from her more feverish Western neighbours.

When the revolutions temporarily triumphed throughout Europe in 1848, it seemed to Aksakov that the total collapse of civilization would shortly follow. No self-respecting man would want to go on living in the dark ages which would then engulf the world. Better an honest death than such a shameful life. 'Let the world perish', he pronounced,

> All our labours and trials have been in vain,
> Every feat of accusation is powerless,
> Every honest struggle is mad.

[1] I. Aksakov : *Sochineniya*, vol. 2, pp. 695–700.

So perish, treasures of the soul,
You fall in an unequal fight,
The senseless lie reigns over all.
Dissolve, sustaining powers, *you are not needed*,
Soul, fall asleep—it is high time.

The subsequent suppression of the mushroom popular parlia-
ments, followed by the perfunctory restoration of European
thrones, failed to convince Aksakov that the vital forces of
Europe would revive. But his doubts extended equally to the
blunt and inflexible repressive policy pursued by the government of Nicolas I after 1848. 'The madman fell, abandoned to
his dreams,' he wrote in a transparent political poem (January,
1850):

But he still lives, diseased and suffering; he could not die in his
  sleep . . .
And we work on, without faith in our work,
Secretly we believe in nothing,
Rush into battle, court our own ruin,
Trying to cheat fate and defy all reason . . .

The Crimean War fulfilled many of his dark forebodings, but
his buoyant nature recovered from the blow and soon found
solace in his pioneer work on the Slav Committee. Here was at
last a fresh outlet for wounded and embittered national self-
respect, and an opportunity to vindicate the vague surviving
Slavophil beliefs in Russia's helpful mission to the outside
world. During the seventies the Slav Committee rapidly out-
grew its modest beginnings as a charitable organization to
help the Balkan Christians. When the rebellion against the
Turks began in Herzegovina (1875), the Committee published
in the Russian Press, without a word of comment, the appeals of
the Serbian and Montenegrin Metropolitans for aid. Donations
promptly poured in from all parts of Russia, and huge sums of
money were raised, exceeding the most optimistic expectations
of the organizers. As Aksakov expressed it, 'the boundaries of
the Orthodox world began to widen before the eyes of the
people.' Then followed the unequal struggle of the little Serbian
principalities against the vast Asiatic army of the Porte. Russian opinion was inflamed by the crusading spirit. After the first
Russian volunteer had been killed in action, hundreds of others
promtly offered their services to the Serbian army. At first the

volunteers were chiefly noblemen, but soon the Slav Committee, and its many local branches, were flooded with letters from old soldiers and simple peasants, begging for help and advice in fulfilling their desire to join the 'holy war'.

Elements of religious hysteria and personal despair mingled with healthier motives in promoting this outburst of Slav solidarity. Readers of Tolstoy's *Anna Karenina* will recall the chapter, describing the painfully melodramatic scene on the station platform, as the stricken Count Vronsky leaves for the Balkan front in charge of a trainload of volunteers, equipped and maintained at his own expense. Similar scenes occurred in fact.

Indeed the rôle of Russia as a political liberator was fraught with ambiguity. Although their Slav 'big brother' might alone be strong enough to rescue them from Turkish cruelty or Hapsburg interference, many of the Balkan Slavs, whether Orthodox or not, felt far more drawn towards the peasant socialism of the Russian *narodniki*, and were, like them, enemies of Tsarist power. The far-sighted statesman Gorchakov, who fought against the pan-Slav policy of Ignatiev, frankly disbelieved that the Slav peoples had any sympathy for 'autocratic Russia', and he exercised a steadying influence on Russian foreign policy. Balkan intractability became still more manifest in the eighties, when picked nationalist Bulgarians, educated in Russia and at Russian expense, far from being converted to the beneficial discipline of Orthodoxy and Autocracy, showed stubborn determination to build up their infant country on more egalitarian and independent lines. The parallel with Tito's Jugoslavia is suggestive.

The news of the humiliating concessions due to be made by Russia at the Congress of Berlin (1878) roused Aksakov to a fever of indignation. In a widely publicized speech to the Slav Committee, he openly attacked the Russian government's policy, while characteristically appealing to the Emperor to override his bad advisers. 'We have met here,' he announced, 'to bury the freedom of the Bulgars, the independence of the Serbs, that great and sacred cause handed down to us by our ancestors, by our own vows—to bury Russian glory, Russian honour, Russian conscience. Is it possible that the Turkish armies imprisoned near Plevna in the Caucasus, the winter advance of Russian armies through the Balkans, and the heroic

exploits of our soldiers, which amazed the world, our triumphant advance to Istambul, the extraordinary victories, paid
for by hundreds of thousands of Russian lives, those incalculable
sacrifices, that sacred surge of national spirit—can it be that
they are all a myth, an abortion of our inflamed fantasy, perhaps even a fabrication of Moscow fanatics? Did you, victorious
Russia, voluntarily turn yourself into a defeated suppliant?
Hardly restraining their ribald laughter, and with contemptuous
irony praising your political wisdom, the Western Powers, with
Germany leading, have impudently torn from you the victor's
wreath, and put on you instead the fool's cap and bells. And
you, obediently, almost with sympathetic gratitude, bow your
long-suffering head in front of them!'

'It must be a lie,' he interjects. 'Whatever may be happening
in the Berlin Congress, however deeply Russian honour has
been insulted, its pledged Preserver is alive and powerful. He
too is its Avenger! If our blood boils at the mere sight of the
newspaper headlines, what must the Tsar of Russia feel, responsible to history for Russia's fate? Did he not solemnly announce
to the deputations who greeted him on his return from the
Danube, 'the sacred cause will be carried through to the very
end!' War is horrible, and the Tsar's own heart cannot lightly
call for a renewal of death and bloodshed from his self-sacrific-
ing subjects—but neither can these sufferings be bought off by
concessions made at the cost of honour and conscience, Russia
does not want war, but still less does she want a shameful peace.
Ask any Russian from the common people, would he not prefer
to fight to the last drop of his blood?

'The duty of loyal subjects demands that we should still believe and trust. But it demands too that we should not remain
silent during these lawless and unjust trials, sowing dissension
between the Tsar and his country, between the Tsar's mind
and the national spirit.'

Aksakov's protest proved to be in vain, though it seems to
have eloquently voiced the feelings of many inarticulate Russians. The peace terms with Turkey dictated to Russia by the
Berlin Congress inflicted a crushing defeat on the Empire's most
popular line of foreign policy at home. It seemed for a moment
as though the shame of the Crimean War had been wiped
out, that the Golden Cross would shine again over the dome
of St. Sophia, the Crescent be driven back to the mainland

of Asia, and ancient Byzantium resurrected to bring unity (and perhaps peace) to a hitherto unknown extent throughout South-Eastern Europe. Then came the concerted intervention of the Western Powers, and Russia's military victory changed abruptly into humiliating diplomatic defeat.

Aksakov was right in talking of the rift between the Tsar and his country. In that bitter national setback Alexander II's prestige sank heavily. Had the issue been otherwise (if the original Treaty of San Stefano had also been accepted as the final peace settlement) there was a chance he might have escaped assassination in 1881. As it was, the Emperor paid the full penalty for his personal responsibility. The active period of the Slav Committee and the Russo-Turkish war of 1878 marked the apogee of Aksakov's public influence. But he fought on, undeterred by his many defeats, started his last journal, *Rus*, in 1880, and in 1886, the year of his death, he was still conducting a vigorous campaign against the clumsy ineptitude of Russian diplomacy in Europe.

V

Two unspectacular but none the less remarkable members of the Slavophil group ought properly to be included in this survey —A. Koshelëv (1806–1883) and Yury Samarin (1819–1876). They were both men of proven ability, balanced judgement and wide international culture. Koshelëv possessed a rare combination of fervour and restrained common sense, which he showed in the following statement about Slavophil aims: 'The Slavophils refused to retaliate when they were ridiculed by Westernizers. The latter gave us our name, but that did not express the essence of what we stood for. We cherished no desire to revive ancient Russia—all that was slander invented by the enemy camp. Nor did we set the peasant on a pedestal and bow down to him. But in that primitive creature we searched for what was peculiar to the Russian man, for what he needs most, for what ought to be developed in him. Time has proved that we were right.'

Even more than the other leading Slavophils, Koshelëv admired England intensely, though for qualities which are under a cloud today. He visited London for the International Exhibition of 1851, and wrote with enthusiasm about this display of

English 'wisdom, vitality and strength'. He thus recorded his three main conclusions: (1) that no people in the world had gone further than the English in almost all branches of industry. . . . 'Whatever one may want to learn, it should be studied in English schools'; (2) 'Louis Blanc's teaching and that of most Frenchmen, demanding more and more interference by the government in industrial affairs, is victoriously refuted by England's example to the contrary'; (3) 'This country, the most aristocratic of all in its traditions and culture, has simultaneously set its mind on producing and extending the use of cheap goods in order to raise the well-being of the masses.'[1]

Like many of his friends, Koshelëv felt far more drawn to Orthodoxy as a traditional phenomenon of Russian culture than as an attractive form of Christianity. The doctrinal and authoritarian sides of Orthodoxy both left them cold, though its symbolic ritual moved them. Being enlightened Europeans to the marrow of their bones, their personal attitude to religion was none the less sincere when they treated it as one aspect only of an unfathomable mystery. It is symptomatic that they esteemed Spinoza more highly than the fashionable French and German philosophers, though little could be said publicly or written about Spinoza, because his natural piety had caused him to be officially banned as an 'atheist'. Koshelëv, however, revealed a lot when he said : 'We all admired Spinoza, and found his works infinitely superior to the Gospels and other sacred writings.'

An outspoken opponent of Russian claims to a monopoly of the true Christian faith, he observed that, while Christianity had been known to inspire admirable personal conduct, it was absurd to imagine that it could transfigure any organized society. *A fortiori*, the State as an institution could not possibly be Christian, or modelled on Christian lines. While religion might refine and discipline personal action, it would, if translated into political action, cease to be religion at all and become a menace. Koshelëv distrusted the exaggerated hopes which K. Aksakov attached to Russian theocracy. 'You found your structure on absolute rules. I believe that no absolute rules can exist in human society. In its immutable eternal aspects the world enters into the sphere of the church ; only in the spheres of change, movement and struggle, does it belong to society. State laws must therefore

[1] A. Koshelëv: *Zapiski*, Appendix, p. 25, Berlin, 1884.

flow from circumstance and change with circumstances. France tried to make brotherly love an immutable law, but she entangled herself in such a ridiculous experiment.'

Yury Samarin was a far more influential figure in his lifetime than the amiable and perspicacious Koshelёv. Born in St. Petersburg, where both his father and mother held posts at the court, he learned French before Russian, and received a classical education (in Greek and Latin) at Moscow University. At first he aspired to become a university professor. He remarked later that the tasks of learning are insignificant and petty compared with the tasks of life. Khomyakov saved him from foundering in Hegel, and finally, deferring to his father's wishes, he entered the government service in the Ministry of Justice. He spent eight years in various official posts and served on the government committee for settling agricultural problems in the Baltic provinces. But his letters from Riga expressed indignation at the systematic maltreatment of the native population by Baltic German officials. The German party at the Court made the most of his alleged insubordination, and by their malicious intrigues succeeded in getting Samarin imprisoned in the Fortress of Peter and Paul (1849). There he was cross-examined in much the same high-handed and arbitrary way as members of the socialist Petrashevsky circle had been.

The muddle-headed and futile revolutionary conspiracies of that period appalled Samarin, but so did the morbidly suspicious and clumsy rigour of the government; he recognized that both were symptoms of some horrible underlying instability, which could no longer remain concealed. 'Of course this is madness,' he observed, 'but madness does not occur without a reason. What strikes me most forcibly in all this disorder is not so much the painful evil and absurdity of Communist ideas, such as they are, but the absolute void which must exist in many hearts and minds to enable these ideas to find a place in them. That negative evidence is what alarms me most. I can explain such a void following after the humane atheism of the eighteenth century, the chaos of the French Revolution, the cult of material gain under the bourgeois rule of Louis Philippe; it needed centuries to produce this in France. But for a Russian, from the moment he leaves school, to find himself in exactly the same position, to start life without an atom of religious feeling, or any sense of responsibility towards his family or his country,

that is what surpasses my understanding and what after a
hundred years will be hard to believe.'[1]

Despite his temporary fall from favour, his honesty and
manifest ability partly disarmed official prejudice against him,
and Samarin took a prominent part in the preparatory com-
missions concerned with working out the conditions of emancipation. Together with N. Milyutin he was even directed to
compose the original draft of the Emancipation Edict. But
Panin, the Minister of Justice, found its terminology too 'liberal',
and handed it over to the Metropolitan Filaret for final revision.
Samarin spent the latter part of his life administering his estates,
and working on the recently established organs of local government. Perhaps he inspired respect in so many diverse quarters
because he belonged to a type of human being even rarer in
Russia than in Europe—the thoughtful, independent-minded
and disinterested man of affairs. A letter he wrote to a French
deputy in 1840, demonstrates that, young as he was, he had
reflected deeply and profitably enough to arrive at some firm
conclusions about making the most of such constructive qualities as his country possessed. 'Dazzled by the brilliance of the
West, we forgot our own past, we became first French, then
German. In the West, religious problems were no longer *à la
page*. The latest intellectual influence there bore a grudge
against our social order. It strove to destroy our principle of
government—our absolute monarchy. It wanted to persuade us
that we were groaning under tyranny; it tried to infuse us with
its own hatred of despotic rule—a sentiment legitimate and
reasonable elsewhere, but absurd for us to share.

'A whole generation which we still mourn,[2] allowed itself to be
seduced. It had misunderstood its own country, it had loved the
West too blindly. Then came a pale and lifeless cosmopolitan
era through which we had to pass in order to attain a renewed
sense of our own national character. It is true, for us everything
lies in the future, but that future can only be the result of our
own past. Russia has spent about ten centuries on the defensive,
warding off blows from outside. Her influence on the West has
up till now been merely a physical one, but the time will come
when she will act there through the force of her ideas.

'What are the principal distinguishing features of our national

[1] Y. Samarin: *Sochineniya*, vol. 12, p. 340, Moscow, 1911.
[2] The Decembrists.

character? They are our religious feeling and the principle of our absolute monarchy. Only religious unity saved our nation. We have experienced no foreign conquest, no feudal class, no social contracts. An absolute power guides us forward without hideous revolutions or religious wars.'[1]

History does not record how the French deputy responded to this covert Russian challenge to French intellectual supremacy. He may have winced over its downright but wholly undefined recourse to religion and monarchy. Samarin's insistence that these were poles apart from the Western type of religion or feudal monarchy, such as the French had known, would nevertheless have fallen on deaf ears. What was self-evident to him could only be unintelligible to a precise French mind. In fact Samarin interprets the peculiarities of Russian religion in an original and penetrating way. 'What is the mystery of our people's religious life? Since they cannot read, the scriptures do not exist for them. The only link between the Church and the individual remains in the church services and in those few prayers which are passed down orally from father to son. But it appears (and I have personally convinced myself of it) that the people—at least in our parts—do not understand a single word of the Church Slavonic language, not even the 'Our Father' prayer which they repeat mechanically with omissions or changes, depriving it of any vestige of sense. Yet there exists within their unenlightened consciousness, as in Athens, an altar dedicated to the Unknown God. For all of them the active presence of a providential will in every incident of life is such an indisputable fact that, when death draws near, these people open their doors to it as they would to a familiar and long-expected guest. In the most literal sense they surrender their souls to God.'[2]

Samarin had the insight to perceive what the liberal Paul Milyukov emphasized later, that the Russian common people had this much in common with the intelligentsia, a fundamental indifference to the official teaching of the Orthodox Church. But he did not therefore share Milyukov's approval of universal secular education as the social panacea; nor did he jump to Belinsky's conclusion and claim triumphantly that Russians were the most atheistic people in the world. On the contrary, he

[1] Y. Samarin: *Sochineniya*, vol. 12, 62 ff., Moscow, 1911.
[2] *Ibid.*, p. 132.

believed the people to be far more genuinely religious than their Church, even though they were less Christian than pantheistic. The habits of the Russian peasants proved to him that they had kept the roots of faith alive, that they were constantly aware of a divine providence surrounding them. That faith remained the precious key to the only better world they knew, an imaginary world of beauty and revelation. 'The sphere of revelation is a world in the same way as that combination of things existing in space and time which we usually call the universe or the world. The first of these worlds is no less fruitful in content than the second. It has its own depths. To explore it demands no less persistent concentration than to master the mysteries of geology or chemistry.'[1]

Samarin had quarrelled with Herzen and broken with the radical Westernizers in 1847; by that time he had come to the conclusion that the root of all contemporary social evils lay in the unchecked spread of greed for money and power over people. That motive derived from the West, and whether it took a bourgeois or a socialist form made little difference to its essentially destructive character. Russian society, he said, had caught the infection, and was sinking into a morass of useless exaggerated luxury and a widespread craving for lazy comfort. Insatiable material greed became most dangerous, when it not only triumphed over every better instinct, as it seemed to be doing, but also claimed the crowning justification of logic and historical necessity. Faced with this prevailing current of opinion, so contrary to his own, Samarin tried to discover some inscrutable ulterior purpose, which the fanatics of materialism might unconsciously be serving. 'Perhaps', he suggested, 'a few generations are doomed to blindness, in order that their narrow rational obsession may prepare a material basis for some further steps forward. Therefore they are not only blinded, but proud of their blindness, unaware of mystery, unstirred by the beauty of the world, for them nothing more than a web of cause and effect which science has not yet fully elucidated.'

In a curious letter to Gogol (March 1846), Samarin describes his own struggles to overcome the psychological paralysis induced in him by modern Western thought. 'My illness is one common to our time, though no cure has yet been found for it—a one-sided development of the mind, killing emotion and

[1] *Ibid.*, p. 133.

crippling the will. I think, speak of, and defend in words one course of action, but in fact I submit to another course. I have convictions, but no faith or love. I admit that I do not suffer from it, for I live quietly and can forget that half my soul has dried up or been struck dumb. The strongly aroused activity of thought, irritated by constant contradictions, concealed from me the deathly slumber of my other faculties. But when I came to Petersburg I realized to my shame how weak and cold is mere conviction when pitted against the pressure of organized society. That was my worst moment.'[1]

Samarin suffered a lot from the intrigues of Petersburg society, from its German bias and its morbid suspicion of Moscow Slavophils. Perhaps this bitter personal experience accounts in part for his curiously weak defence of absolute monarchy as the only remaining responsible moral bulwark against self-seeking hypocritical cliques, manoeuvring for power. 'Our society', he wrote, 'persecutes sincere conviction as a crime and rewards cowardly informers for their feats. Only the iron hand of government can save Russian thought from persecution by Russian society.' In 1844 he told K. Aksakov that his work in Petersburg had brought him into contact with an entirely new circle of influential but obtuse people. 'I see that what we accept as known, proved, and obvious, is still for the majority of educated people entirely unknown, unproved, and even incomprehensible.'

His estrangement from the political phobia of Westernizers in no way prejudiced Samarin, any more than his fellow-Slavophils, against the immense potential value of modern Western science. He was far better informed about the course of European affairs than many of his opponents, and he built up an extensive knowledge of European law, administration, and European economic thought. In 1849 he wrote to Khomyakov: 'Since we last parted, I have been constantly studying political economy and I have absorbed up to fifteen fairly fat volumes. I am now sure that this science (or rather, this method of inference from the historical development of public economy in the West) does not deserve either that hostility, with which so many of our respectable people have for some time regarded it, or that immense importance attributed to it by those who regard society as a limited liability company, national life as a

[1] Y. Samarin : *Sochineniya*, vol. 12, p. 241.

commercial enterprise, and the human being as a digestive process. It is a necessary science and may be a very useful one. As regards its practical application to Russia, except for some of its suggestions (*e.g.* the superiority of voluntary labour to compulsory labour, the advantage of free trade, the damage done by any artificial stimulation of industry), I think that it can guide our attention to certain aspects of our national life which might otherwise escape attention.'

Samarin's discriminating interest in economics led him into violent conflict with Chernyshevsky. He deplored that the latter's crude positivist arguments had already convinced so many unbalanced students that the whole of organic life was nothing more than a chemical process and that all psychological phenomena derived from physical data by the action of natural law. During the last years of his life he did his utmost to refute the monstrous misconception that a so-called science of spiritual values could profitably follow the same methods as a branch of natural science. Unfortunately he also started to use a variety of unconvincing religious arguments, which prejudiced his otherwise sound and reasonable case.

In 1864 he visited London and insisted on seeing his former friend, Herzen. They entered into a passionate dispute which lasted till the early hours of the morning, and on parting they flung themselves into each other's arms and embraced in the best Russian fashion, forgetting momentarily that they were sworn enemies. Ten days later Samarin wrote a vehement letter to Herzen, urging him to recant. 'Your propaganda affected a whole generation like a ruinous unnatural habit, inoculated into a young organism, not yet formed and strengthened by maturity. You have dried up their brains, weakened their nervous system, made them incapable of concentration, self-restraint or energetic work. Could it be otherwise? You have no solid ground under your feet . . . only the revolutionary ways and habits, which I can call by no other name than a revolutionary itch. You have in you two men. One is a free spirit recognizing the responsibilities inseparable from personal freedom, but the other sees in himself an autonomous product of chemical combinations. The time has come for you to choose between what you have taught and what you truly love and respect.'[1]

[1] *Rus'*: No. 1, 1883, pp. 36–39.

The longer he lived in the West, the more sensitive did Herzen become to the distant charms of Slavophil persuasion. That eloquent appeal to him was only one of many efforts made by Samarin to win the co-operation of his few mentally alert compatriots. After the launching of Alexander II's series of administrative and judicial reforms, he had announced: 'Now our task is no longer to change and reform institutions. . . . The time has come for us to create not institutions, but people. . . . One way is by the direct spontaneous action of one person on another in that limited sphere where personal influence can work. We must mould and bake people like bricks.'

Nevertheless, the major part of the organized and influential Russian intelligentsia remained staunchly faithful to the scientific brand of materialism which German masters had first taught them. This involved a radical zeal, which was more than conservative in the rigid inflexibility of its methods, though quite unprincipled in the fluidity of its historical content. Loyalty to Chernyshevsky automatically excluded serious consideration of his opponent Samarin, or any of the other Slavophils. It was enough that their twin idols, 'science' and 'history', belonged to Chernyshevsky's period and were fixed in a compact scholastic mode of interpretation.[1] They blinded themselves to the disconcerting novelty that Western science, as it advanced, was simultaneously revolutionizing its own earlier methods, and therefore soon outstripped that system-building phase of its history, on which Chernyshevsky, Dobroliubov, and Karl Marx had all been nourished.

[1] It should be noted that this Hegelian interpretation, which the Bolsheviks have inherited, can also be flexible to the extent that it is unprincipled. Its historical opportunism contributes aptly to the justification of every change in policy, and can even be stretched to explain some of the contradictions between Soviet statements and Soviet actions. The tactical importance of this fluidity is revealed in Stalin's recent re-definition of Marxism: 'Marxism is the science of the laws of natural and social development, the science of the victory of socialism in all countries. . . . In its growth Marxism is bound to be enriched by new experience, new knowledge. It recognizes no unalterable conclusions or formulae. It is the enemy of all dogmatism.' (*Pravda*, 2 August 1950).

N. G. CHERNYSHEVSKY

From a photograph taken in Irkutsk in 1864

CHAPTER VI

N. G. CHERNYSHEVSKY

I

THE powerful figure of Nicolas Chernyshevsky started to dominate the movement of Russian thought in the 1860's, but his fame did not flare up and quickly die down again like that of his more amorphous radical contemporaries, Dobroliubov and Pisarev. From that time onwards till the present day, he has exerted an almost magnetic attraction over the Russian intelligentsia, and hence over every stage of Russian social change. Such enduring influence is all the more remarkable because it is out of proportion to Chernyshevsky's merits as an original thinker. Outside Russia he remains almost unknown, hardly even an object of curiosity, and none of his works—except one American edition of *What to Do*—have ever been published in English. Perhaps a reference to the Russian proverb 'In a place without fish even a crayfish is a fish', will cause some condescending Europeans to murmur that Chernyshevsky could only appear to be a giant in Russia because he was there a Gulliver in an intellectual Lilliput. That is a tempting way to satisfy the Western elect who turn up their noses at any manifestation of Russian 'originality', but it evades the issue of Chernyshevsky's lasting magnetism and belittles his undoubtedly great qualities of mind and character.

It is true that he suffered martyrdom for his beliefs, and that Russian youth is temperamentally prone to hero-worship, but this motive is insufficient to explain his grip on them. So many other Russian intellectuals whose daring independence also led them to living death in the Siberian mines, or to fade away in the dungeons of the Peter and Paul Fortress, have none the less sunk into complete and well-deserved oblivion. Perhaps his indomitable integrity of character, more consistent in underlying feeling than in articulate thought, his acute controversial ability—fortified by encyclopaedic knowledge—the firm example which he set in pursuing every implication of what he preached, are a combination of features rare enough to have won for him respect and admiration as an intellectual leader, in whatever country he was born. But most of all he rose to fame through his ability to fuse these qualities with a robust uncompromising flair, promptly transmuting his whole range of thought into coherent plans of action—and plans which seemed strictly relevant to the most urgent Russian needs. He made herculean efforts to piece together a scientific understanding of European society as a whole. But they were always harnessed to that single driving purpose—a plan to transform Russia. He faced the perennial Russian tangle soberly and as he found it, indeed with such scant enthusiasm for uniquely Russian characteristics that Dostoevsky attacked him as one of those traitors who 'jeered and spat' at their own country.

Like the majority of Russian Westernizers, Chernyshevsky started his intellectual career by plunging into German philosophy. He studied Hegel more thoroughly than Kant, fell under Hegel's dialectical spell—so fatally flattering to would-be intellectual leaders—and ignored the sobering limitations set by Kant's more scrupulous theory of knowledge. He emerged from Hegel into Feuerbach, whose hazily abstract materialism he then allied with Fourier's naïvely voluptuous social objectives, hailing with somewhat uncritical excitement his discovery of this modern social bible. Thus far he had remained a dogmatic and derivative rationalist—but, one might say, a synthetically derivative one—for he fitted together pre-fabricated parts with fresh initiative and zeal, and fired with the intention of constructing a completely new building adapted to the rigours of the Russian climate.

He thus became a pioneer of progress in his native land, mainly in three respects. He first focused the attention of his more intelligent contemporaries on ugly social and economic sores from which so many Russians were suffering with averted eyes, or with eyes turned helplessly to heaven; and he first expounded the march of historical determinism as a factor ascertainable in laws of social progress applicable to Russia as well as to the West. But simultaneously, brushing aside the niceties of consistent logic, he reiterated his staunch belief that personal self-interest is the mainspring of human conduct, and consequently of all human improvement. In this respect he proved to be a loyal disciple of Belinsky and the English Utilitarians. He thought he had rushed well ahead of them again when he asserted, that among reasonable men (and to him all men appeared to be as kindly and reasonable as he tried to be himself) self-interest was bound by some inscrutable historical law to blossom into a more and more enlightened sentiment. This highly purified egoism would in course of time become a habit and would even turn into an inherited characteristic. By gentle stages, rather than by violent shocks, it would lead us towards the goal of an orderly world inhabited by altruistic mortals, all politely saying 'After you, please', and competing with each other only in feats of spontaneous self-sacrifice and exemplary industry. In order not to create an exaggerated impression of Chernyshevsky's naïveté, it is only fair to add that his undaunted social optimism, apart from its flavour of purely imaginative charm, was modified by his recognition that the course of history has familiarized us with catastrophic backslidings.

Chernyshevsky started his journalistic career when in 1854 he joined the staff of the *Sovremennik* under the editorship of the business-like poet Nekrasov. His own contributions soon raised the political reputation and influence of that journal to the highest level it ever reached. Through its pages, and in spite of censorship, he swayed an even wider public than the completely untrammelled Herzen in the fight which they both waged, first for the liberation of the serfs, then for a bold and equitable reform of land-ownership and rural administration. When over a period of years, the glaring economic defects of the Emancipation Edict roused throughout Russia a crescendo of indignation and disappointment, Chernyshevsky was already wasting away in the enforced silence of his remote Siberian exile. But his vigorous writings, sanctified by the halo of his personal example, had done much to inspire the formation of the first 'Land and Liberty' group, and continued to inspire the later *narodniks*. Finally, notwithstanding the Marxist war of extermination against the *narodniks* and their Social Revolutionary successors, Chernyshevsky, as a personality, surprisingly enough found favour with the new masters, partly as a so-called Russian precursor of Marx, and partly as a Marxian *sans le savoir*.

Some Christians who highly appreciate Aristotle have done their best to prove that he was a Christian, or would have been had he not suffered the misfortune of being born before Christ. For a similar reason, it seems, some patriotic Russian Marxians are reluctant to admit that so eminent a Russian sociologist as Chernyshevsky was not a member of their faith. Thus they have

tried to canonize him as a Marxian John the Baptist, a forerunner who preached an approximation to the true gospel in
the Tsarist wilderness. It stands to the credit of Plekhanov, for
long the revered father and popularizer of Russian Marxism,
that he defended Chernyshevsky against the claims of these
over-zealous disciples, and insisted that, despite his high intellectual merits and brief glimpses into the Marxian revelation, he
remained to the end an unrepentant Utopian socialist, who
never scaled the heights of dialectical materialism. None the
less, a later twist of ideological caprice has condemned Plekhanov, the most orthodox of Marxians, to fare less well among
the Bolsheviks than his 'Utopian' predecessor. Since he was
formally excommunicated from the Bolshevik party as a *petit
bourgeois* Menshevik heretic, his opinions remain under a cloud
in Russia, though he has, of course, been assigned a limited
historical rôle.

Marx had himself told the Russian socialist Lopatin that he
considered Chernyshevsky to be a truly original thinker. In fact
he seems to have been the only Russian thinker for whom Marx
had enthusiastic words. Lenin in his turn started to sing the
praises of Chernyshevsky and picked him out as a 'remarkably
profound critic of capitalism', from whose works 'breathes the
spirit of class-warfare.' He commended him to all and sundry as
a 'great teacher' who had served many as 'a guiding star leading towards Marxism.' The subsequent Soviet cult of Chernyshevsky is a very instructive and topical study. Most noticeably
since the early thirties, the highly serious Soviet periodicals
have devoted a cumulative spate of articles to Chernyshevsky in
a multitude of aspects. The Large Soviet Encyclopaedia in
its long and ponderous article about him sums up somewhat
equivocally : 'He has found the place that he deserved in the
pantheon of predecessors of Marxist-Leninist economic theory.'
His most voluminous biographer, Yury Steklov, was officially
rebuked in 1932 for having exaggerated the picture of Chernyshevsky as a pioneer of scientific socialism in Russia, and was
informed that the latter had no need of such a false and flattering appraisal. But more recently the pendulum has swung in
the opposite direction. In 1947 the leading Party intellectual
G. Alexandrov was harshly attacked by the fiery Party philosopher Zhdanov (d. 1948) for having failed to devote proper
attention to the most important Russian predecessors of Marx,

and in particular for having said nothing about the originality and foresight of Chernyshevsky in his (Alexandrov's) history of nineteenth-century Western philosophy. The Soviet Academy of Sciences announced in 1948 that Chernyshevsky's works will be published in a new Library of Philosophy which they are planning, and a number of volumes have already appeared.

After such a chorus of flattering attentions from Old Testament Marxians and modern Bolsheviks alike, it is a trifle bewildering to find that the paradoxical monarchist, V. Rozanov, expressed a still more glowing enthusiasm for Chernyshevsky. In his *Fallen Leaves* (1913) he wrote: 'Reading him, you feel you will never tire, never stand still; he had only a handful of ideas, but of promise a whole sheaf of lightnings. . . . He was a Disraeli, who was allowed to go no further than being a novelist. Damn it, that is fate, and not so much his alone, as Russia's fate! More astonishing still, had he entered the world of affairs, we should probably have escaped the misery of theoretical Nihilism. . . . Never since Peter the Great have we encountered such a figure, whose every hour is breathing, whose every minute is alive, and whose every step is taken with solicitude for his country. It is inconceivable how our lifeless flabby state mechanism, which knows not where to find energy and workers, did not avail itself of that steam engine, that electric dynamo.' Rozanov, however, blames Chernyshevsky for not having swallowed his pride, for not 'kissing the hands of all the generals' provided they gave him a responsible government job. It is tempting to speculate how a deliberate mastery of this courtier's technique might have changed Chernyshevsky into a great administrator, a second Speransky under Alexander II! At least the present outcome is significant and it might justify more contemporary curiosity about Chernshevsky outside his native land—not only did he find the most diverse chorus of admirers in the past (for he was much more than an intellectual drill-sergeant), but his thought, susceptible to various interpretations, continues to play a part in the formation of Soviet minds today.

When contemporary Bolshevik writers place Chernyshevsky as a worthy forerunner of Marx and Lenin, they simultaneously know how to condemn the features in which he differed from them as 'grave errors', 'idealistic follies', excusable only because of the dark age in which he lived. So anxious indeed are they to dismiss these follies categorically, that they tend to run away from the danger of analysing them, nor do they point to the probability that Chernyshevsky, like Herzen, was familiar with the early works of Marx. He had almost certainly read *The Communist Manifesto*, Bakunin's translation of which was published in Herzen's *Bell*, and the first volume of *Das Kapital* was sent to him in Siberia in 1872[1]; yet neither before nor after Siberia did he express a single authenticated opinion about Marx's work. This is all the more remarkable, since Alexander II's discriminating censorship permitted the publication of Marx's *Kapital* in Russian. To mention and discuss Marx need not therefore have compromised Chernyshevsky. We might escape some chronological obsessions if we regard him as a contemporary rather than as a predecessor of Marx (he was only ten years younger) ; and it seems plausible to infer from his silence on the subject that he was not profoundly impressed by Marx, though he undoubtedly shared a number of his ideas, derived by both from Hegel, Feuerbach and John Stuart Mill— and none the less rejected some of Marx's most important conclusions. Clearly he approached Marx in method by bringing into the limelight the rather obvious but insufficiently analysed economic basis of society; he shared Marx's harsh dogmatic temper and his readiness for violence ; he even sympathized with Marx's own extremely low opinion of Russian political capacities (that unflattering estimate is discreetly soft-pedalled by most Russian critics both of Chernyshevsky and of Marx). But the points in which he flatly contradicts Marx, far from being mere regrettable accidents, seem to be among the cardinal parts of his teaching. This should be evident from the chronological survey of Chernyshevsky's own mental evolution which I now propose to sketch.

Inability to see Chernyshevsky as a necessary link in the chain leading towards Marxism may provoke his present ideological watchdogs to repeat their familiar retort about the futility of trying to turn back the wheels of history—a convenient medieval way of evading further argument, by insisting that argument must not conflict with an article of faith. The only general answer to this kind of argument, and on a parallel devotional level, is to suggest that those who have faith in Chernyshevsky at the present historical moment, need not, and

[1] Y. Steklov: *N. G. Chernyshevsky*, vol. 1, p. 270, Moscow, 1928.

do not, have any similar faith in Marx. Indeed they resort to Chernyshevsky for qualities which Marx never possessed. The fact that many educated Russians still obviously find him more attractive than Marx is an encouraging symptom of their unimpaired discernment. Only the Party purists demand that this feeling must be interpreted as a logical desire to explore preliminary stages on the high road to Marx. But there are still many people—and contemporary Russians will be among them —who remain unmoved by doctrines of economic predestination. They are bound to become aware, if they study enough of Chernyshevsky's neglected writings, that his thought is far more complex, honest and far-sighted, less *monolithic* in its points of contact with Marxism, less *dated* in its divergences from Marx, than many of his Soviet commentators appear to realize, or are able to admit.

II

Chernyshevsky was born in 1828 in Saratov, where his father served as a highly respected local priest. He received his early education in the local ecclesiastical seminary, where he showed such exceptional ability that he gained admission to St. Petersburg University—a rare achievement for a commoner seminarist at that time, and one which proved that the educational ladder could even then be climbed to the top by persistent and outstanding talent. At the university he plunged with wholehearted zeal into a broad study of European philosophy, history and literature. But he soon found to his dismay that his chosen subjects—far more than any others—were distorted and cramped by the perfunctory official manner in which they were taught. Natural and military science were encouraged and relatively unshackled, as useful practical and limited subjects, which did not pry into forbidden questions. But in all subjects alike, any fresh interpretation or free research, which ran counter to the line laid down by the Government, was rigorously banned from the university curriculum.

Chernyshevsky's professor in philosophy, a hidebound pedant of German origin, displayed a cautious ingratiating cast of mind, which might find sympathetic response, *mutatis mutandis*, in a Soviet university today. This professor treated philosophy, not as a search for some form or demarcation of objective truth, but principally as a weapon for defending Government policy from any breath of hostile criticism. Airing his views in the *Journal of the Ministry of National Education* (September 1834), in an article which reminds one strangely of Soviet Party philosophers laying down the latest ideological requirements in the journal *Bolshevik*, he described the study of philosophy as a very important activity 'because it can preserve us Russians from the ruinous consequences of false education, that monstrous birth of our period, which like a moral disease infects and damages more and more the social body of decrepit Europe'. His view of false education had at least the merit of crystal-clear simplicity; it meant any education other than that promoted by the Russian Government at that time. It should be noted that in 1826, after the Decembrist revolt, the government abolished the Chair of philosophy at Moscow University. In Petersburg, where the ever-watchful eyes of the Tsar could better guard against the seductions of philosophic thought, the Chair was allowed to remain, but it was carefully filled, according to the Prussian example, by a philosopher whose outlook favoured the autocratic state and orthodox religion.

No wonder that Chernyshevsky, like many other intellectuals of his time, felt crushed under this ossified mental environment and goaded into uncompromising rebellion against it. But the conflict within him appears to have been complicated, gradual and continuous. While he was still a believing Christian he wrote indignantly to his pious father about the lectures of the Petersburg Theology professor: 'Can an intelligent man, understanding the present position of Christianity, and of the Orthodox Church in particular, who realizes that it is no longer a matter of fighting Greek or Roman paganism, or Papism, which were all discredited long ago, but of struggling against vague deists and Hegelians—knowing that most of his hearers are not too firmly grounded in Christian teaching as a result of their bad education—how can he waste time in futile commentaries and meaningless rhetorical phrases about what was written in the preface to some Greek Father's book? Not one fresh word, not a single clearly demonstrated argument, only naked empty speeches, explaining nothing and leading nowhere! It is pitiful and terrible when one reflects that these hundreds of young people, hearing not one efficient word in support of their religion, lacking the strength or the desire to study the sources for themselves, will have to remain stuck either in their Pharisaical faith or in their sincere unbelief—and may even turn into sceptics for life!'

Could this be the same university, the intellectual centre of a mighty Empire, which Chernshevsky had pictured in such glowing colours from the quiet backwater of his provincial Saratov? His letters to his parents are soon sprinkled with scathing comments about 'learned people of whom we have a far greater number than literate ones', about the Latin professor who would find life unbearable without the existence of irregular verbs. He reluctantly came to the conclusion that if he had spent one hundred roubles on books to be sent to his home in Saratov, he could have learned more and spent much less of his parents' scanty income than he had done by uprooting himself in order to live precariously in expensive Petersburg and listen to useless stereotyped university lectures. He consoled himself with the thought that the famous critic Belinsky, his idol at that time, had fared none the worse for having left Moscow University without a degree and without passing a single examination.

Acutely disappointed by the gross intellectual stagnation which he so unexpectedly found in the capital, he began to reflect more searchingly about the total effect which the novelty of higher European education had produced in Russian minds. 'Has any scientific genius ever arisen in Russia?' he wrote to his friend Pypin. 'People complete their course of study, and off they go! But hardly one soul loves learning for the sake of learning, and not merely as a means of winning a diploma. And can it be that only whatever is unfit for Europe is brought over from there to us? Look at the list of members of the Academy, of professors at the university; more than half are foreigners. But, above all, what have Russians contributed to the sum of human knowledge? Alas! nothing; and what has learning imported from abroad contributed to Russian life? Also nothing. Thank heaven, European science is young, only one and a half centuries old! At least Leibnitz, Descartes and Newton really lived in the seventeenth century. . . . But is it possible that our Russian mission in life is confined to maintaining a standing army of one and a half million soldiers, to being able to conquer Europe if we want to, like the Huns, like the Mongols? Surely the existence of such peoples is a wretched one. Rabid and raging, they passed across like a storm, destroying everything, burned, imprisoned, plundered, and that is all. *Are we also destined to be like they were—to be all-powerful in the political and military sphere, but barren and futile in every other aspect of national life?*

If that is so, it would be better never to be born than to be born a Hun, Attila, Genghiz Khan or Tamerlaine, or one of their warriors or subjects. Let us hope for the contrary, that Russians will not enter political history as plunderers, as Huns and Mongols—but as saviours—saviours from the yoke of the Mongols whom we held back, whom we walled off from Europe —and from the other yoke, that of the French and Napoleon. We should also become conciliators and saviours in the world of science and faith. Let us swear to be so—but what is the use of an oath? Does God need words and not will-power? Let us decide firmly and with all the strength of our soul to work in order to end that epoch in which science was foreign to our mental life, to stop science from remaining a stranger's cloak, a melancholy monkeyhood for us. . . . If we can thus contribute not to the ephemeral glory but to the eternal good of our country, what can be higher or more desirable than that?'[1]

The abortive European revolutions of 1848 broke out while he was still studying at the University. He followed them with passionate concern, and their failure seems to have pushed him towards any extreme course which held out better hopes of putting revolutionaries into power, regardless of their methods and ultimate aims. 'From February 1848 till now,' he wrote in his diary (8 September 1848), 'I feel more drawn to politics and believe more and more firmly in an ultra-socialist outlook. The chief object of my worship is Louis Blanc (whom I have hardly read at all) and to whose following I belong. Feuerbach, Proudhon and Ledru-Rolland also appeal to me, but the latter seems rather, or very much, out of date.' We may well wonder how he came to worship Louis Blanc when he had neither met him nor read his works, but this is typical of Chernyshevsky, who, though he read voraciously, never hesitated to make up his mind from a rapid general impression. Nevertheless, the French thinkers' juristic maze of subtle distinctions, and their preoccupation with the form rather than the functions of government, intensely irritated him. Even when he agreed

[1] Y. Steklov: *N. G. Chernyshevsky*, vol. 1, p. 18.

with them, they struck him as superficial, pedantic, and side-tracking the main issue: 'Gentlemen, you think the matter depends on the word republic, but there is no power in that word. What matters is to relieve the lower class from slavery, not to law, but to the inevitability of things, as Louis Blanc says—so that it may eat, drink, marry, educate children, feed its family, grow civilized, and not turn men into corpses or desperadoes—and women into prostitutes for the sake of money. I do not care a rap for those people who shout Freedom, Freedom—and there it ends. Freedom for what? The word is spoken and written down in the laws, but it is not brought to life. It is no question of whether there should be a Tsar or not, but a question of social relations, of whether one class should suck the blood of another.' (Diary, 18 September 1848.)

Chernyshevsky confided to his diary many of the inner conflicts through which he was passing at this time. I will illustrate them by quoting two obviously sincere passages, both written within a year of each other. It is only fair to their author to observe that the second of these entries flatly contradicts the first, and that the first contradicts itself: 'I begin to think that a republic is the best and only form of government worthy of an adult human being. This opinion is taken from the French, but I add to it my former ancient deep-rooted conviction that there is nothing more ruinous for the lower class than the domination of any one class over another—and my hatred in principle for any kind of aristocracy—for the quintessence of such a government rather than for its form and rule. . . . You want equality, but will there be equality between a weak person and a strong one, between rich and poor, between a developed mind and a primitive one? No, and if you admit conflict between them, then of course the weak, poor and ignorant will be enslaved.'

To improve this situation, which he admitted to be natural, but which his unconquerable Christian conscience condemned, Chernyshevsky prescribed the following strangely conservative remedy. 'Therefore I think that the only, and possibly the best form of rule, is an autocracy or better still a hereditary limited monarchy, but one which understands its function, that it must stand above all classes, and is specially created for the protection of oppressed people, whose interests it defends. It must act with energy and conviction, and it must know of course that its rôle is temporary and dual; first, it

must champion the lower class, not in the sense of discriminating against the other classes, but because the lower class needs
more protection in matters of taxation, legal proceedings, etc.;
secondly, because it is obliged to prepare for the realization of
future equality—not formal but real—of that class with the
higher one—equality in means of living, in order to raise it up
to the level of the higher. Peter the Great acted thus in my
opinion, but such a power must realize it is temporary, that it is
a means, not an end.' (18 September 1848.)

But now let us turn to what he wrote on 20 January 1850.
'About a year ago, I thought it would be best of all if autocracy
sustained us in its embrace till the end of the development of
the democratic spirit within us, in order that when popular
government started, government *de facto* and *de jure* would pass
into the hands of the lowest and most numerous class. Thus we
should be saved any transition between autocratic rule (ours in
any case) and a government which would observe and develop
the interests of the mass of the people. Evidently I then believed
that an autocracy sincerely tries to prevent the higher classes
from trampling down the lower ones, that it is the opposite to
aristocracy—but now I am convinced of the contrary. The
monarch, especially an absolute monarch, is only the pinnacle
of an aristocratic hierachy to which he belongs body and soul.
It is the same as if the top of that pyramid were the monarch
himself. So now I say, "Perish!—the sooner the better; let the
people enter into their rights unprepared, or prepared only by a
time of struggle. Until you fall, they cannot be prepared . . . but
at present they regard their main oppressor as their protector,
and think he is a sacred being." '

There is nothing intrinsically new about Chernyshevsky's
struggle to resolve his political doubts. It follows the same
pattern as that of many other vigorous Russian personalities
who revolted desperately against a leaden weight of frustration
which they felt in themselves and tended to ascribe exclusively
to defects in the Russian social order. It is idle to speculate on
whether Chernyshevsky, had he lived today, would have seen
Stalin and the upper crust of the Communist party in the same
lurid light as he saw Nicolas I and his somewhat less inflexible
bureaucracy. But in several ways his vague revolutionary ardour
with its childlike optimism about the rosy future, is more akin
to Bakunin's anarchist dreams than it is to Marx or Lenin.

He also shares Bakunin's weakness in detailed constructive innovation. And although he called himself at this time a red republican, he seems already to have felt the anarchist's temperamental revulsion against any authoritative state or governing class. When questioned about his immediate political aims, he replied that if he were in command he would at once announce the liberation of the serfs, dismiss half the army and very soon curtail as much as possible the whole administrative and governmental power.

Having taken his bachelor's degree at Petersburg University in 1850, he returned to his native Saratov with an appointment to teach the Russian language and literature at the local high school. But his mind had by then matured and hardened; firmly convinced that he had a militant mission to influence events, he was determined to find a battleground wider than the humdrum routine of a provincial teacher's life. In 1853 he returned to Petersburg, and the following year saw the delivery of his doctoral dissertation 'The Aesthetic Relation of Art to Reality'. This was a dreary though closely-reasoned essay written in the stuffy and tortuous polemical jargon so fashionable at that time. He later admitted that it was almost entirely a rehash of Feuerbach's left-wing Hegelianism (censorship forbade the mention of Feuerbach's name). But the dissertation caused a stir in radical circles by its bold uncompromising tone. Nekrasov met Chernyshevsky shortly afterwards, and in 1855 he invited him to become Assistant Editor of *The Contemporary*. This editorial post served as his spring-board to fame and to subsequent ruin.

III

Though Chernyshevsky had started his career as a student of literature and philosophy, he impressed his admirers most by his encyclopaedic and readily applicable knowledge of European history and political economy. Fundamentally he appealed to them in his self-imposed rôle of an intrepid reformer and man of action, an original teacher, who had broken with narrow academic specialization without succumbing to a diffuse and tepid dilettantism, as too many of his contemporaries did. Seen in this light, his enthusiasm, mental brilliance and moral courage temporarily covered up his many errors of judgement.

The latter were of course visible to his official opponents, but they were properly understood only by a few of the more impartial and far-sighted intellectuals, as they were by Turgenev. Much of what he wrote for *The Contemporary* was journalism, and is quite unreadable today, but it was efficient journalism for its time, reaching the more polemical Russian equivalent of the best *Times* leader standard in England. Now that the feverish topical controversies in which he was embroiled have long since died out, Chernyshevsky's sporadic flashes of insight stand out all the more sharply as an example, and perhaps a warning, to his more fortunate successors. A fair-minded modern student of Chernyshevsky's writings cannot fail to be struck by his integrity, consecutive clarity in argument and cool-headed sobriety under extreme provocation, as much as by his fanatical one-sidedness and mule-like obstinacy. The former qualities, which seem more admirable in the long run, are unfortunately rarer among Russian revolutionary thinkers than the latter, which we know well enough.

By the time he joined *The Contemporary*, Chernyshevsky had already decided to be a fighter, if necessary a martyr, for the cause of radical social reform. And in his own emphatic way he had already divided reformers into two groups, distinguished, *not* by divergent political programmes, but by differences of temperament, tactics, and intensity of conviction. He had no doubt about the group to which he himself belonged. 'Some,' he wrote, 'seeing their efforts blocked by a handful of people who derive advantage and profit from the existing state of affairs, think it is necessary to persuade and convince these people that they should act differently and co-operate with the aims of the reformers. But others conclude that eloquence and truth are powerless in dealing with any person when they oppose his own advantage, and that sincere progressives must maintain only one unchanging attitude towards such people, an attitude of *implacable hostility*. These are the revolutionaries.' This last remark sounds thoroughly up to date, and may help us to account for Chernyshevsky's present popularity with the Communist party.

The reading public of *The Contemporary*, regardless of its politics, was quickly swayed by the burning sincerity, practical bent and clear responsible tone of Chernyshevsky's articles. His main contribution in 1856 consisted of his *Essays on the*

Gogol Period of Russian Literature, which he modestly and rather misleadingly described as a restatement of Belinsky's teaching. In spite of their literary title, these essays were full-blooded socialist propaganda, quite thinly disguised. They preached, but much more categorically than Belinsky, the strict duty of imaginative literature to serve as an intellectual weapon for inspiring life with principles of social conduct. Their tone was lofty, but monotonously harsh and indignant; they often betrayed the spiritually hollow ring of the Puritan killjoy, though they were certainly devoid of Puritan humbug. By overstating the case for Gogol and pouring cold water on Pushkin, these essays may be held partly responsible for pushing so many younger Russian writers under the crushing influence of Gogol in his most perverse and gloomy style, obsessed with morbid self-analysis and piling up repulsive realistic detail from the ugliest underworld of Russian life—not the exuberant and sensitive Gogol who wrote *Taras Bulba* or the whimsically poetic Gogol of *The Old-world Landowners*, but the bitter frustrated Gogol of *The Overcoat*.

Chernyshevsky, who had previously shown such fine discrimination in his critique of Tolstoy's *Childhood*, was by this time irrevocably vowed to the conduct of a crusade against what he called the epicurean tendency in literature. Even the Radical Nekrasov showed misgivings at this point, and began to puzzle how he could continue to run Chernyshevsky in double harness with his far more eminent non-political literary contributors, who included Tolstoy, Turgenev and the poet Fet. In one of his letters to Turgenev, Nekrasov stated bluntly, 'Chernyshevsky is an efficient and useful fellow, but extremely prejudiced; he despises, if he does not hate, the more elegant kind of literature, and has managed in the course of a single year to give the whole paper an impression of one-sidedness and monotony.'

Turgenev, after several meetings, began to detest Chernyshevsky, decribed him as a snake and his disciple Dobroliubov as a cobra. He ended by refusing to write another line for *The Contemporary*, after a far-fetched review by Dobroliubov of his novel *On the Eve* had appeared in its columns. Though Herzen, whom he visited once in London, respected him far more than Turgenev did, he nicknamed Chernyshevsky and Dobroliubov 'the jaundiced ones' and wrote of them in *The Bell*: 'In spite of eighteen centuries of Christian contrition, the world is prone to pagan joys and will not stand indefinitely those Petersburg Daniels, solemnly reproving people because they can dine without gnashing their teeth, or, while admiring a picture or a piece of music, can forget the miseries of this world.'

IV

In 1857 Chernyshevsky handed over the entire literary side of his work to Dobroliubov, with the avowed object of devoting himself wholly to the political and social sections of *The Contemporary*. The impending abolition of serfdom was the main topic of the day. He approached this thorny subject as much from an economic as from an ethical standpoint. In considering only the economic advantages of emancipation, he maintained, there should be enough sound reasons to disabuse those short-sighted landowners who imagine that their profits depend on the preservation of serfdom. Yet the argument of greater economic efficiency, which finally convinced so many people, never satisfied Chernyshevsky as sufficient in itself. He always set equitable distribution higher than maximum output. This later became a vital principle of Russian agrarian socialism, and one which he was the first to formulate clearly. In refusing to admit that human welfare should ever be sacrificed to intensified production, he constantly argued that it was better for the *degree* of economic development to remain lower so long as it belonged to a healthy *type* of development.

This priority of moral over economic conviction is alone sufficient to explain why Chernyshevsky could never be a full-blown Marxian, and how he found himself defending the *mir* and the *artel*, ancient semi-autonomous institutions normally loved by patriarchal conservatives, but which for a long time charmed many Russian socialists as well. In substance, both the feudal economy of the past, and the large-scale industrial economy of mid-nineteenth century Europe, seemed almost equally odious to him. 'The whole difference between a slave and a hired workman', he wrote, 'is that the slave receives compensation in kind and the hired workman in cash; the slave gets lodgings, the workman gets money, out of which he must find a lodging. . . . Whether the value of the product of his labour is high or low, affects him as little as it does a slave. . . .

Therefore we can conclude that while there is a huge moral and juridical difference between a slave and a hired workman, there is no specific economic difference in their relation to production. If the labour of a hired workman is more productive than the labour of a slave, it is due to the fact that a free person is superior in his moral and mental development, and thus he works more intelligently and conscientiously.' (*Sovremennik*, No. 1, 1860.)

At such moments Chernyshevsky blissfully forgot that any expansion of the elementary Russian economy demanded a vast labour-force of unskilled drudges. He praised Peter the Great unstintingly, but he omitted to mention that St. Petersburg was built at the price of the exhaustion, sickness or death of thousands of state serfs, who laid its granite foundations in bare unhealthy Finnish marshes. Without claiming that all the tasks of slaves could be performed in future by machinery, he argued that the growing complexity of the machine will no longer tolerate the cruder handling of a slave. But here he seems to have drawn no distinction between the elementary common sense needed to operate a modern fool-proof machine, and the elaborate training plus initiative needed to design or make one. Since he looked forward to a future when every Russian would sing at his work—what Fourier charmingly named 'le travail attrayant'—one is tempted to wonder what he would have thought about the indispensable part still played by convict labour in the more highly mechanized Soviet economy of today.

At times Chernyshevsky was candid enough about the chinks in his own doctrinal armour, especially on the economic side. For instance, in the same article, at the outset of an argument to show that compulsory labour of any kind was contrary to natural economic laws, he hastily corrects himself by adding that to talk about natural economic laws makes very little sense, nor need what is natural be any recommendation. Then he follows this up by relapsing rather lamely into an outburst of categorical assertion about the deeper human instincts governing economics: 'Personal interest is the main motive force of production. This personal interest consists in striving to possess things. Thus the energy of labour, *i.e.* efficiency of output, is commensurate with the producer's right of ownership over the product. It follows that production is most satisfactory when the product is the property of the producer. . . . Everyone digs more zealously in his own kitchen-garden than in a stranger's.' ('Capital and Labour', *Sovremennik*, 1860.)

To do Chernyshevsky justice, he never suggested that this crude labour theory of value could be usefully applied to modern large-scale industry, where the final product can only be the result of many people's contributions to a multitude of processes. He applied it solely to agriculture in Russia and in order to strengthen the case for a larger number of private peasant holdings, so that every member of the *mir* as a communal agricultural worker should simultaneously become a small landowner. He none the less vigorously defended the *mir* as a stabilizing counter-weight against cut-throat competition, as 'a traditional organization which could maintain the beneficial principle of communal land-ownership and save us from the terrible ulcer of proletarianism in our village population'. In 1861 he went so far as to plead that the government should enact further laws to save the *mir* from disintegrating, and he observed regretfully but honestly: 'The commercial-minded peasant of today will certainly try sooner or later to buy a decent piece of land as his full hereditary property.'

Chernyshevsky's views about the distribution of wealth contain some revealing side-lights, though in principle they do little more than echo the stale and discredited felicific calculus of Bentham. 'The most satisfactory way of distributing goods', writes Chernyshevsky like a faithful disciple, 'is that by virtue of which a given quantity of goods produces the maximum quantity of well-being or satisfaction.' None the less these trite parrot-like statements do not vitiate his enduring belief that a reasonably just distribution ('to each according to his needs') of available capital and goods, was a worthier aim than any vulgar self-satisfied surfeit of national prosperity. He deprecated, for instance, the ugly and lop-sided industrial expansion of early nineteenth-century England. 'For a democrat our Siberia, where ordinary people live well in their own way, stands much higher than England, where the majority, with all its wealth, live badly.' Of course he had heard accounts of England's squalid poverty and the child-labour in her new industrial slums. But it was equally inconceivable to Chernyshevsky (who had never seen any) that poor artisans, after becoming prosperous, could continue to live just as crudely and wretchedly as some of the prosperous merchants or officials whom they envied. Preoccupied with the exceptional economic inequalities of a relatively rich nineteenth-century Western Europe, he shut out from his mind the living heritage of her more civilized past, and failed to open his eyes to the expanding economic amelioration which European and American industry were building up for the future benefit of the whole world. His natural moral indignation at the ugly contrast between superfluous wealth and grinding poverty, between gluttony and starvation, merely provoked him to make a drastically Puritanical economic prescription: 'Until all members of society have their basic needs satisfied, any labour used in producing things which satisfy more refined needs, less necessary for health, is used unreasonably, superfluously and unproductively. Every working day used for the satisfaction of caprices or luxury is a loss for the production of things which satisfy essential needs.' Herzen, despite his respect for Chernyshevsky, could not abide him in this rôle of a 'Petersburg Daniel', a Savonarola denouncing the glorious Medicis. It is true that Chernyshevsky found it hard to distinguish between genuine spiritual culture and the frills of idle luxury, between creative beauty and insolent ostentation.

Notwithstanding his contempt for immoderate wealth, he was most emphatic in attributing every social evil to the root cause of poverty. Moreover he found the underlying cause of poverty, not in the improvidence of the poor, nor in the incalculable rigours of nature, but in a man-made social and economic system which deprived the poor of incentive to improve their lot by working harder. Not the personalities, but the system was to blame, for it corrupted even the most personally honest people who struggled against it. One of his suppressed articles makes a very plausible attempt to identify this 'system' with the Russian Government, but in the end it partly defeats his intention, for after lifting the lid off governmental institutions, it unexpectedly fastens the maximum guilt on the Russian methods and motives underlying them.

'Whoever says "poverty of the people" also says "the government is bad." . . . Our government servants are irresponsible to everyone and everything in the world except to their superiors. Since they are absolutely dependent upon them, they are absolutely at their mercy. If a man has no choice, but is forced to act against his conscience in any case, he may as well do so

with profit to himself. . . . Therefore it must be made possible
for government servants to carry out the law with impunity.
And, in order to achieve this purpose, government service must
cease to be shrouded in secrecy; it must be open before the
eyes of society, so that society can express its own opinion about
every official action of every official person.' Russians have
been called a lazy apathetic crowd, Chernyshevsky protests,
but how can you expect productive energy from a person who is
never allowed to show energy in protecting his work, personality or property from arbitrary interference. 'You cannot bring
up a man to be alert in the fields, if in his own hut he is confined
to scratching the back of his head and crossing his legs. He will
be just as much a clumsy oaf when his hand is on the plough.'

'Of course our people are poor, and does not everyone know
that public well-being will only develop when people become
industrious and frugal? But a man can only work zealously
when no one interferes with him or deprives him of the fruits of
his labour. He can only be frugal when he knows he is saving
for himself and his family, and not for the sake of some beast of
prey. If he has no such assurances, a man will hurry to spend—
probably on vodka—what little money he can gain.'[1] It is
rather odd to find the famous revolutionary praising such traditional *bourgeois* virtues, and condemning any governmental
'system' which discourages their pursuit, but perhaps that goes
to show how artificially Chernyshevsky has been understood.

In discussing agricultural reform, Chernyshevsky confessed
that he had changed his mind and grown ashamed of his own
previously exaggerated praises of the *mir* (*Sovremennik*, No. 12,
1858). He admitted that the mystic Slavophil adoration of the
mir, as some sacrosanct uniquely Russian product, had become
a farce. Other European countries possessed similar institutions
when their society was still patriarchal or feudal. Other Asiatic
countries possessed them still. It was no credit to Russians that
they had preserved intact this relic of antiquity, while it had
vanished wherever education advanced. That only helped to
prove how backward Russia was. The *mir* itself was hardly free
from blame for the wretched state of Russian agriculture—the
ignorance and apathy of the peasants, the lack of liquid capital,
the abominable roads—but, despite all that, the *mir* had a

[1] 'Zapreshchënnye Tsenzuroi Teksty N. Chernyshevskovo', *Literaturnoe
Naslyedstvo*, No. 3, p. 90, Moscow, 1932.

compensating balance of merit which could not be secured in any other way. It automatically prevented speculative merchants from buying up agricultural land from poor or greedy villagers. It guaranteed a piece of land for every peasant to till, a subsistence which might rise to plenty in abundant years; though of course it could neither ensure a good harvest nor prevent sporadic famine.

'We are disgusted', wrote Chernyshevsky, 'by the observations of our out-of-date economists, who say that our bad agriculture could be remedied by the application of a local poultice —the abolition of *mir*-ownership and the substitution for it of personal land-tenure. We must first take steps to secure efficient administration and honest law-courts; then even *mir*-ownership will not hinder the improvement of our agriculture, because then our poverty will disappear, and those conditions will come into being without which no system of land-holding can ever be made satisfactory.'

V

Chernyshevsky's revolutionary zeal did not prevent him from occasionally praising the Tsar's wisdom. He wrote in *The Contemporary* (No. 2, 1858): 'The one deed of abolishing serfdom will bless the period of Alexander II with the highest glory in the world. He will be the only sovereign in Europe who voluntarily freed his own subjects.' But two years later Chernyshevsky switched over to the opposite extreme in a furious letter which he wrote to Herzen in London : 'What does this mean?' he demands; 'Instead of fierce denunciations of falsehood, there are borne to us from the banks of the Thames hymns of praise to Alexander II. . . . The liberal landowners, liberal littérateurs, liberal professors, lull you with hopes in the progressive aims of our government. . . . But this is how the matter really stands. At the end of the reign of Nicolas I, everyone sincerely loving Russia came to the conclusion that only by force could human rights be seized by the people from the Tsar's grip, that only those rights are stable which are conquered—for whatever is given as a gift can also be taken away again.'[1]

[1] The authenticity of this letter has been disputed, but we have the authority of M. Lemke in attributing it to Chernyshevsky. (Herzen: *Polnoe Sobranive*, vol. 10, p. 224.)

Herzen had the good grace to print this angry letter anonymously in *The Bell*, and in an accompanying editorial he printed his own answer. Those who read both must have felt at once what a deep spiritual gulf separated the aristocratic rebel from the plebeian revolutionary. 'We differ from you,' wrote Herzen, 'hardly in our ends but in our means, not in our principles but in our manner of operating. . . . Your integrity is understandable to us, it is close to our heart. . . . But we will not call for the axe as the *ultima ratio*, so long as there remains one vestige of reasonable hope for a solution without the axe. The further I look into the western world, into the chain of events which brought Europe to us Russians, the more there rises up in me a disgust for all bloody revolutions; sometimes they are inevitable, and the social organism thus rids itself of chronic diseases by acts of violence and flaming hatred. But we Russians are not in that state; we do not need to be; where have we that vicious circle which can only be cut with the axe? Deficient confidence in our own constructive powers, that is our worst misfortune, and most remarkable of all—that lack of self-confidence exists equally in the government, the nobility and the peasantry.'

Chernyshevsky followed the same course as Herzen, and a number of the Slavophils, in strenuously advising the Government to hand over extra land to the peasants without piling up on them still heavier financial burdens. But the Government finally adopted the contrary principle, according to which all land added to the *mir* out of the landlords' estates had to be redeemed by the peasants through yearly payments spread out over a period of forty-nine years. They could escape these payments only if they accepted a lot about one quarter of the standard size—the paupers' lot, it was called. Moreover the state peasants (about one half of the total) were granted larger holdings than the landlords' peasants, who bitterly resented such arbitrary discrimination. It is indisputable that the redemption dues were a mill-stone round the necks of the already disgruntled peasants, many of whom had pinned their hopes on a much more sweeping and less half-hearted settlement.

Nevertheless Chernyshevsky was asking for trouble when, nettled by the Government's neglect of his warnings, he started not only to attack in print the economic provisions of the settlement—which sensible people almost unanimously found

inadequate—but also to vilify the personal character and motives
of the landlords and Government committees. The man who
foamed at the mouth about serfdom, pronounced it to be the
sole cause of the Stenka Razin and Pugachëv revolts, who indiscriminately branded all Russian landlords as idlers and parasites, and all local government officials, including the law-
courts and the police, as riddled with corruption, could hardly
expect mercy from the authorities when the time came for them
to strike. Several landowners denounced Chernyshevsky in
letters to the Ministry of Internal Affairs. They accused him—
and the accusation was true—of stirring up class-hatred in the
country, of doing his utmost to inspire the peasants with ground-
less suspicion and distrust for the intentions of the Government
committees. The Ministry thereupon ordered the Censorship
Committee to produce a report on the activities of *The Contemporary*. The censors, whether deliberately or not, had given
Chernyshevsky enough rope with which to hang himself. Their
cautious report confirmed that this journal had been in places
carried away by 'Western sophistries', especially by 'that
striving to reduce to economic terms all the principles of existence, not excluding the moral ones'. Meanwhile the March
issue of *The Contemporary* had appeared without a single word of
comment on the Emancipation Edict (5 March 1861)—except a
perfunctory factual statement in the internal review section.
Chernyshevsky had reached the stage at which he preferred to
express his resentment by stony silence.

The extent to which he was implicated in underground
agitation against the Government, and whether he wrote or
inspired the illicitly printed 'Appeal to the Landowners'
Peasants', are matters of controversy. His most conscientious
recent biographer, Yury Steklov, has no doubt that he wrote
this inflammatory document. But his open activities as a
journalist more than suffice to explain his arrest in 1862, and,
from the Government's point of view, his treasonable intentions
justified his trial and deportation to Siberia, where he remained in exile for twenty years. He was finally convicted on
the general charge of 'plotting for the overthrow of the existing
order'. The more specific charges brought against him could
not be substantiated,[1] and much of the evidence for them is said

---

[1] But this could also prove Chernyshevsky's skill in covering up his
tracks. (See M. Lemke, Herzen: *Polnoe Sobraniye*, vol. 16, p. 75.)

to have been fabricated by the police.[1] The sinister reputation
of the Tsarist police is thus confirmed once more, but at the
price of diminishing Chernyshevsky's stature as an active
revolutionary.

VI

In their natural desire to do full justice to martyred free-
thinking Russians prior to the Soviet period, Soviet historians
sometimes create the misleading impression that the Tsarist
censorship was infinitely more cramping than their own. In
Chernyshevsky's case—leaving out of account his own skill in
circumlocution—the censors treated his articles with quite
surprising leniency. Of course a number were suppressed and
many more were cut, but he was far from being silenced, even
when his articles were acutely embarrassing or hostile to Government policy. Oddly enough, among the suppressed articles,
first published since the October Revolution, there is one which
contains a glowing personal tribute from Chernyshevsky to the
censorship staff. Perhaps the censors stopped it through fear of
what might happen to themselves by drawing such embarrassing
attention to their leniency.

Chernyshevsky starts this article by quoting from a letter
written to the official *Journal de St. Petersbourg*. 'In addition to the
disease of silence, we suffer from the paralysis of indifference to
public affairs. We even transform both these defects into comfortable qualities, so long as we remain enclosed behind our
Chinese wall. Consequently the revulsion which we feel against
speech, and against the printed word in general, is only equalled
by the immensity of our bad faith when we blame governmental
rigidity, or the so-called exaggerated severity of the censors, for
our own inexcusably tepid and spineless attitude, and its fatal
effect on our social interests. It is all the more incomprehensible
and strange that such apathy should prevail in a young, physically and morally healthy country, with an enlightened Government always standing in the vanguard of progress and moving
in advance of the masses.' Chernyshevsky then proceeds to
agree with the subsequent argument that torpid Russian citizens ought to grow more public-spirited—but how can they
possibly do this, he protests, when the Government has no

---

[1] 'The Chernyshevsky Affair' (from unpublished sources) by M. Lemke:
Byloe, No. 4, 1906.

intention of acting on their advice, and does not even want to hear it? He concludes by paying this handsome tribute : 'One must do full justice to the generosity with which the censors fulfil their difficult task. One must even admit that many of them are noble-minded to the point of being ready to risk or sacrifice their own careers. Everyone who has constant dealings with the censorship comes away with the most favourable opinion of the enlightened patriotism of the individuals to whom it is entrusted.'[1]

In a reference to the same letter, he suggests another likely reason for the torpor of the Russian public, and supplies an international stock-market illustration which sounds a little shocking from a socialist pen; 'Till quite recently the Russian Government was primarily military in character—enforcing discipline, unquestioned obedience to orders. But the present industrial period exacts more confidence from the public, more participation from them in governmental affairs. For example, the prices quoted for the government bonds of Austria, France and England stand in direct proportion to the part taken by their societies in public affairs. Thus English prices for 3 per cent. bonds stand twenty points higher than the price of 5 per cent. Austrian bonds.'

Still more striking evidence of the censors' generosity to Chernyshevsky is the fact that, while imprisoned in the Fortress of Peter and Paul, he was allowed to write and publish his famous novel *What to Do* (1863). Almost the only work of Chernyshevsky's, then as now, widely read by Russian students, it is usually called his masterpiece, and remains the most vivid and compact expression of his social gospel. Most of its ideas can be traced back to Fourier, Robert Owen, and John Stuart Mill —whose *Principles of Political Economy* Chernyshevsky translated into Russian—but its tone and application to typical Russian characters are uniquely his own. In spite of its plainly didactic structure, the novel radiates a firm and serene confidence in a happy future for Russia. With generous naïveté it pleads that human beings could rapidly be transformed into a brotherhood of kindly and industrious angels as soon as hunger and poverty no longer harassed them. Its childlike sincerity breathes the charm of an ancient Russian folk-tale. It contains no broken champagne bottles, no nights with gypsies, none of the

[1] *Zvenya*: Sbornik Materialov, vol. 5, 347 ff., Academia, 1935.

murky tortuous spiritual torments which we expect to prevail in Russian novels of that time. The only extremist character is the noble ascetic Rachmetov, and even he is sane and straight-forward. Though he never emerges into the foreground of action, he serves very aptly as a sharp foil to the mild reasonable people around him, who all brim over with a rather forbiddingly self-conscious mixture of enlightened self-interest and benevolent consideration for others. Rachmetov sleeps on a plank covered with nails in order to test his powers of endurance; he is fiercely abstemious and refuses to eat any food more refined than the plain fare of the poorest peasant. Yet we discover what a human Russian he is, when enjoying a meal with a friend, he conquers temptation by yielding to it, and devours with relish all the pastry and cakes in an enormous dish.

Chernyshevsky's contemporary, the critic Shelgunov, observed with acumen that Rachmetov was clearly intended to represent a towering Titan of resolution, who planned an exact use for every moment of his day. While such an individual might well seem awe-inspiring and exemplary to Russians, they ought to realize that the whole North American continent was already full of precisely such efficient hard-working men, who try to prove by every action of theirs that 'time is money'. Therefore those people to whom Rachmetov appeared such a demi-god, such an unattainable ideal, could hardly have achieved a very high moral standard in their own social organization.

But Rachmetov is even more revealing as the type of man whom Chernyshevsky clearly admired most highly, who appealed to his deepest instincts. Far from being a down-trodden proletarian moulded by the iron laws of production, he is a decidedly eccentric landowner, an adept of strenuous self-imposed discipline, but above all a law unto himself. Yet he towers above every other character in the book as the motive force of Russian society, its brightest hope for the future. His creator extols him in almost lyrical terms: 'You are few in numbers, but only through you can all human lives blossom; without you they will wither away. Though you are bound to be few, you alone enable people to breathe; without you they will die of suffocation. There is a great mass of honest and good men, but such men as you are the rare bouquet in good wine; from you arises the strength and the aroma. For you are the prime movers, impelling others to move; you are the essential salt of the salt of the earth.' My imagination was stirred when some years ago in Moscow a Soviet intellectual told me that Rachmetov should be regarded as a forecast of the Bolshevik hero of today. For surely it is only going one step further to acknowledge that the Bolshevik hero still comes nearer to life in fiction than he does in fact, and most successfully in fiction written by a non-Marxian long before the Bolshevik régime appeared on the horizon.

With all due respect to the eminently masculine originality of Rachmetov, it should be observed that Chernyshevsky was also one of the few militant male feminists, that he expressed advanced views about women's civic equality with men, and advocated both experimental marriage and divorce by mutual agreement. His emancipated women are formidable figures. Vera Pavlovna, the heroine of *What to Do*, preaches and practises the virtues of co-operative enterprise. In her sewing-room the girls enjoy their work, do what they want to do, and let others do the same. They all work for their own profit, and share any increase in profit. Yet she opposes the 'You must be cruel in order to be kind' arguments advanced by her revolutionary husband, Lopukhov. 'This theory, which I cannot accept,' she exclaims, 'condemns people to a life which is merciless, cold and prosaic.' 'No, Vera Pavlovna,' he reassures her, 'the theory is cold, but it teaches people how to find warmth. The theory is merciless, but if people follow it, they will cease to be pitiful objects of idle compassion. The surgeon's knife must not bend; otherwise you would have to take pity on the patient under the operation, who would be no better off for all your pity. The theory may be prosaic, but it discovers the true motives of life.'

We cannot hope to fathom the thoughts of contemporary Soviet readers of Chernyshevsky's novel. They are less likely to be carried away, for they will be on their guard against idealistic pitfalls, about which they have received warning in advance. But the novel, as a feat of moral exhortation, certainly took the younger generation of the sixties by storm. It became their bible, and one which many of them interpreted in the most literal and drastic sense. Earnest young men blew out their brains, improving on the example of the young husband who simulated suicide in order to make room for a worthier friend who had won his wife's affection. Strong-minded adolescent girls of every class vied with the heroine Vera in launching small co-operative societies, and they flocked in embarrassing numbers to study practical subjects like medicine at the over-crowded universities.

VII

In his youth (1849) Chernshevsky had dreamed and written about his intention to invent a machine of 'perpetuum mobile', 'which must revolutionize the world and make me the greatest benefactor of mankind in material improvement, which people need most of all now . . . When the curse of winning bread by the sweat of his brow is removed, man's real moral and spiritual task will begin.'[1] Such thoughts sound less fantastic in the present atomic age, and encourage one to believe that some 'Utopians' may have more scientific prescience than so-called 'scientific socialists'. But Chernyshevsky's touching faith in moral improvement as the inevitable sequence to a well-filled stomach has so far proved to be a deceptive mirage in the few countries which have reached that enviable economic level, whether by socialist or other methods.

The magic word 'scientific', in the sense of indubitable and exact knowledge, was worshipped by a number of mid-nine-teenth century social thinkers apart from Marx, whose disciples have strenuously sought to monopolize it. Chernyshevsky used the same word persistently as the hall-mark of his own brand of socialism. Kropotkin tried to prove that his version of anarch-ism was the only scientific socialism. So the dispute continues to rage, except, curiously enough, among exact scientists, whose hypotheses long ago abandoned similar dogmatic pre-tensions. Like other left-wing Hegelians, including Marx, Chernyshevsky had embraced Hegel's dialectical method while rejecting his respect for the existing social order. But he had not swallowed Hegel's Prussian passion for the mighty organic state. Though he approved of centralized government, the anarchist's vision of free associations of producers, jostling each other in a political void, seems to have been nearer to his heart. Nevertheless he accepted the dialectical law of historical pro-gress, derived from Hegel, as neither more nor less than the discovery of a natural law, a law of human growth, but as

---

[1] 'Chernyshevsky and Fourier': *Sovremennii Mir* (November 1909).

scientifically correct and inevitable as the laws of gravity and chemical combination.

Fired by this belief, Chernyshevsky advanced the sweeping argument that the political and moral sciences were only younger than the exact sciences, but not different in kind. He made this the central theme of his article 'The Anthropological Principle in Philosophy', which purported to be a review of P. Lavrov's *Essays on Questions of Practical Philosophy*.[1] 'The word science,' he said, 'does not in English cover all those branches of knowledge which it includes for us and other continental peoples. The English describe as sciences—mathematics, astronomy, physics, chemistry, zoology, geography—branches of knowledge which are termed by us exact sciences. They do *not* so describe history, psychology, moral philosophy or metaphysics. One must admit there is a huge difference between these two spheres of knowledge, in the degree of certainty with which they can answer questions. If you say, the human organism needs air in order to live, no one will argue with you. But say, poverty injures the mind and heart of human beings— and a lot of clever people will retort that poverty sharpens the mind and educates the feelings. Others will retort, just as firmly, that poverty is the main source of ignorance, vice and crime.

'But now,' Chernyshevsky warms up, 'natural sciences have advanced so far that they provide the means for arriving at exact decisions in moral questions as well. Present-day psychology, for instance, can say with certainty that a good or bad action is the direct result of some moral or material fact, or combination of facts. Psychological truths, like the truths of the natural sciences, can be discovered by the most exact analysis of the facts—truths as authentic as the revolution of the earth round the sun. These ought not to be accepted without the strictest verification, but once they are accepted they lead to conclusions warranted by the facts, and leave no path open for retreat, or for any repetition of absurd mistakes . . . Irritable changeability, hesitation, do not belong to the spirit of the new ideas; on the contrary, instability of conviction, moods of alternate scepticism and over-confidence, can only occur where there is inadequate knowledge of the ideas worked out by contemporary Western science. When the time is ripe, and those

[1] *Sovremennik*, No. 4, 1860.

people striving to re-create Western Europe show themselves to be unyielding in their philosophic convictions, that will be a sign for the rapid triumph of new principles in European society.'

Clearly the priest's son, in turning atheist, had shed nothing of his militant religious temper. He allayed the pangs of his renegade conscience by fortifying his new faith with the same rock-like certainty as the Christian dogma had possessed for him until he turned his back on it. Kneeling to Western science as the latest revelation of Divinity, how could he admit the blasphemous thought that political and social sciences (if they could correctly be named science at all) might be bound by the infinitely more complicated nature of their data to remain perpetually experimental and tentative? Nor did he face the more mundane but awkward moral issue. By trying to invest politico-economic principles with the same type of absolute and predictable certainty as the laws of physics and chemistry, he twisted them into blind mechanical movements, ethically neutral forces, obliterating what he elsewhere held sacred, the imperative human urge to value and judge for itself.

In some of his essays on political and economic organization, Chernyshevsky betrayed no less acutely his haunting sense of self-contradiction and honest doubt. The introduction to his translation of J. S. Mill's *Principles of Political Economy* castigates social scientists for their unfounded self-satisfaction and cock-sureness.' 'The laws which govern historical development have been discovered, the rights of man ascertained, the formulae of ways of life necessary for his well-being are established. Is there a single person dealing with moral and social science who does not talk in that strain? And almost the whole profane crowd believes them. This loud self-praise indulged in by philosophers, publicists, historians, etc., is a strange contrast to the modest testimonials of natural scientists about the state of physics, chemistry, etc.'[1] In his article on Guizot's Memoirs (*Sovremennik*, No. 2, 1858), he champions a more empirical application of radical policy, though in the last resort he is keen on breaking heads which remain too dense to be persuaded. 'A radical policy', he wrote there, 'does not consist of adherence to any single definite form of political organization, but it rests on

---

[1] N. Chernyshevsky: *Neizdannye Teksty*, 94 ff., Saratov, 1928.

the conviction that the worst faults of a certain society can only be remedied by a complete reconstruction of its foundations, and not by the correction of details. In North America a radical would be a monarchist, in China an advocate of European civilization, in India an enemy of the caste system. Of all political parties, only the liberal is irreconcilable with radicalism; because the latter sets out to change with the aid of violence, and for the sake of reforms is ready to sacrifice freedom of speech and all constitutional niceties. . . . Liberals alone refuse to recognize that legal rights have no value for a man until he possesses material means to benefit by them. Liberals fuss about all sorts of abstract rights, but make no attempt to uproot poverty and ignorance, and thus enable people to use these rights.'

The latter remarks would sound strangely out-of-date today in any realistic verdict on the practical achievements of later nineteenth-century liberals, not only in Europe, but even in Russia. They nevertheless illustrate that implacable hostility to compromise, which constantly makes Russian political thinkers and Russian politicians so exasperating to their European opposite numbers. And Chernyshevsky's own impatience with liberals is comprehensible, when we recall that the Russian liberals of his day were mostly ineffective orators who clung blindly to absolute *laissez-faire* in political economy. *Laissez-faire* never suited Russia, where no private individuals normally took the initiative unless the Government gave the lead, and where huge Government monopolies such as the wool trade (started by Peter the Great to clothe his army) had been long-standing institutions. Chernyshevsky satisfied himself with condemning *laissez-faire* as a principle which was basically immoral and unsound, for the simple reason that it *a priori* denied the Government any right to control or even to influence economic growth. Judging it solely by its effect on his own environment, a mid-nineteenth century Russian could quite excusably conclude that liberalism was a sickly exotic plant. No Russian thinker, until much later, was able to see it in the light of its European champions, as a militant faith in an indispensable degree of compromise and co-operation between reforming policy and inherited custom, a faith for which its supporters might strike as hard as others did for any extreme course of action.

VIII

It is remarkable that, in spite of his invincible prejudices against the more resourceful and flexible type of modern European mind, Chernyshevsky remained from start to finish a Westernizer, who never faltered in his belief that Europe was in every respect more civilized and 'advanced' than Russia, and that Russia could do no better than follow her example, especially in learning from her political experience. He displayed his maximum of sense and insight by the resolute way in which he countered the specious argument—almost as prevalent then as it is today—that Russia was destined to take over the torch of civilization from an exhausted Europe. Having mastered the Russian intellectual's indispensable technique of using learned themes as a camouflage for political messages, he spoke out vigorously on this subject under the skilfully antiquarian cover of his article on 'The Causes of the Fall of Rome' (*Sovremennik*, No. 5, 1861). 'People like to assert that the capture of Rome by barbarians saved a dying world. The Roman world had exhausted its potentiality, ceased to develop, and fallen into an advanced stage of decay. Unfortunately this historical judgement has been used to justify various foolish dreams about contemporary society. Western Europe has outlived its time, spent its vitality. Western peoples are unable to pursue their social progress. The world must therefore be renewed by their fall; fresh forces are due to replace them.'

After this argument comes the exultant boast: 'Here we stand ready to renew the world. What fine fellows we are, to be sure!' In this way our national vanity is inflated and strengthened by pseudo-learned arguments. And when we arrogate to ourselves the rôle of barbarians, Goths and Vandals, we conveniently manage to forget what barbarians really are. A barbarian is a creature still wallowing in the most abysmal ignorance, standing somewhere between a wild beast and a man of developed mind, but much nearer to the former. If power falls from the hands of developed people into the hands of barbarians, what hope remains for progress or increase of knowledge? How can social life benefit, if institutions, good or bad, but at least human, with some element of reason, are overthrown and exchanged for bestial habits? What do people mean when they repeat: 'The Roman Empire lost its vitality'?

Had the people composing it lost their human qualities? Young men still took the place of old ones. They were not born without heads or stomachs. Do they mean that society, the soil on which grow the manifestations of social life, dried up or lost its fertility? If that is what they mean, answered Chernyshevsky, then their minds are clouded. 'Individuals age, but society is always being replenished by new people. Botanical metaphors, like "flowering", "taking root", "fading away", are too often used by historians in a cloud of indiscriminate rhetoric which obscures a proper understanding of the issues at stake in human society.'

To clinch his argument, Chernyshevsky draws a striking parallel between the Roman Empire in Europe and the British Empire in India, using terms which might later have won him unsolicited applause from Rudyard Kipling or even from Winston Churchill. 'Is the vitality of India being exhausted by English rule?' he asks. 'Of course the people are ignorant and live poorly; the impositions on them are heavy. But were they any better off before the English came? On the contrary, conditions were then much worse, and now they are growing steadily better every year. Roads are built, savage customs are abolished, the natives are learning the rudiments of law. Civilization is still weak, but it grows. The English themselves tell you that India will reach a stage when it no longer needs British rule, and will then become independent. What the English foretell about the future of India had already happened, but prematurely, in the provinces of the Roman Empire. There the people suffered under the exactions of arbitrary rule and of the Imperial prefects. But however bad was the state of affairs prevailing in the Roman Empire, it was made incomparably worse by the barbarian conquest. Excellent Roman civil and criminal codes were overthrown by the arbitrary caprice of greedy and bloodthirsty barbarians. These conquering barbarians murdered, plundered, and ran riot in an orgy of sheer boredom. The destruction of the Roman Empire by a mass of savages was as much a geological catastrophe as was the destruction of Herculaneun and Pompeii by a volcano, or of Lisbon by an earthquake. The widely-held opinion that the ancient world died of senile decay, that its removal was necessary for human progress, simply contradicts the facts. . . .

'Moreover this opinion has another side, flattering to the

tribes that conquered Rome. Just as the ancient world was lifeless and stagnant, so were the barbarians bursting with vitality
and capacity for growth. What foundation is there for this
claim?' Chernyshevsky then pours scorn on all the familiar talk
about personal freedom in the Teutonic tribes, about the
pristine virtues of the citizen not stifled by the state. 'We have
seen the free Franks of Clodwig, the free Huns of Attila, the
free Mongols of Genghiz Khan. Each is free to rob and murder
as he pleases until his *Ataman* cuts off his head. Such freedom is
nothing but an alliance of chaos and despotism. . . .

'Out of this banditry which lasted several hundred years,
feudalism at last emerged. Was this the special feature contributed to civilization by the barbarians? Here at least some kind
of law and order was maintained. Compared with the wretched
sixth or seventh centuries, feudalism stood for progress. But it
was neither more nor less than plunder turned into a system,
civil war subordinated to rules. Free people took oaths of
allegiance to powerful neighbours, to whom they abandoned
part of their property in return for protection against other
bandits. But similar relationships had arisen all over the world
in a time of troubles. There was nothing unique about the
Western form of feudalism. Similar connections existed between
weak and strong Rajahs in India, between the latter and their
Emperors. It is now well-known that some kind of feudalism
arose in many parts of the world, but only as a transition period
between the most complete savagery and the lower stages of
legal order. Towards the end of the Middle Ages feudalism gave
way to a more centralized form of government. But this centralized state did not fully overcome feudalism till the seventeenth
century. In the Roman Empire a similar form of organized
state had already existed in the third century. Thus fourteen
centuries were spent in trying to raise civilization back again to
the same height from which the barbarians had originally
knocked it down.'

I have quoted Chernyshevsky's argument at length both
because it reflects so categorically his modest view of Russia in
relation to the superior achievements of Europe, his understanding of the unpredictable ebb and flow in human civilization, and because this aspect of his teaching has received scant
attention from his Soviet commentators. Boastful, aggressive
Russian patriots, whatever their political colour, filled him with

misgivings. 'I do not speak only of the Slavophils,' he wrote, 'They are few in numbers and one meets too many people who indulge in cheap mockery of them without noticing that they themselves belong to the same deep-rooted tendency from which the Slavophils spring. These vain, conceited obsessions are unfortunately the result of a feeling shared by almost the majority of our society, and expressed by many people who influence the thought of the public. We are called on to renovate the life of the civilized world, to inject into it higher elements which it is powerless to work out for itself. Scrutinize carefully our most-invoked Westernizer. In this respect he often seems to be a Slavophil.'[1]

Chernyshevsky bore no grudge against the Slavophils and frankly admired the personal character of their outstanding leaders. In 1855 he wrote : 'We never shared and never felt the smallest desire to share the views of the Slavophils, but with all their errors they are among the most cultured, noble and gifted people in the whole of Russia. Whoever knows them only through the polemics conducted against the old "Moskvityanin" does not really know them.' And two years later he announced : 'When we consider how many of our so-called Westernizers suffer from confused ideas of what is good or bad in Europe, and how till now many of them mistake the worst things for the best, we must admit that the criticism of the European way of life advanced by the Slavophils is far from useless in clarifying our minds.' (*Sovremennik*, March, 1857.)

But while he spared and even revered the Slavophil leaders, he reserved his most scathing invective for the majority of the Slavophil rank and file. 'They possess', he wrote, 'an extraordinary capacity for discovering that every filth peculiar to our country is something excellently designed for the revival of Europe. One claims as a great virtue our patient submission to every kind of outrage ; Europe has endured too few of these, and should therefore be stimulated by undergoing similar trials ; others find a hidden treasure in our mode of family life in the peasants' dirty hut, in husbands beating their wives, fathers beating their sons (or fathers being beaten by their sons when the former grow old and decrepit), in filial obedience to parental orders about marriage, regardless of the desires of bride or bridegroom. Others are proud of our long severe

---

[1] Chernyshevsky here refers to Herzen.

winter, and find that Western Europeans are enervated by too little frost. But at this point even they give up the battle. . . . People endowed with common sense, even the most zealous searchers, can find nothing whatsoever in our institutions and way of life, except the *mir*, which might usefully be spread abroad. Moreover, Europeans know much better than we do what institutions they need, and how to organize them. . . . We are far from admiring the present state of affairs in Europe, but none the less we believe she need borrow nothing from us. Europe has her own mind, much more developed than ours, has nothing to learn from us, and does not need our help.'

According to Chernyshevsky any major revival of which the leading western countries stood in need would emerge from within themselves. So would any major calamity, but he did not enlarge on this, for he was never a prophet of doom. If he had been, he would have agreed with the substance of Dean Inge's aphorism : 'Ancient civilizations were destroyed by imported barbarians; but we breed our own.' At home he attacked those barbarians, and identified them, not with the simple untaught people, but with the horde of crooked and arbitrary civil servants bred by the Russian bureaucratic autocracy. While he was immune from that perverse psychological streak which finds redeeming virtues in barbaric crudity, and though he was an avowed enemy of mysticism in every shape, he nevertheless clung to a mystical superstition about the still untested political wisdom of what he termed the slumbering masses. But here too he seems always to have looked more hopefully to Western Europe than to Russia for support in maintaining and realizing his faith. And unfortunately his knowledge of Western Europe was almost entirely derived from books, especially from those written by French or German socialists. His reading, though wide, was extremely one-sided, and his experience of the way in which Western institutions worked was virtually nil.

He thus came closest to Marx—and simultaneously to Marxist error—when he insisted that tentative social hypotheses advanced by a few disgruntled intellectuals were leading to conclusions as exact and certain as the laws of natural science. And he disclosed his lack of modern scientific method by prejudging the verdict on social experiments which had not yet been made. Finally he left out of account all the unpredictable factors which complicate every experiment, whether social or scientific, and which sometimes produce results contradicting the hypothesis which the experiment was hopefully intended to vindicate. In this way he himself contributed unwittingly to that swelling current of intellectual arrogance—obsolete from any scientific point of view—an error which he could none the less sincerely deplore when it took shape in the blustering of the stupider Slavophils.

IX

If we turn from Chernyshevsky's methods to his ultimate aims, we are faced with a distinctly bleak commonplace outline of the Socialist good life, which hardly escaped from being smugly petty bourgeois by virtue of its thin theoretical claim to be more genuinely unselfish. His appreciation of the spiritual side of human civilization was morbidly embittered by class-consciousness, as well as unduly sanguine about the moral stimulus to be derived from evenly distributed economic abundance. Nobody can find fault with him for giving priority to the conquest of poverty, the grinding Asiatic poverty of Russia. But he imagined human nature briskly changing for the better, like a snake throwing off its old skin, as soon as all the hungry were fed and all the naked clothed, because at this stage rational education should start to work its miracles on the minds of the masses. Then only would it become legitimate for people to trifle with music or poetry, or to indulge in exalted philosophical arguments after a solid meal. Civilization would spring into a fresh and peerless blossom on the soil of industrious well-fed co-operative societies. 'Reform society, and there will be no more diseases', he confidently repeated in company with Turgenev's Nihilist Bazarov; 'in a properly organized society, it will make no difference whether a man is stupid or clever, bad or good.' 'Yes, I understand', answered Odintsova; 'they will all have the same spleen.'

During his twenty years in penal servitude, though he wrote a lot, Chernyshevsky added nothing substantial to his system of thought. He appears, however, to have found fault with a number of his former European teachers, and in his letters from Siberia he calls Malthus a charlatan, Proudhon a fool, and Comte a futile nonentity, though he continues to admire Ricardo. He conducted a kind of educational correspondence course with his sons, and urged them repeatedly to learn French and German, and to travel abroad. In overpraising European literature he showed surprisingly poor judgement of Russian talent, and in a peculiar outburst of pro-Western prejudice he dismissed Pushkin and Lermontov as weak imitators of Byron.

On the whole, a perusal of his letters from Siberia[1] confirms the impression that his main ideas about Russia and Europe had changed but little since he wrote in his diary in August 1848 : 'History—is faith in progress. Politics—is respect for the West, and the conviction that we can in no way be compared with Western peoples; they are men while we are children.' He lashed out against 'false learning', the mechanical and use-less memorization of a mass of unrelated facts, and he warned his sons against the snares of futile scholastic pedantry, so pre-valent in Russian schools. Let them above all learn to think logically, develop the faculty of judging and acting for them-selves, and the ability to compare one branch of knowledge with another. In some pointed remarks about the Jesuits he obliquely drew his sons' attention to the evil which infected political organizations. To appear to attack the Catholic Church was a sure way of dodging official suspicion, for abuse of Catholic institutions was almost equivalent to a sign of devotion to the Russian Government. 'My mistake in my essay on the Jesuits', he wrote, 'is that I omitted to emphasize that no organized corporation ever served any cause disinterestedly; for every organization always sets its vested interests higher than per-sonal convictions. There may be people who can love and devotedly serve an ideal independently, but they remain ex-ceptional beings, and they can never unite in an organization established for that purpose.'

After his return from Siberia in 1883, he met in Astrakhan the editor of *Russian Thought*, to which journal he planned to contribute regular articles. But the scheme failed to materialize. Loyal friends helped him to earn his living by commissioning him to translate into Russian the ponderous German volumes of Weber's *World History*, a work which he cordially detested. He wrote for *Russian Thought* one vigorous article attacking Darwin, whose 'survival of the fittest' as a formula for human evolution seemed to him nothing but a sinister design to justify for ever

---

[1] *Chernyshevsky v Sibiri*: E. Lyatsky and M. Chernyshevsky, St. Peters-burg, 1912.

the ruthless exploitation of weak people by strong ones. While re-asserting that unrestricted economic competition, far from enlarging the spiritual capacities of the competitors, merely served to admit the most brutal jungle-law as the decisive factor in human relations, he remained cautious and vague as before in prescribing governmental control as a remedy for economic maladjustments.

For industrial organization in Russia Chernyshevsky seems to have favoured some half-way house between the handicraft *artel* and the giant productive monopoly. He obviously believed that the commercial benefits of mechanization would eliminate the primitive small producer and craftsman. And here he foretold, like Marx in the *Communist Manifesto*, a period of ever-increasing misery for the wage-earning artisan—a prediction which has proved to be very wide of the mark, since the poor of industrialized countries have clearly not grown poorer since 1848, but in most countries considerably richer. Be that as it may, Chernyshevsky was equally convinced of the long-term advantages which mechanization would ultimately bring to the wage-earner, and he rightly pointed out that agriculture could not remain isolated from the technical evolution of urban industries. Here he saw further than his *narodnik* disciples, who did not understand the business-like Chernyshevsky who wrote: 'Linked by the increasing profitability of large-scale production, the reasons for differentiating between agriculture and industry will shortly disappear.'[1]

On the administrative side of industry, Chernyshevsky showed more guild socialist than modern Marxian leanings. He had no doubt observed as an object-lesson in Russia that the more the state interferes and controls, the less inclined it is to accept responsibility for what is done. When things went wrong, it preferred to find scapegoats among its intimidated employees. Such a system neither promoted managerial efficiency nor improved the material status of the artisan. He remained none the less hostile to *laissez-faire*, which he called an economic talisman for people with absolute principles, who neither observe facts nor think. Whatever the disadvantages of the state meddling with industrial management, there were plenty of other necessary jobs which only the state could do. *Laissez-faire* could never guarantee that every member of society would get the chance

[1] Y. Steklov: *N. G. Chernyshevsky*, vol. i, p. 568.

of doing honest work, but the state could. And the more immediate and drastic measures it took to abolish poverty, ignorance and vice, the less it would need to interfere at a later stage. No one questioned the right of the state to tax its subjects for purposes which private citizens could not fulfil. On this important subject, Chernyshevsky never substantially enlarged on the vague principles which he laid down in his article 'Economic Activity and Legislation' (*Sovremennik*, 1859). Liking the centralized state as a reforming and co-ordinating power, but distrusting it as a universal employer, he fell back on the consoling, if quixotic, maxim that the more mature human beings become the less government they will need.

It is hardly surprising that twenty years of monotonous living burial in the wilds of Siberia provoked no spectacular mental development in Chernyshevsky. Rather it is a tribute to his immense powers of endurance that his brain still functioned clearly, though his health was shattered and he had faded into a shadow of his former vital self. His son, who met him in Astrakhan on his first return to European Russia, was painfully struck by his father's nervous hurried speech, by his jerky disconnected movements, and his melancholy sarcastic smile. He lingered on for a few years, but was still working when he died in 1889.

Meanwhile a powerful legend had grown up in intellectual and radical circles (the two were then almost identical), based on Chernyshevsky's name and personal example. The glorified martyr proved to be an even more inspiring leader than the living man had been, and both *narodniks* and later Social Revolutionaries claimed to be his faithful disciples. Illuminated by this halo, he captured the imagination rather than the minds of a whole generation of Russian students, who had no more studied his teaching—except his novel *What to Do*—than the majority of Russian students in the following generation had ever grappled with the voluminous writings of Marx.

Perhaps I am only voicing the unexpressed thoughts of some Soviet admirers of Chernyshevsky when I venture to suggest that the intensified governmental interest in him today seems to serve a party policy of promoting national self-esteem—which he would have been the first to deplore—more than a genuine desire to study and assess his merits as an individual thinker, who derived much from a mixed ancestry of international

European origin. A pure-blooded Russian socialist, born ten years after Marx, and expressly admired both by Marx[1] and Lenin (leaving out of consideration how far he agreed with either) provides a solid national asset which can be built upon to fortify the still shaky confidence of Soviet citizens in their native socialist pedigree. We are reminded of far-reaching claims, boosted in all the appropiate Soviet journals since 1946, that Russian citizens were the first and original inventors of wireless telegraphy—(Marconi only exploited it)—the steam-engine, the military tank, 'Soviet' penicillin, the jet-propelled engine, etc. This newly unearthed creativeness in Russian science—much of it admittedly pre-Soviet—has made many puzzled European scientists rub their eyes; it has to be suitably matched by the discovery of pre-Soviet pioneers in other spheres of activity, especially in that of 'scientific socialism', the most important of Russian specialities. The amplified commendation of Chernyshevsky now in vogue fulfils the latter purpose admirably. A divergent interpretation of him, which could hardly be voiced in the Soviet Union, may help a little to redress the balance.

[1] 'I speak of a great Russian critic and scholar with the high respect which he deserves.' (*Pis'ma K. Marksa*, p. 115, St. Petersburg, 1908.)

CHAPTER VII

ALEXANDER HERZEN

I

ALEXANDER HERZEN (1812–1870) stands apart as the most versatile, flexible, passionately persuasive and ironically disconcerting figure in that strange galaxy of original intellectuals thrown up by nineteenth-century Russia. Though he wrote chiefly as an obscure exile living abroad, he wielded over his compatriots an electrifying influence, which at its peak can only be compared with the religious veneration accorded to Tolstoy by his Russian admirers at the beginning of the present century. But whereas Tolstoy (in his popular capacity as a moral evangelist) cast his spell over *exalté* groups of agrarian socialists, back-to-the-landers, vegetarians, Christian sectarians and desperate anarchists, Herzen displayed such an unpredictable succession of dazzling facets that he appealed in turn to the widest variety of normal and abnormal Russians, including Alexander II himself, many liberal statesmen and landowners, a number of revolutionary students, and even through them to some of the wholesomely sceptical and illiterate peasants and artisans.

The edifying story of the student Engelson provides one of the most striking instances of Herzen's magnetic power in making converts. This melancholy young man had decided to put an end to his misery by poisoning himself. While he was sitting in a café, brooding over his unlucky destiny, his eyes turned by chance to an early article of Herzen's in a copy of *Fatherland Annals*. Reading its caustic words about the petty self-indulgence of private grief he suddenly began to feel ashamed that he had yielded so easily to unjustified despair. Instead of pouring out his phial of poison, he ordered half a bottle of Madeira, re-read the article attentively, and became a devoted and lifelong disciple of Herzen. Curiously enough, it was Engelson who later took the initiative in suggesting to Herzen that he ought to produce a regular Russian journal in London.

It is true that Herzen's disciples of one phase easily became

ALEXANDER HERZEN

From a portrait by K. Gorbunov

his enemies in the next, for his mental honesty kept his erratic enthusiasms in check and caused him to change his mind whenever he realized he had been mistaken—and that occurred quite often. The Russian liberals found him too revolutionary in the long run, and broke with him irrevocably when he stood up for the Polish rebels in 1863; the revolutionaries complained that he failed to keep pace with them, and never forgave him for having, as they termed it, 'betrayed the revolutionary cause'. Lenin redressed the balance by providing him with a respectable niche in revolutionary history, when he categorically explained Herzen's dilemma as reflecting the period when 'bourgeois revolutionary democracy had already died (in Europe) and proletarian revolutionary democracy had not yet ripened', and summed up his services—rather portentously— as 'the first sowing of that harvest, which will be gathered in the second onrush of the giant struggle when the proletariat will fight its way through to a union of the socialist workers of all countries'. Herzen, who heartily condemns his socialist successors, the Nihilists of the sixties, would have shuddered at being assessed as a mere link in the consecutive chain of an unfolding social order—a metaphysical view of change which he always hotly contested as demonstrably untrue, apart from being morally undesirable. Fifty years after his death, his memory was honoured in a more concrete way when the Soviet authorities gave his name to one of Moscow's principal streets.

Contemporary Soviet critics do not boggle at Herzen's innate antagonism to Marxian thought; they openly deplore it, and take considerable pains to explain it away as Herzen's 'spiritual bankruptcy'. 'Cut off from the working-class movement, not knowing the laws of social development and the historical rôle of the proletariat, Herzen lost heart after the defeat of the 1848 revolutions.'[1] This patronizing verdict occurs in a major but guarded article which reviewed the Academy of Sciences' edition of his *Selected Philosophical Works* (1946). It omits to mention that Herzen mixed freely all his life with every type and class of international revolutionary throughout Europe and consequently had some ground for forming his own tentative conclusions about the 'laws of social development'. Nevertheless this two-volume edition contains a fairly representative

[1] *Bol'shevik*, No. 9, 1947.

selection of his most important writings, enough to enable a discerning Soviet citizen to form his independent estimate of Herzen. It is the best available substitute for those who cannot grapple with Lemke's twenty-two bulky volumes, which, incidentally, are neither referred to nor quoted there. Popular anthologies, containing selected extracts of Herzen's most turgid remarks about patriotism and humanity, are also current in the Soviet Union. No doubt these are pleasant reading for the multitude—because Herzen, even at his tritest, had a splendid gift of style, but they scarcely attempt to reflect his many-sided personality, still less to trace the stages of his mental evolution.

In the thirties one substantial book[1] appeared, which avowed its object to be the defence of Herzen against 'reactionary counter-revolutionary distortions by the ideologies of bourgeois-landowner restoration'. A lively admiration of Herzen was apparently suspected of being linked with counter-revolutionary plots, and it would seem that such an emphatic and long-drawn-out statement of his proper historical position must have been urgently needed in order to fortify wavering Soviet minds. At least this provides a ray of hope that Herzen's original aims and strivings, rather than the Party's version of what they ought to be, are still debatable and live issues in his native land.

II

Herzen was born the illegitimate son of a wealthy Russian nobleman, Ivan Yakovlev, and a gentle self-effacing German girl of humble origin. His father, an intelligent but saturnine Voltairean, knew French much better than his native language, and, according to Herzen, never read a single Russian book. He tempered his sceptical outlook on human affairs by conforming strictly to the observances of the Orthodox Church, not because he was a believer, but because he thought it was the duty of all well-bred Russians to set a visible and comprehensible example to the lower orders.

Thus the impressionable child grew up among adoring house-serfs in a semi-luxurious, semi-barbaric environment, where the

---

[1] L. Piper: *Mirovozrenie Gertsena*, Moscow–Leningrad, 1935.

most sophisticated European taste and subtle sense of worldly compromise mingled with ancient Russian feudal customs and wild primitive superstitions. But darkened images of saints and Christian martyrs, peering through the chased silver frames of ikons, were never allowed to fill his childish heart with awe and terror. His father's instruction introduced him to the Bible not as a sacred repository of supernatural revelation, but as a collection of moving and imaginative human stories. Nor did the Gospels take first place in his infant education. The Russian aristocracy were never more sensitively alert to the charms of secular European culture than during that period when their share in Napoleon's defeat first gave them a leading place in the councils of Europe. Under his father's guidance the precocious Herzen tasted all the leading literatures of Europe, and at an early age he was absorbed in the stirring study of his country's rôle in recent European history. He tells us in his memoirs, 'Tales of the burning of Moscow, of the Battle of Borodino, Beresina, and the capture of Paris, were my cradle songs, my Iliad and my Odyssey.'

In 1825, at the age of fourteen, he stood with his lifelong friend, Ogarëv, on the Sparrow Hills overlooking Moscow, and together they took a solemn oath to devote all their strength to upholding the cause for which the Decembrists had suffered. At Moscow University, apart from his insignificant routine studies, he passed through the voluntary ordeal of studying Hegel, and emerged unscathed. German learning, he observed, apart from its artificial clumsy language, infected Russians with another deeper defect. 'It caused our young philosophers to spoil their intelligence as well as their style. It made their approach to real life scholastic and bookish, like that learned interpretation of simple matters which Goethe so genially satirized in his dialogue of Mephistopheles and the student. Every direct unconstrained feeling had to be analysed into the appropriate category, and thence emerged as some pale algebraic symbol, without one drop of animated blood.' Hegel's phrase, 'Whatever is real, is rational', had been triumphantly torn out of its context in order to justify subjection to the powers that be. 'But,' objected Herzen, 'once any existing social order can be justified by reason, so can the struggle against that order, if the struggle *exists*, be equally justified.'[1] The famous phrase, so

---

[1] A. Herzen: *Polnoe Sobraniye*: (ed.: Lemke), vol. 13, pp. 13–15.

dear to 'Berlin Buddhists', turned out to be tautological or ridiculously ambiguous.

In fact, Herzen discovered that Hegel's dialectical method, the moment it was logically applied to life, became a monstrous hoax. By asserting that everything real—apart from being rational—is in a predetermined state of endless flux, it merely facilitated the most cynical orgy of casuistry. Sliding glibly from thesis to antithesis, you could reconcile reason with anything you liked, with rigid conservatism at one moment and with bloody revolution at the next. The study of Hegel effectively sharpened Herzen's wits, but it led him to a very decisive rejection of Hegel's conclusions and methods, and it cleared the way for his next intellectual adventure, the plunge into the more stimulating social theories of Saint-Simon and Fourier.[1]

The lasting inspiration derived by Herzen from his university friends formed one of his most happy memories. They are immortalized, together with so much of his vital experience, in the superb memoirs, *My Past and Thoughts*, which he wrote in London in the evening of his life. 'What I have written may contain dreams, a riddle to which I alone hold the key. Perhaps no one except me can hear how spirits come to life under these lines . . . perhaps, but the book is none the less dear to me for that.' These 'spirits come to life' persisted in the undying aspirations formed in Herzen's student days, animating a loyalty which was only intensified by his many subsequent disappointments in people and events. Those three distinct student groups which grew up around Stankevich, the Slavophils, and Belinsky, embraced a unique educated aristocracy of outstanding young men who, in spite of many natural divergences in social origin and personal temperament, were inwardly united by a profound feeling of estrangement from official Russia, and by a vague but genuinely disinterested enthusiasm for revised human values. 'They neither thought nor cared about their social position, their personal profit, their security. They spent their lives, their whole energy, in a pursuit which brought them no personal advantage. Some forgot their wealth, others their poverty. Where, in what corner of contemporary Europe, will you find such hermits of thought, such devotees of science and art, such fanatics of conviction, whose strivings

[1] Excellent short accounts of these two writers can be found in *The Socialist Tradition* by Alexander Gray (1946).

remain eternally young even though their hair turns grey? In Europe today there is no youth, there are no young people . . . The finished self-centred modern Western man is always pleased with himself. He never forgets his personal views, his petty position and individual rights in his own pathetic little sphere . . . Western man was not always like that; he is fading away. The historical wave of natural changes has thrown up on the scene a slimy layer of petty bourgeois, covering over the paralysed aristocratic class and drowning the original national character. . . .

'Blunt pedants and heavy scholars did not understand the nature of our meetings. They saw meat and wine, but they saw nothing else . . . We were not monks, we lived a many-sided life; and sitting at table we set more in motion and achieved no less than those fasting toilers who rummage in the backyards of science. We did not weep over the sins of this world, although we felt its sufferings, and we stood with a smile in readiness, without brooding over the foretaste of sacrifices which lay before us.'[1]

Though Herzen first threw himself into the ideological fray as a whole-hearted Westernizer, he felt a chivalrous sympathy for the leading Slavophils as participants in a family quarrel, and he drew closer to them as the years advanced. 'The fight between us is long over, and we have clasped hands again, though at the beginning of the forties we had to meet as enemies', he wrote in his memoirs; and he commented on Konstantin Aksakov's death (1861): 'It is painful for those who have loved them to know that they are no more, those noble tireless men of action, those opponents who were closer to us than many of our own supporters.' Yet he never drew close enough to be reconciled to 'the feudal slavery of the Byzantine Church'. The Church, and all that it stood for, remained the deepest gulf between them. Moreover, his conception of Russian nationality was more resolutely anti-governmental; he stated it in more precise and historically qualified terms than the Slavophils' ominously fluid and mystic version. 'The idea of nationality is itself a conservative idea, a self-protective one; it carries with it the judaic sense of the unquestionable superiority of a single race, together with an aristocratic urge for purity of blood and rights of succession. Nationality as a banner, a war-cry, can be admirable only when a dependent people is struggling for independence. Thus

[1] *Polnoe Sobraniye*: (ed.: Lemke), vol. 13, p. 100.

national feelings, in spite of their excesses, are full of inspiration
in Italy and Poland, while at the same time they are disgusting
in Germany. For us to concentrate on demonstrating our
nationality would be even more absurd than it is for the Germans; even those people who shower us with abuse do not deny
our nationality. . . . We ought rather to contrast our real
national character with that of our Germanized government
and its renegade servants!'[1]

The last sentence provides the key to Herzen's innate sympathy with the anti-governmental Slavophils who, like some
anti-Soviet Russians of today, protested when they could
against a state-religion which seemed to them to stifle the fresh
young shoots of national life and sturdy independent character.
He found the Slavophils' instinct surer than their reasoning,
because its first impulse coincided with his own craving to
repudiate the crushing bondage of Petersburg Russia. But he
saw the folly of suggesting that they could save the situation by
a return to the more easy-going habits of pre-Petrine Russia,
even if such a course, had it been persistently pursued, might
perhaps have bred less virulent social evil than the existing
system contained.

Herzen abhorred on principle the powerful centralized state,
not for its own creative inefficiency—though that was a minor
reason—but because its unwieldy regimental system was bound
to stupefy the defenceless masses and to brutalize its finest individual citizens, those who could give most to civilized life. The
educated despotic state, with all its subjects trained for government service, and nothing but service, filled him with the maximum of horror; 'Genghiz Khan, equipped with telegraphs,
steamships and railways', that was the nightmare which
Herzen saw taking shape in Russia during the reign of Nicolas I.
But since this Frankenstein monster had been conjured into
life, its makers and victims had first to recognize it for what it
really was, before they could effectively resist or tame it.

The immense growth in numbers and power of the official
class, Herzen repeatedly observed, must be counted among the
most harmful and enduring results of Peter's reforms. Apart
from being an artificial class, cynically uncultured and greedy,
it contrived to cover its misdeeds under a mask of public service,
while in fact it remained abysmally ignorant of everything

[1] *Polnoe Sobraniye*: (ed.: Lemke), vol. 13, p. 122.

except office routine and the craven fulfilment of instructions from above. 'It has turned', said Herzen, 'into a civil clergy which sucks the blood of the people through a thousand dirty mouths.'[1]

An officially fostered and indiscriminate distrust of all new developments in Western Europe darkened the Russian picture still more. Government edicts abruptly switched the course of national education from one scheme to another, according to the prevalent official view of European affairs. The astute ex-serf, A. Nikitenko, thus summed up the situation in his diary (1833) : 'There was a time when no one dared to talk about improving agriculture unless he could quote supporting texts from holy writ. Then the authorities wanted to extend higher education, provided it conformed to a programme prepared by the Ministry of Public Instruction. Teachers of logic had simultaneously to convince their pupils that the laws of reason did not exist, and history teachers had to prove that Greece and Rome were not republics, but similar to absolute monarchies in the Turkish or Mongol style. . . . And now, it is quite another thing. Now they demand from young people that they should learn many subjects—and not in a parrot-like way—but on condition that they read no books, and so long as they do not start to consider for themselves whether it might be more useful for the Fatherland if its citizens had bright minds instead of bright buttons on their uniforms.' Herzen hardly expected that the intelligentsia would find a way out of this permanent impasse. Nor did he believe in cutting Gordian knots. But he expected people to start by drawing a sharper distinction between the horrors of Governmental Russia and the healthy constructive elements which the Government overshadowed. As he expounded later in his poignant letter (1851) to the brilliant French historian Michelet : 'Our Government, which first broke with the people in the name of civilization, hurried, a century later, to break with civilization in the name of Orthodoxy and Autocracy. The Tsar seeks to isolate Russia from Europe, to kill thereby her growing civilization. He is doing his job.'

The demon of national self-satisfaction had thus acquired a spurious sanctity. That was a crime for which Herzen could never pardon Nicolas I. Yet even he admits that the Emperor's bigoted brutality was tempered by unswerving devotion to duty,

[1] *Ibid.*, vol. 11, p. 27.

and by an implacable sense of justice, which did not spare the highly-placed. Superbly confident of his own infallibility, Nicolas was ruining his country with the best intentions in the world. Herzen recounts, in favour of Nicolas, the case of one of the Trubetskoy princes, who was deprived of his title and estates and banished to Siberia, in punishment for having flogged a single serf to death. He also cites a striking instance of injustice redressed through Imperial intervention. This case involved two peasants, who had been punished for a crime of which they turned out to be innocent. The men were publicly retried, presented with two hundred roubles compensation for each stroke of the knout they had received, and given new passports testifying to their innocence. (They had been branded for incendiarism.)[1]

But sparks of justice, lighting up the surrounding darkness, also made it look darker and more impenetrable, and when Herzen read de Custine's famous book, *La Russie en 1839*, its withering indictment did not rouse him to protest against it, as many indignantly patriotic Russians did. Instead he honestly confessed : 'I bow my head ; one feels the terrible truth.' His own mind was moving rapidly towards a course of action, which, for want of any more precise definition, he called 'Socialism', meaning to begin with, a more socially conscious opposition to despotic Imperial rule.

Herzen's eager but elusive quest for socialism, after leading him on a tortuous nomadic trek from East to West, drew him back again to the amorphous Asiatic steppes. It is tinged from the start by an almost mystic yearning for enlightenment, and chastened by a frankly tentative and undogmatic approach. Thus it becomes clear-cut exclusively in negation, and political only by virtue of its unrelenting struggle against the fatal abuse of power in the hands of a self-seeking Government or governmental machine.

Perhaps the most remarkable quality of Herzen, as a prophet of socialism, is that his warnings against the likely perversions looming ahead are more emphatic than any rosy predictions about the benefits which it might bring. If he cherishes any permanent pet aversion, it is against the hard-bitten evangelist, the typically religious mind unleashed in the sphere of political reform. Therefore he deplored those revolutionary know-alls

[1] *Polnoe Sobraniye*: (ed.: Lemke), vol. 12, p. 216.

who retained Messianic illusions about building a new paradise on earth. He regarded them as no better than dangerously competent fanatics, who would fight and toil without ever advancing a single step towards the realization of fruitful freedom. 'We have no logic, only Holy writ attached to earthly things. Both the worshippers of property and its iconoclasts poison and irritate each other more and more. This will lead, where all religious obsessions lead, not to agreement but to bloodshed. . . . It is high time to abandon theories of universal brotherhood,' Herzen protested. 'Explain to me please why it is foolish to believe in God, but not foolish to believe in Humanity? If it is stupid to believe in a kingdom of heaven, can it be wise to put our trust in earthly Utopias? After successfully ridding ourselves of positive religion, we have preserved all our religious habits, and after forfeiting paradise in heaven, we still expect the approach of heaven on earth and boast of it. . . .'

No soothing sophistry could induce Herzen to exchange the dwindling Christian theocracy for another patched-up legend to deify the improving order of the future. The stuffy 'scientific' rationalism of the German socialists, despite its stress on fact and action, seemed to him incurably Utopian, since it offered little more than promissory notes and post-dated cheques on a dwindling or non-existent bank-account. His own religious fervour, if such it may be called, found outlets as markedly un-political as they were untheological. He tells us how at Moscow University the scales first fell from his eyes, when he saw in the midst of his studies how 'the religion of life was conquering the religion of death, the religion of beauty replacing the religion of flagellation, fasting and prayer. The crucified body experi-enced resurrection and no longer felt ashamed of itself.'

III

As for plunging into the political arena, Herzen admitted with-out quibbling : 'Our ideas were vague.' He and his friends ex-tolled the stoic virtues of the Decembrists and the drastic example of the French Revolution ; feeling some qualms about the outcome of the latter, they took Saint-Simon in their stride, passed on to an ideal constitution, an ideal republic, and came heavily down to earth again when they fixed their thoughts on the pressing problems of how to start to make Russian society

less painfully uncivilized. They anticipated Sir William Har-
court's non-party dictum—'We are all Socialists now'—to mark
the inessential differences between English political parties towards the end of the nineteenth century. For them, any ruler
efficiently guided by an altruistic social conscience and sense of
the possible in fighting poverty and ignorance, became to that
extent a Socialist in fact, whatever he might be in name. A
thorough Socialist must simultaneously endeavour to cut down
the sphere of governmental rule. For at that time the one unquestionable goal of a healthy socialist society was to limit and
by degrees to render superfluous the functions of the State.

A terribly remote and even a receding goal—for, unless human
nature was transformed, how could any perceptible improvements in social conduct and institutions be maintained without
the abiding guarantee of law? And how could laws be enforced
except by a strong central government? Herzen saw the dangerous absurdity of pursuing this argument consistently, except
by confining it to a counsel of perfection for wise men who knew
how to be laws unto themselves. Six months before his death
he wrote in his open letter to Bakunin; 'Because the forms of
the state are transitory, it does not follow that the state itself
can be discarded as a thing of the past. How is it possible
to repudiate the state, when the chief requirement for getting
away from it is the attainment of years of discretion by the
majority?'

Meanwhile every generation, in struggling first and foremost
to satisfy its own most urgent appetites, is prone to underestimate its bonds of kinship with the larger unrealized aspirations of
the past. It is guilty of historical ingratitude. 'The Petrashevs-
kists were our younger brothers, even as the Decembrists were
our older ones. The rising generation has forgotten them, repudiated them, as people less practical than they, less efficient,
knowing less well where they are heading for; it is annoyed
with them, and indiscriminately discards them as "superfluous
people", imaginary dreamers. It forgets that in judging characters belonging to the past, a true estimate of their value and
quality depends less on comparing the amount they knew with
the amount they achieved, judged by present-day needs, than
on gauging the energy and sincerity which they put into their
work. . . . Boldly and quite deliberately I say once more about
our comradeship of that time; such a circle of talented,

pure-hearted, intelligent and devoted people I have never met anywhere else. . . . More than once I have heard voiced this strange objection: "You, even more than the Decembrists, were dilettantes of revolutionary ideas; for you, your participation was a luxury, revolution was never a crust of bread and bare existence, a matter of life or death. . . ." I suppose, I answered once, that it was, for those condemned to death.'

'But the refusal to acknowledge people, because they do from inner necessity what others do only when goaded by poverty, strongly resembles that morbid monastic asceticism which values highly only those obligations which are most repulsive to fulfil. The oligarchical claims of poverty to a monopoly of virtue are as unjust as all monopolies. Saint-Simon, a descendant of Charlemagne, Robert Owen, the factory owner, did not become apostles of socialism because they were dying of hunger. Gospel charity and democratic envy both together get you no further than almsgiving or enforced robbery, no further than a re-distribution of property or universal beggary. . . .

'Our childish liberalism of 1826 lost its seduction for us after the ruin of Poland (1830). It was then that one section of our young people threw themselves into a deeper study of Russian history, while another set out to master German philosophy.' Some, like the restless Galakhov, knocked at the doors of the Catholic Church: 'but his lively soul recoiled from that gloomy twilight, from the raw sepulchral prison-like smell of its joyless vaults. . . . Ogarëv and I belonged to none of these groups. Our faith in revolutions in the style of Béranger's songs had been shattered, but we were looking for something which we could not find either in Nestor's Chronicle or in the transcendental idealism of Schelling. In the midst of these strivings, con-jectures, and efforts to overcome our terrifying doubts, we came across Saint-Simon's brochures. . . . Our souls, our hearts opened to that new world . . . Saint-Simonism became the foundation-stone of our convictions, and so it has remained immutably in all essentials.'[1]

Herzen is now no longer ridiculed for having allowed the impulsive and whimsical Saint-Simon to charm his imagina-tion more permanently than the famous system-building German professors, who wrought such havoc on weaker Rus-sian minds. Saint-Simon, despite his engaging streak of madness,

[1] *Polnoe Sobraniye*: (ed.: Lemke), vol. 12, pp. 151–2.

went one better than Plato's plea for philosopher kings. He urged that all sensible men should start to cultivate an entirely new separation of spiritual and temporal authority. The spiritual leadership of mankind should be henceforth entrusted to a select body of mathematicians, scientists, writers, artists and musicians. These brilliant creatures he aptly called the 'flambeaux' of mankind, their torches. Ordinary lesser mortals would learn to feel appropriate gratitude to such enlightened 'natural' teachers, because the majority could not help deriving immense advantage from their 'lumières'. Moreover the 'torches', though few in number, would be elected by universal suffrage—a generous, if risky, concession to the democratic sentiment of the French Revolution.

Of course, all men must work. Every man whose brain is less useful than his body will be obliged to work with his hands. And God ordains (in a vision vouchsafed to Saint-Simon) that all Bishops, priests and other clergy must forthwith cease to speak in God's name, since 'they have ceased to be more learned than the flock whom they would lead, and have allowed themselves to be dominated by the temporal power.' The 'torches' ('The Council of Newton') will therefore take the clergy's place as God's proper representatives on earth.

Herzen seems to have discerned a certain dazzling incoherence in these and other ideas thrown out so abundantly by the fertile Saint-Simon. He never reached the point of recommending that they should be studied as a manual for practical legislators. Also he noticed disapprovingly that both Saint-Simon and Fourier attracted the sorry kind of Russians who were incapable of making up their own minds about anything definite. In spite of all these drawbacks, he was firmly convinced that, by virtue of their more imaginative approach to a science of society, they had left Hegel and Feuerbach far behind. By hinting at a new order of spiritual leadership alongside —and not to be confused with—a new and freer type of economic association—they helped to revive a world which was rapidly abandoning its confidence in either. Herzen found spiritual guides to be necessary, even if they were rare and far from infallible. He felt more temperamentally suspicious of economic leadership, and ridiculed the far-fetched pretensions of some economists to scientific infallibility. But though he disparaged its 'ready-made and compulsory order, its dose of regimental manners', the economic *idée maîtresse* behind Fourier's self-sufficient phalansteries struck a responsive chord in his heart. For it corresponded to something which he knew and treasured in the friendly co-operation of workmen in the small-scale Russian *artel*.

IV

'Leaving the gates of the University, we entered the gates of the prison-house', was Herzen's comment on the next stage of his career. He meant of course the stifling Russia of Nicolas I, as it was felt by energetic, independent-minded and therefore 'superfluous' young men. 'Sensing long ago that we were superfluous on the shores of the Neva, we pursued the sensible course of exile as soon as the cord was loosened', he said. But before they could spread their wings abroad, Herzen and several of his friends had first to taste the rigours of exile within Russia, to pay the penalty for ill-disposed expressions of political discontent. In fact, a roving interest in vague socialist ideas, plus a couple of disrespectful remarks about Nicolas I, were the blackest crimes that could be proved against him—but enough to sentence him to banishment in Perm and Vyatka (1835), and later in Novgorod (1841). Afterwards, from his voluntary exile abroad he looked back on these years of compulsory home exile with something like nostalgia. They turned out to be a tonic, an ordeal, which strengthened his mind and character without impairing his faith in Russian potentialities.

'The consciousness of open persecution supports the desire to resist, enhanced danger stimulates our strength', he said, and could afford to say, about the mild punishment which he suffered, and which provided him with a wholesome instruction course in Siberian local government. Working as a minor official in the Vyatka administration, he learned to prize the sturdy qualities of inconspicuous townspeople and peasants, rescued by sheer geographical distance from the paralysing grip of the huge administrative centres. He benefited also by his opportunity to study at close quarters the revolting Esquimau-faced Governor, Tufayev, 'like a sinister beast, encountered in some primeval forest'.

The erudite Westfalian agronome, Baron von Haxthausen, who toured Russia and met Herzen in Moscow in 1843, later produced a substantial book about the Russian Empire,[1] containing many respectful remarks about its system of land-tenure. In Russia he became almost a national hero overnight, through being the first foreign observer who had systematically *written up* the *mir*. He praised it as 'a small republic, governing tself in its internal affairs, and knowing neither personal property nor proletariat. . . . The Commune is the family enlarged. The land belongs to the Commune. Since every Russian also belongs to a commune, and all the members of it are entitled to equal shares in the land, there are no born proletarians in Russia.' Haxthausen concluded that something like the Utopia of European socialists already existed in Russia, which had therefore nothing to fear from the revolutionary unrest threatening the other countries of Europe.

Various Slavophils had previously said much the same thing as Haxthausen. But owing to a peculiar double-edged sensitiveness to foreigners' opinion about themselves, most Russians attached a far higher degree of importance to the sober German's discovery of their unconscious and unrecognized Arcadia. Herzen, on the contrary, was not carried off his feet at all. Haxthausen's tribute was undoubtedly flattering, and probably honest, but was it well-founded? Moreover, his gratified Russian readers too readily forgot that he had modified his praise by pointing out two radical defects in the communal system. First, its conservative rigidity militated against any improvement in agricultural technique. Secondly, it encouraged the population to outrun their means of subsistence. For, since every surviving son was automatically entitled to a strip of land, the Russian peasant could most easily increase his wealth by enlarging his family. It was all right for Russians to breed like rabbits so long as there remained enough surplus uncultivated land which could be added to the *mir*, but even in so vast a country there were obvious limits, and much of the land was uncultivable or poor. Haxthausen's analysis, and still more the misguided enthusiasm which greeted his book in Russia, stimulated Herzen to set forth his own more critical and mature judgement of the Russian peasant and his local communism.

Despotism above, Communism below, between them the

---

[1] *Studien über die inneren Zustände, das Volksleben, und insbesondere die ländlichen Einrichtungen Russlands*, Hanover, 1847. These two volumes were simultaneously published in French. An English edition appeared in 1856.

hesitating circle of the aristocracy, the effervescent froth of the intelligentsia—that was a bald summary of the *status quo*. When peasants rebelled against their masters, what mattered vitally was not more freedom for themselves but more land for the commune, and they hardly ceased to imagine that they must be serfs of the Tsar. The commune remained the original foundation. But was it a good foundation to continue to build on? 'In reality the commune is far too static;' Herzen argued, 'it vegetates without any internal striving. It receives no impulsion from outside. In giving to every man inalienably a piece of land, it likewise deprives him of any personal responsibility. Is it surprising that our peasant had hardly developed the beginnings of self-respect, or sense of personal possession, when his strip of open field, even his wife and daughter—are not really his own. He is worse off than the urban proletariat, for he is a mere chattel. . . . In what way are we superior to the colonists of Surinam, to the English in India? No, we are inferior, because our peasants as human beings stand much higher than savages. They bear their heavy cross meekly, submissively.[1]

'The Russian peasant is still in the same state as he was when the nomad armies of Genghiz Khan surprised him. Is it decline or infancy, the barbarism which follows death, or the barbarism which precedes life? The peasants, both in Great and Little Russia, have remarkably alert minds, an almost southern vivacity, which is astonishing to find in a northern land. They build their little huts close to each other, preferring them to be burned down together rather than to be scattered. Their fields, without enclosures, lose themselves in an endless distance behind the dwellings. Here is an intermediate existence between geology and history; it has a character, a way of being, but no biography. After a few generations, the peasant rebuilds his pinelog hut, which has gradually fallen to pieces, without leaving any more permanent traces behind it than does the peasant himself when he dies.'[2]

Despite his profound sympathy with the peasant's fate (prior to emancipation) as a downtrodden helot with qualities of rustic charm and immense physical vigour, Herzen's attitude to the future of the Russian masses is fraught with ambiguity. He wants their material and moral standard to improve, but

[1] *Polnoe Sobraniye*: (ed.: Lemke), vol. 3, p. 117.
[2] *Ibid.*, vol. 6, p. 198.

not at the cost of impairing those original virtues which spring from their peasant mode of life, virtues which could never survive under a Western type of urban industrial civilization. Haxthausen had shrewdly observed that the Russian peasant was both enterprising and good at heart so long as he was poor, but that as soon as he acquired money or influence he turned into an arrant rogue. 'The craving for money and distinction are rocks upon which in Russia every character is shipwrecked.' Herzen appears to have felt this same paradox and, much as he hated the brutal side of serfdom, he wrote later, 'Les bonnes moeurs paysannes étaient en partie sauvegardées par le servage'.[1] Turgenev teased him about his worship of that mysterious new idol, the sheepskin cloak, and warned him that the peasant was conservative to the core. The responsive Herzen felt heart-searchings, and sometimes asked himself the same question as the sceptical *narodnik* Nekrasov, pondering over his hazily idealized *moujik*:

> O will you waken, full of power,
> Or bowing to the yoke of fate,
> Have you already accomplished all you could,
> And bursting into song so like a groan,
> Did you in spirit leave this life for ever?[2]

Herzen remarked that the childhood of a nation could easily last for several thousand years. But, he admitted, so could a nation's old age. The Slav peoples with their ancient but changeless peasantry struck him as an example of the former stage, the Chinese and Indians of the latter. A consoling thought —only disturbed by the query whether such a long-drawn-out childhood might not prove to be a permanently stunted and arrested development. As for the *mir*'s adaptability, Herzen in course of time agreed more and more decisively with Ogarëv, Bakunin and the economic Westernizers, that this obstinate relic of primitive communism was an appalling handicap. Herzen has often been called 'the first *narodnik*', but few *narodniks* seem to have shared the disgust which he felt for the stagnant *mir*.

Indeed, the communism of the *mir* flatly contradicted Herzen's recurrent argument that self-respect, creative zeal

---

[1] *Polnoe Sobraniye*: (ed.: Lemke), vol. 20, p. 165.
[2] *Razmyshleniya u Paradnovo Podyezda* (1858).

and careful responsible work could never flourish without a sense of personal property. Though he always stressed the ethical rather than the economic side of socialism, he clearly considered private ownership of property, rightly used, to be itself an instrument of liberation, an indispensable moral incentive. 'We have never denied property, just as we have never made it an article of faith, a theological dogma of absolute right, absolved from any duty in use or abuse.'[1] Undoubtedly his own private fortune served him as a weapon without which his life's work would have been crippled. A poor man could never have published *The Bell* or generously supported so many poverty-stricken refugees. When the Tsar tried to block the transfer of his money from Russia to France in 1848, Herzen successfully enlisted the services of the Paris Rothschild. The reigning member of that international banking dynasty managed to outmanoeuvre the Russian autocrat. Herzen spurred Rothschild's professional pride by telling him that he had to contend with a perfect example of 'that dictatorship on which reaction relies, seizing private property as it pleases . . . Cossack communism is worse than Louis Blanc's!'

V

Two of Herzen's most suggestive early essays date from his period of exile within Russia—*Dilettantism in Science*, and *Buddhism in Science* (1841–1843). He gave the nickname 'Buddhists' to specialists so absorbed in one narrow field of analysis that in the process of splitting intellectual atoms their spiritual faculties became sub-human. 'Buddhists' in the guise of religious and moral doctrinaires he stigmatized as the most dangerous group of all, because, instead of being content with a modest following of fellow 'experts', they thirst to dominate the minds of all and sundry. 'They condemn all selfish conduct with an air of righteous indignation, call egoism a vice, thunder virtuously against it, but without ever condescending to consider what it really is. Egoism glitters in the eyes of the wild beast. It is savage and direct in primitive man; why should it dissolve in educated man? Strange creatures! Instead of basing their whole social wisdom on the fact of human egoism, as an obvious foundation-stone, they try by every means to injure and disgrace it, and to

[1] *Polnoe Sobraniye*: (ed.: Lemke), vol. 20, p. 184.

turn men into insipid good-natured creatures, craving for voluntary slavery!' Herzen recalls the respectable moralist, who having taught his horse to give up the selfish habit of eating and drinking, was none the less furious when it languished and died.

If wallowing in bestial egoism is rightly held to be repulsive in a man, the opposite extreme of self-immolation for a future life, or for the sake of hypothetical superior grandchildren, appears to be a lamentably foolish substitute. However plausible or even admirable the sentiment may sound, its practical application is too often painfully inept. It improves on nominal Christian altruism, from which it derives, only to the extent of being less hypocritical. 'Expectation of rewards in heaven, and punishments in hell, give the best actions a purely egoistic character, and in this way the Christian outlook is much lower than the pagan. The better part of our dim understanding of social obligations is derived from Greek and Roman sources.' But why should we go out of our way to torture ourselves, and inflict torture on others, for the sole sake of an unpredictable future? What right have we to believe that a future we can never see will be better than the present which we know? And, if we look back and survey them, how barren were the results achieved by those who worked on this assumption.

'If progress is the purpose, for whom do we work? Who is that Moloch, who, as the labourers approach him, instead of rewarding them, moves away, and to the exhausted and doomed crowds who cry, "Morituri te salutant", only answers with a sardonic smile that earthly life will be beautiful after they are dead? Can you condemn people to the pitiful rôle of caryatids holding up a terrace on which some day other people may dance? . . . or to be unhappy toilers, who up to the knees in mud, drag along a boat bearing the modest inscription "progress towards the future" on its flag? Some exhausted ones fall on the towpath, others tug at the ropes with renewed force, but the path goes on in the same way, because progress has no end. That thought alone should put people on their guard. A goal which is infinitely far away is not a goal at all, but more like a treacherous decoy. The goal should be nearer. The goal of every generation is itself . . . No, nature never makes one generation a stepping-stone towards the next. She is content, like Cleopatra, to dissolve her pearls in one goblet of wine, so long as she can enjoy the present.'

The last sentence strikes a frankly hedonistic note, which might tempt the unwary reader to identify Herzen with those legendary Russian aristocrats who recklessly gambled away huge fortunes in a single night. It is true that he was a jovial and sociable man, with a touch of wild exuberance which later shocked his Victorian neighbours in Fulham and Putney. But his intensely disciplined mind and discriminating taste abhorred the vulgar excesses of the roué. The stupid and wasteful dissipation of his more fashionable compatriots exasperated him no less than the average European's smug pursuit of the more easily obtainable 'bourgeois' satisfactions. To live for the present never meant, for him, behaving like a glorified pig, or surrendering to every impulse unchecked by reasonable thought for the morrow.

Nevertheless, before joining in the wild-goose chase after impossibly distant targets, he pleaded for a prior consideration of some constant psychological factors, which seemed to recur and emerge in a significant pattern out of the chaotic ups and downs of recent historical change. The leading German and French sociologists, from Hegel to Comte, had all been inclined to invoke history as a store-house of apt illustrations to reinforce their various teleological arguments, while they tacitly ignored examples which might point to the contrary. It was now high time to redress the balance by deciding whether the sum of historical experience did not in fact disprove more than it proved, and render its most valuable service in the negative action of removing ancient stumbling-blocks, in 'debunking' every kind of unscientific prediction.

Would not an honest judge, summing up from the latest available evidence, conclude that the guiding motive of cumulative and comprehensive progress by the whole human race was neither reinforced by historical example nor even intelligible as an idea? Had moral progress not been grossly confused with sporadic outbursts of creative power, sometimes aided by local advances in the technical mastery over nature? Worse still, in Herzen's mind, human obsession with that motive had so far proved to be a source of sterile or destructive illusion. It persisted in modern socialists, not as a 'valuable lie', which made the rigours of normal existence more tolerable, but merely as an obstructive and harassing survival of the primitive Christian superstition that the kingdom of God would be realized on earth.

If people would only devote to their short span of years a love and forethought equal to their worries about a future eternal life in heaven or a future paradise on earth, they would court fewer disappointments, and might learn to build a wiser happiness out of inevitably transitory things. Herzen's own prolonged and unsuccessful political struggle seems to have convinced him that the noblest ideals, even when sincere personal efforts promoted them, were bound to undergo distortion to the point of unrecognizable mutilation, as soon as they became widely diffused. Without ever becoming a sour misanthropist, he ceased to expect wonders from a large number of his fellow-creatures. 'In order to make Reason attractive to the multitude,' he observed, 'you would first have to dress her up as a pretty actress, and then undress her.' It is unjust to infer from this remark that Herzen was either an intellectual or a social snob. He found more fault with the educated multitude than with the ignorant masses. Indeed that standardization of taste in terms of pretty actresses was rather a speciality of the wealthier urban classes. He rightly said about himself: 'I loathe, especially since the misfortunes of 1848, demagogic flattery of the mob, but I hate still more aristocratic slander of the common people.'

In any case the ideals of one generation seemed to be repeatedly deformed and discredited in the process of realization by their historic heirs. They were exploited, but they were not understood. In their original form they stimulated little effective action beyond the lives of their own initiators. Therefore Reason might turn out to be more useful as a prosaic measuring rod for plainly measurable quantities; it should cease to be regarded as an integrating force, potent for good in every human biped, for that was too much like the will-o'-the-wisp pursued by ingenious and superstitiously optimistic eighteenth-century philosophers. 'To be taken over by the future as an element does not mean that the future will fulfil our ideals,' Herzen summed up with sober perspicacity. 'Rome did not bring into existence the Republic of Plato, nor did it realize the essential Greek ideals. The Middle Ages were not a development of Rome. Contemporary Western strivings will enter into the main body of history, will exert their effect on it, in the same way as our physical bodies will disappear in the composition of grass and other bodies. That type of immortality does not please us.'

VI

In February 1847 two huge carriages containing Herzen, his family and various retainers, passed across the Russian frontier. Little though he knew it, this first stage of his voluntary pilgrimage to Western Europe turned out to be the last time he ever saw his native land. His destination was Paris.

At that time France held thoughtful Russians under an irresistible spell, which has long since been cast off. The polished glitter and charm of the French eighteenth-century court, the devastating irony of Voltaire, the pseudo-primitive humanitarian gospel of Rousseau, had each in turn inspired its adept circle of devoted Russian disciples, and each wave of imitative enthusiasm had simultaneously produced a fertile breeding-ground for vulgar travesty. Herzen was only too painfully familiar with the vagaries of Russian Francophils. 'Our *Europe* repeated on a distorted scale all that was happening in European Europe, but with an exaggerated deterioration of quality', he remarked. Undoubtedly *La Dame aux Camélias* and the *outré* feminist novels of George Sand affected the behaviour of Russian society far less advantageously (but far more widely) than the classical French culture which a few aristocrats had assimilated in the age of Catherine and Alexander I.

'The French courtisane dining in a stuffy private room of the *Maison Dorée*, dreams at least of her future *salon*, while the Russian lady, sitting in her luxurious drawing-room, decorated with coats-of-arms, dreams about the public-house . . . our serf-owning *camélias*, our *Traviati* with ropes of pearls! . . . The next phase occurred in the auditorium, where bespectacled students with cropped hair listened to lectures on the secrets of nature. Here one must forget all about camellias or magnolias, forget even that there are two different sexes. The camellias grew up out of vague indignation, revolt against the rules of the household. That revolt reached its natural saturation point. But this time our ladies pursue an *idea*, "the rights of women". No longer carried away by their emotions, they fall instead on a theoretical parachute. They throw themselves into the stream with a guide-book to swimming, and deliberately swim against the tide!'

Until he came to know France at close quarters, Herzen remained content to idealize her image in the romantic haze of distance, reserving his shafts of irony for the discomfiture of Frenchified Russians. The country which had bred the sparkling self-confident intellect of the Encyclopaedists (although a century back) could not fail to attract the vigorous international mind of Herzen, who used a sharper eye than most of his compatriots in distinguishing the features of the painstaking copy from the more masterly original. Fascinated most of all by Saint-Simon and Fourier, he inevitably started by paying more attention to French imaginative aspirations than to their fulfilment in French national life. He tended to confuse exceptional and charming symbolic myths with the unsteady, often sordid, process of French political history, and the lure of France as a focal centre of Europe's intellectual growth became almost identified in his mind with love for France and Paris as the spiritual home of potential revolutionary rebirth. 'Paris, the heart of the world, the brain of history, the international bazaar on the *Champ de Mars*, the beginning of the brotherhood of peoples and universal peace!'

Arriving for the first time in Paris, Herzen recorded his still enraptured emotion : 'I entered the city with reverence, as men used to enter Jerusalem or Rome.' But even his worst enemies would not deny that Herzen's powers of observation were exceptionally acute. He saw through shams, and a few months' residence in Paris quickly dispelled his cherished visions. He was irritated but not surprised to meet numbers of his noisy and gay compatriots sliding over the polished surface of French life, blind to its seamy side; he expected nothing better from the average Europeanized Russian. But it dawned on him with a sense of shock and bitter mortification that French people did not correspond at all to his hopeful conception of them. Unfortunately they fell very far below it.

Neither French refinement and culture, nor French revolutionary vigour, turned out to be anything like the brilliant picture he had formed of them. It seemed to him that both had plainly degenerated, that their nominal adherents were duped by catch-words with meagre substance, that the Paris of his dreams had dwindled into a real city of triumphant shopkeepers, who devoted their fussy bustling energy to 'the unclean worship of material gain and tranquillity'. The criminally greedy Paris of Louis Philippe, immortalized by Balzac, had swamped the original French flair for beauty, clear proportion and distinctive style, and submerged it under a flood of glittering expensive golden luxury. In Herzen's own graphic words: 'Courtisanes set the fashion for ladies; the gambler ousts the educated man; witty social gatherings give place to heavy orgies, in which gold strangles art.'

Some fragments of past magnificence still struggled for survival, but they were weakening, or blended with the present in unpromising hybrid forms. 'The inexhaustible wealth of its long civilization, the colossal supply of words and images, flash through French brains like glimmerings in a phosphorescent sea, without clearly lighting up a single object. A sort of whirlwind, sweeping together the fragments of two worlds before a cataclysm, has drawn them into this gigantic memory, but without cohesion and without science. They move from one phrase to another, from one paradox to another, from antithesis to synthesis, and fail to solve a single problem. They mistake a hieroglyphic for a reality, a wish for a fact. A restless striving without means and without any definite aims; unfinished sketches, undeveloped thoughts, hints, approximations, frescoes, arabesques . . . Those clear connections, of which old France used to be proud, they have lost; they do not seek the truth; it is too terrifying. A false forced romanticism, a melodramatic and empty rhetoric has led their taste astray from everything straightforward and healthy.'

Moreover, the French were living in a fool's paradise, still intoxicated with the consoling self-satisfaction of their formerly superior culture, wilfully blind to the retribution which was overtaking them for their own glaring faults and careless follies. 'What are we to say when the glow of past glory on festering wounds, syphilitic sores and sunken cheeks, is advertised as the blushes of youth?. . . . To flatter the pride of these empty degenerate descendants, to approve their wretched senseless existence—is a crime. To pretend that present-day Paris is the saviour and liberator of the world, to affirm that she is great in her fall, that she has not really fallen—is to fabricate an apotheosis out of the feverish ravings of Nero or Caligula.'

If Herzen had not pinned such extravagant hopes on French moral leadership of Europe his disappointment in the anticlimax of French genius would surely have been less embittered and poignant. He expected the French to set a worthier example and, in spite of his normal scepticism and flexibility of mind, he had been prone to attribute sincere altruistic motives to the architects of French political upheavals. But the damp squib of the 1848 revolution, its final extinction in the blood-bath of Cavaignac, followed by the rise to power of Louis Napoleon, put the finishing touches to Herzen's political re-education. That course of events finally convinced him that his faith in France had been a deplorable mistake and, more important still, that violent revolutions, whether successful or not in conquering political power, had in fact failed to bring Europe substantially nearer to the realization of its social ideals. 'Socialism left a victor on the field of battle will inevitably be deformed into a commonplace bourgeois philistinism. Then a cry of denial will be wrung from the titanic breast of the revolutionary minority, and the deadly battle will begin again.'

More and more he turned away from politicians and the state as the most likely means of securing social improvements. Herzen saw that modern states were almost all turning into powerful industrial bureaucracies which automatically tended to sacri-fice fresh individual aspirations to the practical rules and con-ventions of an orderly ant-heap. That such a rationalized economic order might usher itself in everywhere through following the line of least resistance, and then remain firmly founded on public inertia and impotence, rendered it none the less fatal to further human growth. Bees and ants, as far as one can judge, may go on living for ever in exactly the same kind of social organization. But millions of generations may have struggled and perished before they became fixed in that state of organized equilibrium.'

His life in England provoked Herzen to observe that a people which reaches a state of social organization thoroughly corre-sponding to its needs, has no inner necessity to go further, to fight or to revolt, to produce original personalities. England was turning into a country of white-skinned Chinese. It re-minded him of the immobility of Eastern peoples, but with one important difference. Instead of enjoying ancient ritual and inert Asiatic calm, the majority of Western Europeans were nervous and chronically restless. 'In repudiating originality we have not repudiated changes, so long as these are made all the time and by everybody. Having discarded the traditional costume of our fathers, we are prepared to alter the style of our clothes three times a year, so long as everyone else does the same—and this is done, not for the sake of beauty or comfort, but for the sake of change itself.'

But in change and immobility alike 'the bonds of convention strangle development, when the understanding of good and evil becomes identified with its agreement or disagreement with the accepted custom of the moment. For the essence of development consists in a striving to go further than custom, to improve on it. The collective mediocrity hates whatever is sharp, original, outstanding. And since the average type has less intelligence and fewer desires, the collective stream, like a sticky bog, drags down whoever struggles to rise out of it.' Whether the state which regulated that society was autocratic as in Russia, constitutional as in England or republican as in France, the difference was little more than formal. Conservative and revolutionary politicians alike had proved their spiritual bankruptcy; intellectual pig-headedness and timidity vied with a vain democratic desire to please and cajole the multitude at any price. 'What did you do, revolutionaries frightened of revolution, political tricksters, buffoons of liberty? You played at liberty, at terror and government; you chattered in Assemblies . . . until the real public criminals, surprised at being left alive, praised your clemency. You foresaw nothing. And the best among you paid with their heads for your folly. . . .

'Democracy can create nothing positive. That is not its affair—it will become an absurdity as soon as its last enemy has expired. Democrats only know (to use Cromwell's words) what they don't want; they do not know what they want. . . . Behind the knowledge of what we don't want lies hidden the premonition of what we want. But we no longer count on temptations of the devil, on help from God, on life beyond the grave. The ground is cleared, and that is already constructive, lies are exposed, and that removes a barrier to truth. But there is no genuine creation in democracy and therefore it has no future. The future lies outside politics; it will rise above the chaos of all political and social strivings, extracting from them some threads for the new material, which will make a winding-sheet for the past and swaddling-clothes for the newly-born.'[1]

In his *Letters from France and Italy* (written under the overpowering impression of the 1848 revolutions) Herzen summed up the lessons he had learned from his wandering Odyssey in

[1] *Polnoe Sobraniye*: (ed.: Lemke), vol. 5, p. 443.

Europe. 'Beginning with a cry of joy at crossing the frontier, I ended by a spiritual return to my own country. Faith in Russia saved me on the verge of moral ruin.' At this crucial turning-point in his life, it is salutary to consider why Herzen's first love of European civilization turned by degrees to disappointment, disgust and even loathing. And what fresh virtues did he find in an already Europeanized Russia, which made him clutch at the hope that she could still escape from the enveloping cycle of European movement? How indeed could a moral condemnation of modern Europe turn logically into a defence of modern Russia? The first question deserves to be answered first, and it is easier to answer than the second.

The prosaic anticlimax of mid-nineteenth century political reforms, the misfire of revolutionary efforts, seen in a wider perspective, showed themselves to be minor symptoms of a widespread decline in the standards and ideals of European society. 'On one side the property-owning bourgeoisie, obstinately refusing to part with its monopolies, on the other side the bourgeoisie without property, or with less, who want to seize it from those who have more, but lack the strength to do so; in a word, on one side, avarice, on the other, envy.' Those were the twin motives, both equally sordid, round which the whole European world seemed to revolve. Whenever a new wave of opposition rose to power at the expense of its predecessors, and acquired money or influence, it naturally moved away from the side of envy and joined up on the side of avarice.

Moreover, so long as Europe believed firmly in herself, so long as the future had appeared to be nothing but the natural sequence of her own self-centred development, she could perhaps afford to ignore the inner experience of other continents. But Herzen noticed that the arrogant egoism of many Western Europeans had become in part a shield against the inner ravages of self-distrust and doubt. 'Their superb ignorance about the outside world no longer suits the modern Europeans,' he said, and added significantly, 'Caesar knew the Gauls better than modern Europe knows the Russians.'

The next far-reaching inference which he draws about Russo-European relations is harder to grasp and impossible to substantiate. To Herzen's mind, it was not the spiritually turbulent post-1856 reformist Russia, but the inwardly static post-1848 Europe, which betrayed the stagnant features of a new

Byzantium. For Europe's social organization, not that of Russia, seemed to him to have reached that degree of immutability, beyond which it could no longer satisfy fresh human needs without changing its very foundations, *i.e.* without ceasing to be itself. 'Byzantium could go on living, but she had nothing to live for. She did not really live, but dragged on till her fall.' Europe *appeared* to change, but she did so merely institutionally and outwardly, whereas Russia, apparently more static, was undergoing a dynamic inward change.

Herzen considered that between the new society of Europe (where government should diminish in importance) and the old governments of Europe, there would be about as much similarity—and as much unpredictable divergence—as there had been between Imperial Rome and the Rome of the Middle Ages. 'Imperial Rome, passing through death, became the Rome of the Popes. Instead of triumphal arches, awaiting victorious legions with their "Hail Caesar!", processions of monks passing to kneel before a Roman gallows. . . . When Rome was ripe for the tomb, a man appeared, St. Augustine, who possessed all the culture of the ancient world; he said to those proud Roman citizens, who respected themselves only on that account: "Go; your virtues are for us brilliant vices. Our wisdom appears folly to you." But they did not stone him. On the contrary, they listened to him with stupor and sadness. From that time no further compromise was possible. Either the Christians had to be exterminated, or the old Rome had to be buried.'

Herzen found that the state of affairs in France was most typical of this all-round European decline. France, no longer the 'peuple initiateur', except in 'la mode', but still claiming to lead the world in everything, had turned into Herzen's *bête noire*—a nation of calculating shopkeepers from top to bottom. 'In the days of Beaumarchais, Figaro was outside the law—in our day he is the legislator. Then he was poor and humiliated, and his laughter concealed much anger. Now God has blessed him with all the goods of this earth; he has grown stout and flabby, and he no longer respects poverty, calling it sloth or vagabondage. Both Figaros have this in common—that they are menials; but under the servants' livery of the old Figaro there beat a human heart, while from under the black coat of the new Figaro, the livery peeps out; still worse, he can no longer remove it, as his predecessor could; for the livery has grown into him so deeply that he could not take it off without removing his skin as well! . . . The bourgeois has no great past nor has he any future. He showed some strength in fighting for his own property, but he had no idea how to make use of his victory. The nobility kept its social religion. Principles of political economy can never replace patriotic feeling, the tradition of courage, the sanctity of personal honour. But the heir of brilliant aristocracy and coarse plebeianism, the bourgeois, unites in himself the most glaring defects of both, while he has lost their virtues. He is rich like a grandee, but mean like a shopkeeper.' [1]

VII

We cannot flatter ourselves that, in respect of social motives, Herzen found England much superior to France. In both he considered that the true idealist, a man prepared to lay down his life for some innate belief, had abandoned his place to the adroit merchant, a man of peace, who stood for nothing but his personal comfort and rights and gained his ends by cunning. Honest, cultured and public-spirited merchants remained as incomprehensible to Herzen as they were to Marx. For Herzen, English Protestantism merely reconciled the conscience of a Christian with the activity of a money-lender. He was unkind enough to call *The Times* 'that great eunuch of the London money-changers'. For him, English parliamentary government had developed, through usage and law, into an instrument for imparting to the pursuit of private gain a respectable guise of altruism and public interest. Principally it enabled the rival parliamentary parties to stand with dignity on one and the same place, while creating the impression that they were moving majestically forward. England led Europe in the all-important art of keeping up appearances. 'The whole of contemporary Europe has two deeply embedded characteristics, clearly derived from behind the counter; on the one hand, hypocrisy and reserve—on the other, showing off and display. It is necessary to buy in the cheapest market and sell in the dearest—but at the same time to conceal certain shady transactions, to take advantage in the literal sense of that word, to *appear* instead of *to be*, to behave respectably instead of behaving

[1] *Polnoe Sobraniye*: (ed.: Lemke), vol. 5, 132 ff.

well, to show the outward signs of respectability instead of preserving one's genuine self-respect.'

What ray of hope was left to warm and keep alive a European civilization through which gloom and cold were spreading? All its powers and institutions seemed to be eaten away by a hidden cancer, not one green shoot was sprouting on the withered plant. Intellectual leadership could give no help, for it scarcely existed. Even if it had, who was ready to follow its guidance? Perhaps Herzen was judging from the lesson of his own experience. But European intellectuals had missed their chance of filling the void. They had abjectly discredited themselves and failed in the hour of need. 'I blush for our generation; we are soulless rhetoricians; our blood is cold; only our ink is hot. Our thought has acquired the habit of inconclusive irritation, our language with its passionate words has no influence on action. We reflect where it is necessary to strike, analyse where we ought to be carried away. We are disgustingly reasonable, we look at everything from above; we put up with everything. We are concerned with nothing but generalizations, with abstract ideas, with humanity. We have starved our souls in rarefied spheres like monks who enervate themselves in prayers and fasting. We have lost our taste for real things, detached ourselves from them above, even as the petty bourgeois have detached themselves from below. . . .

'I am horrified by the man of today. Such an absence of feeling, and narrowness of mind, such lack of passion, of indignation, such poverty of thought. How quickly impulses cool down in him, how soon enthusiasm, energy, belief in specific action, are exhausted! And where, how, when did these people spend their vitality and lose their strength? They were corrupted in school, where their teachers stupefied them. They wore themselves out in beer-taverns, in student pranks; they were weakened by mean and dirty vice. . . . Born and bred in the air of hospitals, they faded before they could flower; they exhausted themselves, not by passion, but in passionate dreams. . . .

'No one is to blame: it is not their fault, or ours—it is the misfortune of being born when the whole world is dying. One consolation remains. It is extremely probable that coming generations will be even more degenerate, will grow still more impoverished in mind and heart. Even our deeds will be too much for them; they will find our present thoughts incomprehensible. Nations, like Imperial dynasties, turn blunt before they fall; their understanding is clouded over, they go out of their minds—like those Merovingians dissolving in vice and mixed blood, and expiring in a dazed coma without coming again to their senses—like an aristocracy degenerating into sickly cretins, shrinking in size, warped in features . . . so bourgeois Europe will eke out its meagre life in the twilight of blunted intelligence, in flabby feelings deprived of any conviction, without fine arts, without powerful imagination. Weak, sickly, stupefied generations will somehow drag on until an explosion, an outburst of some kind of lava, which will cover them with a shroud of stone and bury them in the oblivion of chronicles. . . . And then?

'And then spring will come, young life will thrust its way through the coffin-lids, a barbaric infancy full of inchoate but healthy force will replace the old barbarism; a wild fresh power will pulsate in the young peoples and begin a new round of events, a third volume in world history.'[1]

A catastrophic vision of the immediate European future was popular among nineteenth-century Russians. Nor has the course of history proved it to be so fantastically incorrect as Europeans might formerly have hoped. Herzen's contribution to this vision was not inspired by personal spite; he did not desire to ruin Europe for Russia's benefit, as some of his compatriots did, and do today. In his more hopeful moods he looked forward to a time when Europeans would cease to misunderstand Russians as savages, and when Russians would cease to dream about the approaching collapse of the West, followed by the universal rule of the Slav race. And even if the latter development occurred, he seems to have doubted whether it would benefit the world. He quoted a warning speech delivered to the Cortes in Madrid by the Marquis Valdegamas (Donosso Cortes), who pictured a paralysed Europe, dissolving in social upheavals, faced in the East by the Slav world, which was eagerly awaiting the moment when it could pounce successfully on its weakening prey. 'But do not think that the catastrophe will end there. The Slav races in their relationship to the West are not what the Teutons were in their relations with the Roman Empire. . . . From decaying Europe Russia will suck into her

[1] *Polnoe Sobraniye*: (ed.: Lemke), vol. 5, 485 ff.

pores all the poison with which Europe is already infected. *She will herself dissolve from the same decay.*[1]

Herzen pours scorn on the naïve solution proposed by the Marquis, namely that England should return to the fold of the Roman Catholic Church, and thus enable the whole of Europe to be united and saved by the joint efforts of the Pope, monarchical power, and loyal national armies.

Moreover, the Marquis identified European 'decay' with the spread of political socialism and the cynical brutality which accompanied it. In so far as the Russian Empire did in the end succumb to a European brand of socialism, he proved to be right, and this type of Europeanization was precisely what Herzen also feared and fought against. But the Marquis sought the remedy to social decay in an impossible return to the beliefs and feudal structure of the Middle Ages. Herzen compared him to Julian the Apostate. His own diagnosis went far deeper, and his prescription was correspondingly more realistic and less categorical. For him, European socialism, or rather the demonstrable failure of European socialism to achieve what it originally set out to do, was neither more nor less than one warning political symptom of a total decline in European vitality and initiative—a decline which might drag on indefinitely but could only be arrested by an invigoration of heart.

The thought of social revival had sprung from Europe, but it by no means followed that Europe would be healthy enough to bring that thought to fruition. The root of Europe's social decline lay in her 'bourgeois' standard of values. For Herzen the word 'bourgeois' was free from the debased fixation in economic and class categories which it later acquired in Marxian hands. For him it denoted a sterile habit of mind, linked with a craving for an easy, irresponsible life at any price (if possible, at other people's expense) a complex which he found on the verge of dominating every class of European industrial society, including the poorest artisans, and which paradoxically enough reached a ghastly climax under the reign of social-democratic principles. When society ceased to follow any other rule than the calculating ambition and greed of the toughest merchants and shopkeepers, when these same motives spread downwards and gripped the hitherto warm-hearted masses of peasants and craftsmen, then civilization in its former spiritual

[1] *Ibid.*, vol. 5, p. 492.

sense was surely drawing to a close. The notion spread that if all the major nations of the world managed to become equal in gun-power and plumbing, then they would all be equally civilized.

The tragedy of the pathfinders of socialism was that their followers refused to learn from mistakes which they themselves acknowledged. The followers failed to see, as Herzen honestly did, that their relentless pursuit of prescribed political and economic methods, merely accentuated and universalized, instead of eliminating, the most repulsive psychological features of that same bourgeois society which they intended to destroy. Rather than acknowledge that they had been deceived, they hid the unpalatable truth under an attractive coating of words and formulae. As a lifelong connoisseur of international revolutionaries, Herzen knew not only those who specialized in beautiful talk, but also the active ones, like Louis Blanc, who organized revolutions, and those, like Bakmetiev, who sailed away to found model communities in the Pacific Ocean. He summed up his counsel to Europe's socialist leaders in the following lines :

'I do not advise you to quarrel with the existing world, and start some independent self-sufficient life, which would find salvation in itself, even if everything around us perished. I advise you to investigate whether the masses are in fact moving in the direction we imagine, and to go with them, or away from them, after you know whither their path is leading. I advise you to cast aside those bookish opinions with which we have been inoculated since childhood, representing people as entirely different to what they are. . . .

'If you are stronger than they, if you possess, not only something usable, but something which moves other people, it will not be wasted—such is the economy of nature. Your strength, like a morsel of yeast, will immediately cause fermentation in whatever submits to its influence. If you have no such powers, or only powers to which contemporary men do not respond, there is no great harm in that, either for you or anyone else. What eternal comedians we are, what public parts we force ourselves to play! Instead of trying to persuade people that they passionately desire what we want, it would be better to consider, do they at this present moment need anything in particular? And if they want something entirely different, we should then concentrate and withdraw from the public market peacefully, without either violating others or wasting ourselves. Such a negative step might mark the beginning of a new life. At least it would be taken with a good conscience.'[1]

VIII

If Europe, undermined by weak or foolish leadership, sank into dissolution (and Herzen did not want this to happen, though he regretfully thought it probable) if in her final death-struggle she did not drag the whole of civilization down with her, to what new quarter would the world start to look for guidance? Perhaps America would take over the legacy of leadership, but Herzen, after due consideration, decided that America suffered from disadvantages which might be insuperable. She was too far away, too geographically isolated from the rest of the world; she was not spiritually receptive or sympathetic to other peoples' native culture and more complex aspirations; and she was riddled from top to bottom with the same paralysing bourgeois obsessions which her population of European émigrés had imported.

At various times Herzen toyed with the idea of abandoning Europe and taking ship to America, but he never went further than investing some of his money in American government bonds. 'Never,' he wrote, 'has there been such a combination of propitious circumstances for a reasonable orderly free development of society as in the United States of America. The doctrines of the great thinkers and revolutionaries of the eighteenth century, without French wars, English common law, without its class structure . . . everything of which old Europe dreamed, a republic, a democracy, a federation. But the more a country is free from government interference, the more established are its rights of free speech and independent conscience, the more intolerant and uniform the crowd becomes. Public opinion turns into a torture-chamber; your neighbour, your butcher, your tailor, your family, your club, all keep you under observation, and take over the duties of a police officer. . . .

'Can it be that only a people incapable of inward freedom is able to achieve free institutions? Having free institutions without freedom, why not also encourage dazzling comfort for a

[1] *Polnoe Sobraniye*: (ed.: Lemke), vol. 5, p. 483.

mean and clumsy life? The citizen who has made money likes to be eloquent about the comforts of life. All these things are so new to him. But his old habits have stuck. If he spends much money, he spends it on vulgar unnecessary things. He prefers to have a house with many small rooms rather than with a few large well-proportioned ones. Instinctively he likes to take away from other people; he does not want to give.'

Notwithstanding all these transplanted bourgeois defects, Herzen admitted that America had dynamic merits which Russia signally lacked. 'The deadly Russian government, doing everything by brute force, does not understand how to impart that vital urge which would have pushed Siberia forward with American speed.'[1] 'One may be injured in America by the coarse tyranny of public opinion, one may revolt against the worship of material comfort, but at least one remains free from the encroachment of state power. There government has never been held sacred; almost no bureaucracy exists. Citizens are not spied upon; there is no idealization of war and military uniforms. Nevertheless such a republic fails to satisfy the yearnings of contemporary men.'

Herzen concluded, in short, that though America might contrive to build up a comfortable way of life for herself, it could hardly be of a kind to exercise magnetic attraction upon the outside world. Her self-centred moderation would neither draw outsiders to her nor deliberately seek to conquer their minds. 'This young and enterprising people, more active than intelligent, is so much pre-occupied with the material ordering of its life that it knows nothing of our torturing pains. In that country, above all, there are not two different cultures. The people who form the grades of their society are constantly changing; but they move up and down the grades according to the level of their bank-balances. Their contentment will be poorer, more commonplace, more sapless than what was dreamed of in the ideals of romantic Europe, but at least it will bring with it no Tsars, no centralization, perhaps no hunger.'

Having apparently exhausted all other alternatives, despairing of Europe, sceptical about America, bored by the corrupt and servile routine of ancient Asiatic countries, Herzen fell back on Russia. Miracles were possible in that land of glaring contradictions. And miracles were still believed in and desired

---

[1] *Polnoe Sobraniye*: (ed.: Lemke), vol. 12, p. 275.

there. Russia was less encumbered with precious luggage than the West. 'Everything which attaches Western people to the old world does not exist for us—We have nothing to preserve, nothing to cherish, but plenty to hate. In respect of the immediate future, we are more freely placed than the West—let us take advantage of this. We are in certain ways further from Europe, freer than her, through being so far behind her! . . . Europe goes to the bottom because she cannot be separated from her burden—so many precious things collected in a long and dangerous voyage. With us, it is merely artificial ballast. Throw it all overboard—and go full steam ahead into the open sea!'[1]

Let the popular social mascot continue to be called by the same name as the light which had failed in Europe. The name would serve as an advertisement to attract the Westernized intellectuals, until the meaning of the name was transformed by the peoples' fresh interpretation of it. 'The word *Socialism* is unknown to our people, but its meaning is close to the heart of Russians who have lived for ages in the rural commune and the workmen's *artel* . . . I boldly repeat that the mere fact of communal land-ownership and partition of the land justifies the assumption that our black earth is more capable of germinating the seed brought from Western fields—more capable because of the elements composing it, and because on it have piled up less rubbish and all kinds of ruins than on Western fields.'[2]

Turgenev (Herzen's most penetrating Russian critic) reproached him for having confined his diagnosis of contemporary trends to the Western half of the world, instead of applying it logically to the whole race of bipeds unified by modern science. 'You are like a doctor who, after finding every symptom of a chronic illness, announces that the patient will be cured—because he is a Frenchman! . . . You turn away your eyes and stop your ears, and in that ecstasy, which overwhelms a sceptic sick to death of his own scepticism, you rave about " spring freshness " and " purifying storms." . . . That dust-laden wind which is blowing in the West, envelops us too; but since you have lived nearly a quarter of a century outside Russia, you have contrived to rebuild Russia in your head.'[3]

[1] *Ibid.*, vol. 5, p. 113.
[2] *Ibid.*, vol. 11, p. 232.
[3] See *Gertsen i Turgenev*, by V. Baturinsky (*Istoricheskii Vyestnik*, January–March, 1900).

Herzen pined to save Russian socialism from the bleak economic fixation which it had acquired in Europe. Socialism could not prove its superiority over any other system of economic relations merely by producing more goods with less expenditure of effort, and evenly distributing the outcome. If that was the ultimate test, then capitalism and socialism might soon be merely nominal distinctions, and a society of super-efficient, well-fed robots would win the prize. The Russian solution, Herzen hoped, would turn out to be more humane. But it might also prove to be more compatible with the old style of enlightened civilizing autocracy than with the new republican forms, regarded as part and parcel of European social progress.

Most decidedly, Russian society could never benefit by an extension of unstable liberal institutions. 'The liberals, those protestants in politics, have become in their turn the most timid conservatives; behind their revised charters and constitutions, they discover the spectre of socialism and turn pale with terror. Nor is this surprising, for they have something to lose, something to fear. Our (Russian) attitude to public affairs is much simpler and more naïve. Liberals are afraid of losing their liberty—we have none to lose—They are nervous of interference by governments in the industrial sphere—with us the government already interferes with everything in any case—They are afraid of losing their personal rights—we have yet to acquire any. The extreme contradictions of our disordered existence, lack of stability in all our legal and constitutional notions, make possible on the one hand the most unlimited despotism, serfdom and prison settlements, and on the other hand creates conditions in which such revolutionary reforms as those of Peter I and Alexander II can be achieved. . . . We enter history, full of strength and energy, at precisely the moment when all political parties are turning into faded anachronisms, and all are pointing, some hopefully, others with despair, to the approaching thunder-cloud of economic upheaval.'[1]

Few Europeans are sufficiently aware that long before Marx's *economic* criticism of West European society began to captivate an active minority of Russian minds, Herzen, whose name was a household word in Russia, had familiarized his compatriots with a more heartfelt *moral* criticism of contemporary European culture. He seems to have formed his

[1] *Polnoe Sobraniye*: (ed.: Lemke), vol. 5, p, 113.

obscure but uniquely Russian socialist faith as a compensation for his uncompromising spiritual hostility to modern Europe (including both the latest developments of European democracy and the socialist theories of Marx). Whether Russia would be led to social regeneration from above by a new Peter the Great, or from below by a mass explosion, followed by an unprecedented federation of communal *mirs*, eventually replacing the authoritarian state, were for him speculative and secondary questions which the unpredictable future could alone decide. In either case Russian leadership would fail, unless it learned to abstain from following the bad example of the democratic industrial West.

Despite their continuous receptivity to foreign influence, and their numerous foreign rulers, Russians had shown themselves recalcitrant to turning into yet another modern European state. They continued to oscillate between rigid discipline and chaotic disorder. Herzen's own attitude towards this purely organizational question remained deliberately inconclusive. He abandoned his original motto, 'Despotism or Socialism, there is no alternative', when he recognized the foundation-stone of Russian socialism, the *mir*, as a decrepit survival which ruined the peasants' self-respect. He continued to admire some personal peasant qualities *despite* the fatalistic stagnation of peasant communism, and not, like some of the *narodniks*, because he was enthralled by its archaic charm. At one moment he saw a new era opening up for Russia under the rule of Alexander II: 'an autocratic revolution could lead Russia to develop all her inexhaustible powers without shedding a single drop of blood.' At other times he could write: 'I believe in no other revolution in Russia except a peasants' war. He who knows how to unite the sectarian peasants as Pugachëv united the Ural Cossacks will strike to death the icy despotism of St. Petersburg.'[1] In either case he considered the violent, if wasteful, Russian method to be a healthier process than the prolonged internal anarchy which would gradually decimate Europe, where, in the end, among 'mountains of corpses, typhus, famine, fires and desolation, communism will spread stormily, terribly, bloodily, unjustly, quickly. The individual will disappear in a brutal levelling. . . . Factories will stop working, the villages will be deserted, like after the Thirty

[1] *Ibid.*, vol. 6, p. 142.

Years War. Exhausted undernourished people will submit to everything. Military despotism will take the place of laws and orderly administration.' (*Letters from France and Italy*, 1848.) The upheaval in Herzen's social and political outlook, which occurred between 1848 and 1852, coincided with years of personal and domestic tragedy. After discovering that his wife had been seduced by the swashbuckling German poet Herwegh, his relations with her entered into a phase of mutual recrimination. Natalie Herzen's health, never robust, declined rapidly under the aggravated strain. In 1851 his mother and younger son were drowned, when the ship on which they were travelling foundered in the Mediterranean. Shortly afterwards his wife died of pleurisy in Cannes. In 1852 Herzen left France in order to start a new life in England, where he spent the next eleven years.

IX

It has been suggested that Herzen generated his disgust for European ways, together with his mounting esteem for Russian qualities, as a result of some inward psychological reaction to the drama of his private life. He liked to cherish the memory of his dead wife as a gentle long-suffering Russian martyr, an innocent victim of perverse European charlatans. And at this time he first started to champion his own country (its inarticulate personal strivings), to defend it against the calumny and ignorance of hostile Europeans who judged Russia solely by the actions of her brutal government. In his letter to Michelet (1851) he implored him not to malign the genuine Russian people, to learn to distinguish them from 'official Russia, the Empire of façades, of Byzantine-German government'. In Italy where he saw Pope Pius IX carried through St. Peter's Square like a Hindu idol on his throne, he contrasted the theatrical pomp and falsity of Roman Catholic ritual with the finer ceremonies of the Orthodox Church. 'The ritual of our Orthodox Church is infinitely more beautiful and majestic,' he asserted.

Herzen might condone religion to the extent that it created a compensating dramatic beauty, but his mental evolution in no way modified the low estimate which he had formed of Christian benefits. Though he preferred Byzantine to Catholic ceremonies, he drew attention in his memoirs to the argument that Byzantine architecture, ikon-painting, church music and sculpture have hardly reached such high artistic quality as their Catholic counterparts. 'On the one hand this supports the Slavophil conception that the Eastern Church is purer, and nearer to Christianity. On the other hand it bears witness to the incompatibility of Christianity with every living activity, such as art. In the Catholic Church painting served as an emancipation from the former monopoly of religion. That is a great Catholic merit, which the Orthodox do not understand. They do not understand that the abstract and detached life of the Church, *pure* (to use their word), through being cut off from life, is clearly a defect and not a quality. Complete fidelity to such a literal Christianity would lead to a quietist contemplative calm and to a dead Church with a passive inertia.'[1]

Gradually Herzen's powerful mind recovered from the stunning blows of personal loss and irreparably shattered faith in Western Europe. After an interval of cynical despair, it re-opened resiliently to fresh perspectives of effort. The new goal he set himself became a dual one, to keep hope beating in the hearts of his discouraged compatriots, and simultaneously to acquaint Europe with the hidden best of Russia.

He never imagined it would be an easy task to convince prejudiced Europeans that the Russian potential was so immeasurably superior to the Russian actuality, that the muffled and scarcely articulate words of non-governmental Russia were a pledge of dazzling future eloquence. But neither would he have relished Hazlitt's trenchant dictum 'A mute Milton is a euphemism for an ass'. In fact the already pronounced Western hostility to Russian political expansion seemed to preoccupy his mind far more than the still nebulous spiritual mission which might (or might not) underly her undeniably increased political power. 'It cannot be that the two latest agents of all Western historical development, the representative personalities of two worlds, two traditions, two origins—the state and personal freedom—will not strive to arrest, to crush, the third personality, mute, nameless, without a banner, emerging somehow inopportunely, with the rope of slavery round its neck, and roughly pushing through the doors of Europe and of history, claiming the Byzantine inheritance, with one foot on Germany, the other on the Pacific Ocean.'

Though he found a temporary haven of refuge in England,

[1] *Polnoe Sobraniye*: (ed.: Lemke), vol. 3, 142 ff.

Herzen could never settle down and make his home there. He moved restlessly from one house to another, without striking roots or finding peace of mind. English liberal tolerance, which harboured his enemy, Karl Marx, with an equal degree of polite indifference, enabled him to live unharassed by censors and police spies, but English people and ways hardly touched his heart and left him coldly detached and critical. For better or for worse he remained a foreign observer of the English and seldom emerged from the small circle of fellow émigrés and political exiles. 'If it is horrible to live in Russia,' he wrote, 'it is just as horrible to live in Europe . . . I stay because the fight is open here—because there is a voice.'[1]

In a letter written from London to a Russian friend (1855) Herzen remarked : 'Life here is as boring as that of worms in cheese. There is no spark of anything healthy or vigorous.' But in a less jaundiced mood, comparing political England with the Continent, he made the penetrating observation : 'England alone is conservative, because she still has something worth preserving—personal liberty.' And in one of those sweeping psychological generalizations which he enjoyed, contrasting his experience of English and French peculiarities, he is positively flattering to the former. 'The Frenchman is constantly making declarations, interfering in everything, instructing everybody, teaching everybody everything. The Englishman waits, does not interfere at all in other peoples' affairs, and would be readier to learn than to teach, were it not that he has no time— he must be off to his shop. . . . The world of self government and de-centralization, an independent capricious growth, seems so barbarous and incomprehensible to the Frenchman, that however long he lives in England, he never understands her political and civic life, her laws and judicial system. He loses his way in the uncoordinated variety of English laws, as if he were entangled in a dark forest; he altogether fails to notice the tall majestic oaks which compose it, and how much charm, poetry and good sense can be found in this very variety. He hankers after a little code with neatly-swept paths, lopped trees and policemen-gardeners in every avenue.'[2]

The fact remains that Herzen made few English friends and never mastered the English spoken language. Among the few

---

[1] *Polnoe Sobraniye:* (ed.: Lemke), vol. 5, p. 328.
[2] E. H. Carr: *Romantic Exiles*, p. 136.

celebrities whom he met personally, he expressed the most unqualified admiration for the factory-owner socialist, Robert Owen. The model profit-sharing factory which Owen created at New Lanark enjoyed for several years a world-famous reputation. Enterprising industrialists, statesmen, and even sovereigns, flocked to visit it from many lands. One of these distinguished visitors, the Grand Duke Nicolas, was so profoundly impressed by what he saw that he belied his ultra-conservative reputation by promptly inviting Owen to come over to work in Russia. Though Owen found a respectful pretext to refuse, his imagination seems to have been stirred by this signal honour from such an unexpected quarter. Herzen records a conversation in which Owen said to him: 'I expect something great from your country; the ground is clearer there; priests are less powerful, prejudices have not piled up so densely—and how much vigour!'[1]

He deplored the fickle and callous incomprehension which the philistine English public extended to Owen's unique achievement, consigning him to oblivion as soon as his feat of industrial organization had ceased to excite by its novelty. After attending a public meeting addressed by Owen in his old age, he confided this painfully vivid impression to his memoirs: 'One could not see without deep veneration that old man, slowly with halting steps advancing on to the platform, where formerly he had been greeted by the enthusiastic applause of a brilliant audience, but where his pale grey hairs now evoked nothing but indifference or ironical laughter. The crowd was almost ready to pelt him with stones, but it too has grown more philanthropic; stones have gone out of fashion; now they prefer to throw mud, to whistle, or to write slanderous articles in the newspapers.'

Outside this small circle of political radicals, Herzen made brief encounters with some literary lions of the day, among them George Henry Lewes and Thomas Carlyle. The latter wrote a vehement letter to Herzen (April 1855). It deserves to be quoted for the rather surprising light which it throws on an English intellectual's response to Herzen in his judgement of current Russian affairs—an appreciative response, though it diverged sharply from the aim of Herzen's own 'eloquent discourse' at that stage of his career. 'I have read your eloquent discourse on Russian revolutionary affairs. It reveals a potent

---

[1] *Polnoe Sobraniye*: (ed.: Lemke), vol. 16, p. 468.

spirit and high talent. . . . For my part, I must confess I never cherished, and have now less than ever, the least hope in "universal suffrage", under any of its modifications; and if it were not that in certain deadly maladies of the body politic, a burning crisis may be considered beneficent, I should much prefer Tsarism itself, or Grand-Turkism, to the sheer anarchy (as I sadly reckon it to be) which is got by parliamentary eloquence, a free press and counting votes. . . . In your country, which I have always respected as a vast and mysterious birth of providence, whose thoughts are still unknown, there has been evident down to this time one talent, in which it excelled, giving it a potency far beyond any other nation, the talent (indispensable to all nations and all people, and inexorably demanded from them under the threat of punishment), the *talent of obeying*—which is much out of fashion in other quarters just now. And I never doubt, or can doubt, but the want of *it* will be amerced to the last farthing, sooner or later, and bring about huge bankruptcies, wherever persevered in.'[1] Herzen tactfully avoided starting a stormy controversy, and contented himself with the mild rejoinder, 'The talent to obey the dictates of our conscience is a virtue, but the talent to fight, rather than to submit against our conscience, is also a virtue.'

Notwithstanding their sharp clash of opinions, Carlyle's ebullient personality seems to have impressed Herzen favourably. He referred to him as 'a man of immense talent, though extremely paradoxical', and repeated with gusto Carlyle's caustic reply to him when he complained about the severity of the French censorship; 'In forcing the French to be more silent, Louis Napoleon did them a considerable service. They have nothing to say which is worth printing, but they want to go on talking. Napoleon gave them that right.'

X

One of Herzen's most arduous tasks in London consisted in orientating himself among the motley crowd of revolutionary exiles, his chance companions in misfortune. He found, to his surprise and mortification, that the majority of them showed mental ability well below the average, and that incurable

---

[1] E. H. Carr: *Romantic Exiles*, p. 371, Appendix B. Herzen's own version of the letter is given in his Memoirs, vol. 6, 675 ff.

obstinacy in dispute and petty personal vanity intensified their meanness of understanding. For most of them revolutionary activity had meant a job, for want of a better one, a means of livelihood, a social position—and little more. They had been banished, or fled abroad, because they failed to find a foothold in their native lands. Among them Herzen diagnosed sick fanatics, monomaniac careerists, corrupt adventurers, and a few single-minded voluntary beggars. The latter group alone contained some men, devoid of personal ambition, who had genuinely sacrificed their lives to the unprofitable service of revolutionary ideals. And they were not political theorists, but magnetic personalities and men of action. Indeed it is significant that, apart from Garibaldi, a lonely lion-hearted hero who stood apart, the only revolutionary figures who irresistibly attracted Herzen were the Polish aristocrat Worcell and the brazen Italian condottiere Orsini.

'The German emigration,' he said, 'could be readily distinguished from all the others by its heavy boring and quarrelsome character. It had neither enthusiasts, hot heads or hot tongues.' Karl Marx already towered above his colleagues as the most domineering organizer and intriguer. Soon after Herzen's arrival in London, he started to spread rumours that the eccentric Russian gentleman was in reality a camouflaged Russian government spy. This was the same malicious libel with which Marx had pursued Bakunin ever since 1848. Though Marx had never set eyes on Herzen, he hated him platonically as a potential rival and because he was a Russian. Herzen, with more substantial reason, reciprocated this hostility, and the more civilized political émigrés in London shared the disgust which he expressed for the Germans' coarse manners, their colossal vanity, bitter intolerance and sordid petty internecine feuds.

An unprecedented and comic event first focused public attention on the gulf which separated the German socialists from all the other groups of émigrés. In February 1854 the American Consul-General in London received instructions to organize an official dinner for representatives of the international revolutionaries, and to sound their political opinions. The presence of the American Ambassador, Mr. James Buchanan, a future President of the United States, imparted an urbanely diplomatic decorum to the conversation. Herzen, with more than his usual caustic humour, devoted some pages of his memoirs to describing 'the red banquet given by the defenders of black slavery'. He, Mazzini, Ledru-Rolland, Kossuth, Worcell and Garibaldi took their places as the guests of honour. Herzen's place-card bore the inscription, 'The Russian Republican'. But the Americans, in their naïve wisdom, had refrained from inviting a single German, though every other national group was represented. After the Ambassador's early departure had somewhat thawed the formal atmosphere, they all drank the toast of the 'world republic'. Herzen thereupon raised Russian prestige with the American Consul by asking for another cup of the extremely potent brew of Kentucky whisky punch. 'Why yes,' the Consul-General observed, with a sardonic glance at the more abstemious Europeans, 'it is only in America and in Russia that people know how to drink.'

The convivial atmosphere generated at this dinner-party appears to have promoted at least one practical project, the formation of an international socialist committee in London. In order to round off this organization, founder members chivalrously invited the hitherto boycotted Germans to participate. Marx duly attended the first meeting and immediately lodged an objection against the proposed election of Herzen as a member. On being asked to explain his objection, he contented himself with the reply that he did not know Herzen personally, but it was enough to know that he was a Russian, and a Russian who supported Russia in everything he wrote. If we may believe Herzen's memoirs, the English, French, Italian and Polish delegates then voted unanimously against Marx's resolution, with the result that Marx rose to his feet, walked out of the committee and never returned. Thus one more attempt at international organization split against the old rock of national pride, and provided us with an early example of that technique in negotiation to which Marx's followers have so often proved their fidelity. On a later occasion Marx refused to attend a public meeting in London to commemorate the 1848 revolutions, for the sole reason that Herzen was also billed to be present. 'I will nowhere and at no time appear on the same platform as Herzen,' he wrote to Engels, 'since I do not hold the opinion that "Old Europe" can be rejuvenated by Russian blood.'

Marx not only cherished morbid suspicions that virtually

every Russian must be a rabid pan-Slav under his skin, but he remained blind to any possible distinction between pan-Slavs and other breeds of Slavophil. He went so far as to write to his friend Kugelman that Herzen, although a rich man himself, received yearly 25,000 roubles for propaganda from the 'pseudo-socialist pan-Slav party in Russia'. In this case Marx's calumny, though literally quite untrue, bore some remote relation to distorted fact. The curious incident from which it originated is described in some detail by Herzen himself.[1] In 1858 a young Russian landowner, called Bakhmetiev, had turned his back on hopeless Russia, and set out with the vague intention of founding a model colony on some sunny Pacific island. He broke his journey in London, where he deposited with Herzen a sum of eight hundred pounds, requesting that it should be used at the latter's sole discretion. Bakhmetiev thereupon set sail for the Pacific Ocean, and was never heard of again. Herzen deposited this money in a London bank, but he never touched the capital during his lifetime. After his death it passed to Ogarëv, as his co-trustee. Later the whole sum was formally handed over to Bakunin, and by him to the ingenious murderer Nechaev, who refused to give any receipt for it to Bakunin on the plea that his 'revolutionary honour' should suffice. There is no vestige of evidence that Herzen ever received a subsidy for his journalistic work from any outside source, nor is it likely, since he had an ample private fortune. His diary mentions only a few small donations to the 'general fund' from various sympathizers.

XI

To celebrate the New Year of 1855 Herzen arranged a private banquet for his family and close friends. When the merry-making had subsided, he read aloud the dedicatory letter, 'To my son, Alexander', prefixed to all editions of his post-1848 confession, 'From the Other Shore'. That preface began with the words, 'We do not proclaim a new truth, we abolish an old lie. Contemporary man can only build the bridge; another, the yet unknown man of the future, will walk across it. The religion of revolution, of the great social transformation, is the only religion I bequeath to you. It is a religion without a paradise,

[1] *Polnoe Sobraniye*: (ed.: Lemke), vol. 16, p. 643.

without rewards, except consciousness of itself, except a conscience' . . . and it ended: 'I give my blessing to your journey in the name of human reason, personal liberty and brotherly love.' The reading and the occasion chosen, seemed to symbolize, more than anything else, Herzen's own modest dedication to the modified cycle of endeavour which he saw opening before him, a self-imposed pursuit of duty 'without glory and without rewards'. The young Alexander embraced his father and burst into tears, and the guests were deeply moved. Later they all went out for a walk in the frosty night to recover from the emotions of the celebration.

Herzen had not long to wait for his next phase of action. The news that Nicolas I had died flashed like lightning through the heavy gloom of the Crimean War. The event filled Herzen with joy and hopeful anticipation. The war he had waged against Tsarism in the person of Nicolas I yielded place to a conditional alliance with his successor. He immediately wrote a letter of admonition to the new Tsar : 'Your reign begins under an auspicious star. You bear no blot of blood upon you. The Russian autocracy can be revolutionary. It is all-powerful for good or evil. Peasant democracy remains conservative.' On that account, Herzen argued persuasively, the way still lies open for a unique and orderly social revolution to be conducted on the Tsar's initiative. 'Give us free speech, give the land to the peasants, wipe out that shameful blot, serfdom,' he concluded.

Only a few months previously Herzen had travelled to Plymouth to visit the Russian prisoners of war who had been landed there from the Crimea. 'According to their own words,' he wrote, 'these men were never so well lodged in their own barracks as in the building which is called the prison at Plymouth. Will it be believed? The only fear which these unhappy men entertain is to be obliged to return to their former life. Their captivity under the English flag they regard as a deliverance.' Like most Russian soldiers, they were of many different races or racially mixed. Many of them were Poles, Finns or Jews. Their dread of forced repatriation impressed him painfully.

From 1855 onwards Herzen's fame spread like a snowball over Russia. His personality was magnified into a fantastic legend there, and his writings became a potent and pervasive social stimulant. A new fear was born there, a new administrative conscience awoke, a new idol was worshipped—Herzen. The first number of his intermittent journal *The Polar Star* burst upon the world from London (August 1855) only five months after the death of Nicolas I. Its spectacular success impelled him to embark on a far more ambitious venture, his free Russian newspaper *The Bell* (1857). Soon this was passing rapidly from hand to hand throughout the length and breadth of Russia, defying the vigilance of the Tsar's security police. Permission to leave Russia was then, as always, granted with caution to a select minority of 'suitable' citizens. But almost every Russian who set foot in England deemed it his duty to call on Herzen, who regaled his visitors with excellent food, wine, and brilliant inexhaustible conversation at almost any hour. For a Russian traveller to leave London without having visited the famous Herzen became almost as unthinkable as for a tourist to leave Rome without having seen St. Peter's Cathedral.

Though it made heavy demands on his purse and time, Herzen thoroughly relished the unique position he had acquired as unofficial Russia's Ambassador at large, and he noted with χ satisfaction in his Memoirs: 'Our gallery of live rarities from Russia was without any doubt more extraordinary and interesting than the Russian section of the Great Exhibition.' One of the most remarkable visitors he describes (and among the few who never tried to borrow money from him) was the young Prince Yury Golitzin, who turned up in London (1860) with a pet crocodile which he had acquired en route in Cairo, a young lady he had abducted from Voronëzh, and six serf domestics who desired to see the world. Though he had only a few pounds in his possession, and no means of obtaining money from Russia, he immediately rented a large house in Porchester Terrace, in front of whose permanently open doors he kept a carriage harnessed night and day to a pair of fine grey horses, in case he should feel inclined to go for a drive. This enterprising nobleman possessed considerable musical talent and at one time had conducted a serf orchestra on his father's estate. Nature had also blessed him with charm, ebullience, and the physique of an Assyrian god, so that his social success in London was assured. Herzen took a fancy to him, and he composed a *pot-pourri* of Russian folk-tunes for an *Emancipation Fantasia*, played at the huge evening reception Herzen held to celebrate the Edict of

1861. But since his complete financial insouciance could not avail to hide from him the ugly insistence of his creditors, he was obliged to launch some more fashionable and lucrative orchestral concerts, devoted to popular Russian music. Unluckily his incurable generosity prompted him to invite all the musicians to sumptuous dinners. After a few months Prince Golitzin faced the inevitable penalty and found himself sitting in a debtors' prison. Once a week he was allowed to emerge in faultless evening dress, and conveyed under police guard to conduct a further series of orchestral concerts, from whose financial proceeds he started to pay off his debts.

In June 1859 Herzen received a more politically important visitor. Chernyshevsky travelled to London (his first and last visit to Europe) hoping that he might persuade Herzen to come into line with the more radical policy of *The Contemporary*. It is possible that they also discussed the practicability of printing *The Contemporary* as an addition to the Free Russian Press in London, in case the government banned its publication inside Russia. Herzen made such an offer publicly after Chernyshevsky's arrest. But neither would budge from his personal standpoint. Their discussion led to only one positive conclusion, that the two leading Russian 'progressives' fundamentally disagreed and distrusted each other. His visitor struck Herzen as shifty, reserved and insincere, though he made a better impression on the good-natured Ogarëv, who recorded that his ugly face became attractive when it lit up with an expression of gentle thoughtfulness.[1] Chernyshevsky complained that *The Bell* confined itself to protest and exhortation, whereas it ought to expound some clear-cut political or constitutional programme. Herzen, while frankly admitting his empirical policy, stoutly defended it on grounds of practical wisdom.

For the time being, he said, his demands went no further than a series of liberations—'of the serfs from landowners, of their backs from the rod and the lash, of the printed word from censorship, of the law-courts from administrative rulings'. He saw only Utopian folly in planning further ahead, since the future alone could show what the next stage demanded. It was enough to deal with the burning social grievances of the moment. After the long winter of Nicolas I, time was needed to thaw the blood in the veins of his former subjects, to let the constrained

[1] *Polnoe Sobraniye*: (ed.: Lemke), vol. 10, pp. 18–20.

heart beat freely once again. Frozen minds could not reason wisely. Herzen acutely sensed the limits of practicable political action, and the danger of energetic busybodies who would do more harm than good by attempting to do too much too suddenly. 'We fear the spread of Russian Germans and Germanized Russians, wearing the same old clothes with an added patch of political economy, centralizing in the French way and bureaucratizing in the German way. Merely because they are more efficient than the nobility, more honest than our own officials, they may end by reconciling us to everything that we loathe and despise.' In his intense desire to see Russia break free from the moral tutelage of a weakening Europe, to assimilate European scientific advance, her vigorous and virile reasoning power, without succumbing to the demoralizing course of her political development, Herzen was bound to remain a hostile enigma to his rival. He stuck to his attack on Chernyshevsky's policy stated in the article 'Very Dangerous' (*The Bell*, 1 June), which had probably hastened the latter's journey to London.

Nevertheless, even before 1861, Herzen was beginning to lose his original faith in Alexander II's ruling capacities. His determined opposition to Chernyshevsky was not a sign of his conversion to government policy. It seemed to him that the Tsar, like Faust, had invoked a spirit beyond his powers and taken fright at it. His leading article in *The Bell* about the long-awaited Emancipation Edict showed scant enthusiasm. 'The first step is taken! They say it is the hardest. We await the second with hope. We should like to have awaited it with complete confidence, but everything is being done so shakily, so half-heartedly, so clumsily! . . . No relaxation is in store for the government, nothing but hard work. Alexander II has done a lot. His name stands higher than that of all his predecessors. He fought for human rights and sympathy against the grasping crowd of self-centred scoundrels, and he defeated them. But woe if he stops! The beast is not killed. He is only stunned.'[1]

Faced by an unpredictable course of events unfolding within Russia, Herzen's task as a builder of public opinion from outside was further complicated at this juncture by the stormy incursion of Bakunin. That irrepressible *enfant terrible* suddenly appeared on Herzen's London doorstep at the end of 1861. After spending eight years in Austrian and Russian prisons,

[1] *Ibid.*, vol. 11, p. 59.

followed by four years in Siberia, he had escaped through Japan and taken ship from San Francisco to London. Herzen's gradual Slavophil orientation had drawn him into a sympathy with Bakunin far closer than their relations in 1848. But Bakunin came back into the world like a ghost from the past. Like a sleeper awakened, he expected to find everything in the same position as before. In 1862 *The Bell* started to publish articles by him on the well-worn theme, 'Long live peasant Russia and the classless intelligentsia'. His manifesto 'To my Russian, Polish and Slav friends' was issued as a special supplement to *The Bell*. But it only reiterated the old policy (tried without success in 1848) of disrupting the Austrian Empire in order to create a free Slavonic federation of minor states.

Herzen had persistently refused to sanction terrorism and political assassination as a revolutionary policy, but Bakunin wore him down into accepting as a painful duty to write approvingly in *The Bell* about the newly founded Russian secret society 'Land and Liberty'. The precarious alliance of these two volatile friends reached breaking point in 1863. Bakunin, in an effort to recruit support for the Polish revolt, had accompanied an illicit shipment of rifles from London to Stockholm, and announced himself there as a representative of 'Land and Liberty'. Invited as guest of honour to a public banquet, he allowed his vainglorious imagination to run riot, and boosted this struggling little underground society as a vast organization embracing all classes throughout Russia, organizing its own finances, administration and police, and ready soon to raise its own army. He finally proclaimed that 'Land and Liberty' had entered into a formal alliance with the Polish National Committee. Such a ludicrous parade of baseless pretensions roused Herzen to the highest pitch of indignation. He threatened to disown Bakunin publicly in the pages of *The Bell*. Though he later resumed intermittent personal relations with his old friend, this painful incident marked the end of their political co-operation.

Apart from its compromising entanglement with Bakunin, *The Bell*, by taking the side of the Poles in 1863, had already forfeited the support of the moderate Russian liberals, many of whom were veering towards the rising tide of mystic nationalism, or, like Turgenev, had abandoned hope in Russia as a viable political entity. Even more unmistakably, *The Bell* was losing its grip over the second generation of radical intellectuals. Its steadily sinking circulation confirmed the harsh fact of flagging interest all round. Whereas in the days of its glory *The Bell* had been able to print and distribute several thousand copies, in 1864 its circulation dwindled to a few hundred.

XII

In the same year Herzen left England and decided to settle in Geneva, in order to come into closer contact with Russian revolutionary movements on the Continent. Switzerland swarmed with young nihilists of both sexes, who were studying every conceivable subject at the Swiss universities. But they were not what Herzen hoped they might be. These uprooted creatures, so totally unlike the Moscow students of the forties, filled him with misgivings. He was prepared to pool his resources with generous-minded ardent young patriots, however naïve and inexperienced. But he shrank from nervous spiteful people, who quivered like mimosas at every imagined affront to their dignity, and he found it hard to remain on speaking terms with cocksure 'scientific savages', bursting with self-importance and half-baked knowledge.

The young Karakozov's attempt to assassinate Alexander II rescued Herzen from an untenable compromise. *The Bell*, true to its principles, printed some restrained but frankly deprecatory remarks about 'this fanatic'. But the Geneva nihilists had decided to glorify Karakozov as a martyr, and they seized the opportunity to rise in rebellion against Herzen. The method they selected was to print an open letter to him, containing a crescendo of insults, rising to a final assurance that 'Mr. Herzen' with his 'blood-stained wealth' ought to have recognized long ago that he was 'a dead man'. Herzen was quite alive enough to have countered this outburst of petty personal abuse with a far more crushing and objective irony, but he preferred to remain silent. Only a year later he recorded his private opinion, when, not without a note of candid self-reproach, he summed up this misguided rising generation in one devastating phrase—'the syphilis of our revolutionary lusts!'

Meanwhile he faced the unpalatable fact that he had lost his Russian audience beyond recall, but he made one final effort to capture another more receptive reading public. In 1868 he started to publish *The Bell* in French, with an occasional Russian supplement. After a short trial of one year, this last experiment petered out. Public indifference, more deadly than active hostility, stifled Herzen's voice. When *The Bell* finally ceased to ring, Turgenev wrote to console him: 'Do the French want to know the truth about anything, let alone about Russia?'

In January 1869, less than a year before he died, Herzen wrote his *Letters to an Old Comrade*. These form an immensely self-revealing document, and they are prescient to a degree which superstitious people would call clairvoyance. In a series of distinctly modified political judgements they range over all the major issues still at stake. From their foaming torrent of eloquent digressions and hints it is possible to extricate the tentative conclusions he had drawn from his active and tempestuous life, soberly surveyed in retrospect. The nightmare fiasco of the 1848 revolutions still haunted his conscience, but no vestige of doubt about its final lesson troubled him any longer.

'We saw the grim example of bloody rebellion in a moment of despair and anger flaring up on the barricades; we saw that it carried no banner. The conservative world suppressed this rebellion. . . . But what would have happened if the victory had gone to those who fought on the barricades? Within twenty years would not those stern fighters have exhausted everything they held in their hearts? We cannot find a single creative organic thought in their legacy, and surely economic blunders lead, not obliquely, like political ones, but directly and more irretrievably to ruin and paralysis, to death through starvation. Our time is indeed the time for completing our study of what must precede the work of realization, even as the theory of steam preceded the construction of railways.'

Herzen goes straight to the point. An unhealthy political offshoot had been nipped in the bud, but it was a bud which could never have blossomed. More important still, when a national voyage of exploration (undertaken without sufficient knowledge) turned out to be heading unwittingly for the rocks, the navigators could only avert disaster if they observed in time the danger signals, and altered course before they entered the whirlpool centre of the hurricane, before they sank to the

bottom together with their crew and precious cargo. Even
then the skilful steering, which could retrieve political blunders,
would be useless in a state of economic chaos. The best pilot
must be baffled by a rudderless ship.

'An abstract plan of tasks to be fulfilled provides no way out,
no methods, not even an adequate medium for action. You cannot conquer these by force. The whole bourgeois world blown
up by gunpowder, when the smoke disperses and reveals the
ruins, will start again with different variations—*another bourgeois world*. . . . Not a single one of those foundations on which
the present order stands, which should collapse and be re-
created, is sufficiently worn-out and shaky to be uprooted and
thus finally annihilated. The state, the church, the armed
forces can be refuted with as much logical exactitude as metaphysics, etc. In a certain scientific sphere of thought they stand
condemned, but beyond these academic boundaries they continue to control all the moral demands of human habit. . . .'

'Let every conscientious man ask himself this question: is he
ready? Is he so clear in his mind about the new organization
towards which we are moving, through the medium of those
vague general ideas of collective property and social solidarity?
Does he know the process (apart from sheer destruction) which
will accomplish the transformation of old forms into new ones?
. . . A radical economic change, through the sobriety of its
principles, has an immeasurable advantage over all religious
and political revolutions.

'By denial alone, however intelligent it may be, one cannot
possibly win a victory over false dogmas, over beliefs, however
crazy they may be. To proclaim, "Do not believe" is as arbitrary and fundamentally as clumsy as to proclaim "Believe!"
The old order of things is stronger by virtue of its instinctive
established acceptance than through any material force which
upholds it. That is evident in places where it is kept going not
by terror and violence, but rests firmly on "unconscious
conscience", undeveloped mind and immaturity of new ideas,
as in Switzerland or England. . . . There is no need to prove
to property owners and capitalists that their ownership is sinful
(an idea alien to our contemporary outlook), but we need only
see that the absurdity of its contrasts, through having penetrated the consciousness of the 'have-nots' is making its continuation *impossible*. . . . The most desperate miser would not

prefer to be drowned with all his money, if he could save himself and a part of it by throwing the rest overboard. But for that it is indispensable that both the danger and the possibility of being saved should be equally apparent. . . . The coming order must be not only a sharp-edged sword, but a preserving force. By striking down the old world it must at once save everything within it worthy of salvation, and take over into the future whatever is varied, original, alive, whatever does not seek to interfere. Woe to the revolution which is poor in spiritual force and sickly in imaginative feeling, which out of the immensity that has passed and been acquired will create nothing but a dreary workshop, whose sole object is enough to eat and drink!' . . .

'An international union of artisans, of all their organizations and representatives, would have to achieve that non-interference of administrative government with work, which government fails to exercise in its dealings with property. . . . Habits which hold people in half-compulsory chains, will in the long run not withstand logic and the growth of social consciousness. . . . But breaking them by force risks killing the whole organism as well. Because the forms of the state are transitory—(this was a shaft aimed at Bakunin's indiscriminate anarchism)—it does not follow that the state itself is a thing of the past. And how can one repudiate the state, when the chief prerequisite for getting away from it is the attainment of years of discretion by the majority? . . .

'We know what it means to mistake the stage and state of human maturity. Universal suffrage, given to an immature unprepared people, served it as a razor with which it nearly cut its throat. And if the existing conceptions of government and law are still strong, the deeper-rooted conceptions of family, property and inheritance are even stronger. . . .

The refutation of private property as such is senseless. . . . The revised opinion about it as a kind of transition from personal to collective wealth is confused and vague. Property, especially landed property, means to the Western man liberation, independence, dignity, enhanced social status. . . . 'The problem of inherited property is exceptionally hard. Except a few celibate fanatics, like monks, not even the poorest peasant will agree to renounce unconditionally the right to bequeath something to his appointed heirs—hardly in the name of obligatory brotherhood and love for everybody!

'Twenty years have passed since then.[1] Vengeance has gone over to the other side—vengeance has descended from above! The *nations* have swept everything else before them, because they understood nothing, neither before nor after. Inside them the whole centre is crushed and trampled in the mud. . . . But that long oppressive interval has given us leisure to observe and reflect, enough time for passions to cool down, for thought to grow more detached. . . .

'As if words were not deeds, as if the time for words could ever pass away! Our enemies have never separated words from deeds, and often inflicted an even fiercer punishment for words. That forced contrast between words and deeds does not withstand criticism. It is a melancholy confession that every-thing is explained and understood, that there is nothing left to talk about. . . . To be in the right in a struggle may not help a lot. Justice is victorious only in divine judgement! But we need place little hope in supernatural intervention. . . .

'The path we follow is not predestined. On the contrary, it alters with circumstances, with understanding, with personal energy. . . . In order to be blind instruments of fate, scourges, executioners of God, we should have to remain in mental immaturity, ignorant simpletons or wild fanatics. . . . What civilized people forgave in Attila, in the Committee of Public Safety and even in Peter, they will not forgive in us. . . . For us there only exists one voice, one power, the power of reason and understanding. If we are deaf to this voice and resist this power, we shall cripple science and kill civilization. . . .

'Those very masses on whom the weight of existence bears down so heavily, with their Macedonian phalanx of artisans, seek words and understanding; they feel no confidence in people who preach the aristocracy of science and call them to arms. And, mark my words, their preachers do not share their feelings, do not belong to them; they belong to schools, to books and abstract learning. These elderly students have strayed much further away from the common people than their so-called enemies have done. Priests, aristocrats, policemen, merchants, employers or soldiers, now all stand nearer to the common people than do their own intellectual leaders. . . .

'I am not a bit frightened of the word "gradualness", wretchedly debased though it has been by the unsteady shaky

[1] Since 1848.

steps of various reforming governments. . . . One learns mathematics gradually, so why should final conclusions and thoughts
about sociology be spread like an epidemic of small-pox, or
abruptly injected into the brain like medicine forcibly poured
down a horse's throat? . . .

'Neither you nor I are traitors to our convictions, but we are
both at odds with a problem. You rush ahead as before with a
passion to destroy, which you call a creative passion . . . breaking down obstacles and respecting only the history of the future.
I no longer believe in the former revolutionary paths, and I try
to understand the social movement in the past as in the present,
in order to learn how to keep in step with it, without either falling
behind or rushing ahead to such a distance where people do
not and cannot follow me. And, one more word. To tell all that
to the people we live among, demands, if not more, at least as
much courage and independence as it does to pursue extremes
in everything.'[1]

XIII

Of all the heavy blows which fate administered to Herzen,
perhaps the most stunning was to watch his own fame and
ascendancy fading away while he was still alive. At the crucial
moment his former disciples turned impatiently aside from his
difficult and deliberately inconclusive teaching. They started
listening to louder or more seductive voices, and quickly, with
characteristic instability, surrendered themselves to the com-
pelling thrall of the newly born anarchists, social revolutionaries or Marxians. Since Herzen's career as a Russian publicist
suffered such an abrupt eclipse, it cannot be a matter for surprise that European students of political thought have paid
scant attention to his contribution, except as that of a picturesque and transient figure who never occupied the centre of the
stage. Influenced perhaps by the subconscious desire to treat all
Russian ideas as an inferior and distorted reflection of their
own, they have only too readily acquiesced in the perfunctory
verdict of subsequent Russian 'progressives'. Together they
pushed Herzen into an inconspicuous pigeon-hole in the archive
of back-numbers, long ago superseded by the triumphant onrush of more 'scientific' modes of political thought.

Only since the ultra-progressive mountain gave birth to a

[1] *Polnoe Sobraniye*: (ed.: Lemke), vol. 21, 433 ff.

quite unexpected animal, since that feverish intellectual gestation astonished many adherents as well as opponents by its sinister outcome, the way has been opened for a more discerning approach to Herzen, no longer as a discarded stage of the onward socialist march, but as a far-sighted and generous figure spanning both Russian and European political thought, and a still living psychological link between the two.

Zealous intellectual recruits, trained from childhood to bow the knee before an irresistible forward movement of universal history, now face the disconcerting discovery that native local variations, rooted in the past, manifest a more potent character and vitality than many skin-deep though universally diffused contemporary trends of thought. They see how ancient, often unrecognized instincts, like submerged undercurrents, rise suddenly to the surface and impart violent motion to stagnant pools or sluggish uncertain currents. The mutually antagonistic types of *de facto* national socialism, which since Herzen's death have emerged not only in Germany and Russia, but throughout the political world, have proved the essential accuracy of his political foresight, and of Péguy's cognate argument that there are at least as many different socialisms as there are important nations.

He showed a similar clairvoyance in prophesying that unchecked German national power and internationally infectious German modes of thought would be the central agents in spreading world disaster. 'And now, Bismarck, it is your turn,' he exclaimed a year before the Franco-Prussian war. 'And you Mazzini, Garibaldi, the last of God's saints, fold your hands, be calm. You are not needed now. You have done your work. Now give place to madness, to the craze for blood, with which Europe or reaction will destroy itself. What could you do with your hundred republicans and your volunteers with two or three boxes of smuggled rifles? Now there will be ponds of blood, oceans of blood, mountains of corpses. . . .

'Ah, conservative gentlemen, you did not even want such a pale republic as the February one, you refused the sweetened republic served up to you by the confectioner, Lamartine. You did not want the stoic Mazzini, or the hero Garibaldi; you wanted *order*!'

In the long run, systematic programme-builders of social reform, together with more traditional national leaders, by becoming equally brutal, despotic and sterile, became equally anathema to Herzen. Either he found their aims to be illusory, or he saw that they relied for their attainment on spiritual factors operating beyond the sphere of political experiments, yet factors which conservatives and socialists alike ignored or crushed in their bigoted obsession with legal order and economic regulation.

He himself belonged by temperament and sympathy to the spacious internationally-minded generation of the forties. He differed most profoundly from his successors, by keeping not only his tactics but his outlook, up to date, by fully admitting his many theoretical mistakes whenever they conflicted with the verdict of subsequent experience. Far-reaching as they were, these conscientious adjustments failed to bring him into line with the harsh, embittered generation of the puritanical Russian sixties. After making every attempt to do them justice, he could not help judging them to be more deeply mistaken than he had ever been, incurably vindictive and one-sided, and therefore less capable of learning or profiting from trial and error.

While ready enough to compromise over inessentials, he would never capitulate, and he refused to admit that the blatant triumph achieved in popular esteem by those rivals, who had roughly pushed him from their path, sufficed to prove that they were right. He confined himself to suggesting that victory might more easily be won by those who were in the wrong. 'Victrix causa Deis placuit, sed victa Catoni.' And was such a devastating battle worth winning at all? An almost suicidal Pyrrhic victory, its outcome would soon start to disappoint the victors. He predicted that it might usher in a new dark age of repressive human regimentation, which would provoke in turn reactions of convulsive and defiant anarchy. Or perhaps, if it managed to extinguish the last sparks of spiritual vitality still kindling the embers of resistance, it would bring European history to an ignominious end, to a state of crystallization in the *semper idem* of a vast human ant-heap. While he faced the increasing likelihood of their temporary triumph, neither of these alternatives could for a moment enlist the support of Herzen, who had known and striven for a quality of social achievement which was altogether different in kind. The official Soviet view of Herzen (substantially the same as Lenin's) may quite conceivably satisfy the majority of his

Soviet admirers. Even those who feel that it omits too much need not quarrel with its neat historical summary of Herzen, as a dynamic link between the aristocratic Decembrist rebels and the rising generation of proletarian revolutionaries. For those to whom history alone is God, events take the place of judgements. So far as that estimate of Herzen goes, it hardly strays from a bald statement and justification of the course of political events in Russia. But the moment it tries to go further, by pinning Herzen down to the part he played in those preliminary skirmishes for power, with a cursory patronizing review of the errors inseparable from his backward historical position, the argument peters out in a cramped and congested string of faded clichés.

Indeed, Herzen's significance as a recurrent and almost world-wide intellectual type is hardly less striking than his function as a transient figure on the Russian political stage. Standing mentally astride two worlds, with one foot firmly planted in each, he became an intensified personal incarnation of that unresolved conflict between the Europeanized Russian and the 'Russified' European, and his life throws a searching sidelight on the similar but broader conflict then taking shape between the westernized oriental and the Westerner entangled in the East, in a world where neither could flourish any longer without interdependent economic systems.

Having good reason to condemn the Russia which he knew from bitter experience, Herzen became the knight-errant of a theoretical Europe which he knew only through books and pictures. But, having settled in France, and finding that French political practice had turned into a hideous travesty of the theories which it pretended to promote, he switched over to a feverish denunciation of Europe as a whole. His disenchantment with a close view of the European political scene discouraged him from penetrating far beneath the surface. That explains why his poignant anti-European invective, though it often hits the mark, is marred by an air of incomplete reality, as if it were an outburst of rhetorical revenge against a phantom which had enticed and mocked him. And though he retained his hatred and disgust for the 'disciplined Tartars' who ruled Russia, and his scepticism about her stagnant peasant communes, he desperately built a new idol out of a fabulous future Russia, invented by his fertile imagination.

To do him justice, Herzen confessed to the vice of theoretical volatility, but that never prevented him from continuing to indulge in it. He and his contemporaries, he complained, managed to be bold and adventurous exclusively in the sphere of thought and dispute. They had no chance of proving their efficiency in the conduct of human affairs. Being aware of this gap in his experience, Herzen always sought first to elucidate dark situations, to stimulate, help and warn his compatriots, rather than to lead and command them. Because the new would-be leaders of the Russian people shared no such scruples, he feared from the start that their methods would pervert their aims. '*Young Russia*', he wrote, 'is not Russian at all.[1] . . . It is another variation on that theme of Western socialism, which pronounces social desiderata in the form of a call to arms. Those who write for it live more in the world of books and comrades than in the world of facts, are more at home in the algebra of ideas than in the workshop, where the friction and temperature of the moment always modify simple mechanical laws.' Herzen resembled Bakunin in his conviction that the masses would not benefit merely because the stick with which they were beaten was called a popular stick. He felt sure that formerly worthy peasants or artisans, after they had seized supreme power and degenerated into Government officials, would become at least as 'bourgeois' in their behaviour as the class which they had driven out. He therefore turned his back on the modern state as a Western evil, and tried to console himself with the visionary rising sun of an unprecedented Eastern civilization, illuminated by the setting sun of the West. At least he recognized himself to be a fallible creator of legends, and he repeatedly stated that the fulfilment of what is loosely called socialism would turn out to be a quite unpredictable combination of theoretical demands transformed by stubborn facts.

Last but not least, Herzen has been criticized by socialists with economic training for having ignored the intricate requirements of modern industrial civilization. A federalist, a convinced though gradualist republican (after his abortive flirtation with Alexander II), a believer in regional self-government,

---

[1] *Kolokol*, No. 13, July 1862. The secretly printed appeal *Young Russia* urged the revolutionary party to seize the Emperor's autocratic power and retain it, in order to reconstruct the whole social and economic order.

village industries, and the multiplication of small landowners, keeping the *mir* as a humanitarian safeguard against pauperism, Herzen conceived Russia as a slowly developing agrarian nation rather than as a potential industrial giant. In this attitude, except for his republican goal, he resembled the more sensible Slavophils.[1] Like them, he failed to foresee that the pressure of increasing population would force the pace of industrial growth as a means of alleviating intolerable poverty.[2] Disappointed by what he had seen of industrial civilization in Europe, he felt himself ill-equipped for the task of precise economic diagnosis, but he admitted the need for it. His steady belief in the application of science to social improvements remained unshaken by his outbursts of mystical ardour. Towards the end of his life, notably in his first open letter to Bakunin, he pointed hopefully to the sober semi-mathematical methods proper to the newly maturing science of political economy. He welcomed its direct and closely-reasoned approach, its prompt applicability to urgent needs, and even more its freedom from devastating religious and patriotic passions, but he never identified it with a breakneck race to turn Russia into a nation of regimented mechanics.

[1] A. Koshelëv (see p. 162) came close to Herzen and anticipated Stolypin, when he urged that the more enterprising of the emancipated serfs should be encouraged to turn into independent farmers, in order to broaden the basis of the landowning class. Unlike the conventional Slavophils, he was content to reduce the *mir* to a kind of philanthropic institution for backward peasants.

[2] Between 1861 and 1905 the peasant population of European Russia, not counting those who worked in towns, had jumped from 50,000,000 to 78,000,000.

CHAPTER VIII

KONSTANTIN LEONTIEV

I

BITTERLY attacked or fundamentally misunderstood by most of his Russian contemporaries, for long unknown to the outside world, Konstantin Leontiev (1831–1891) is barely recognized today as one of the most far-sighted and consistent political thinkers of his epoch. Believing that civilization would degenerate or collapse without the leadership of monarchs and aristocrats (provided they scrupulously fulfilled their duties), he understood best a monarch like Peter the Great, who burst upon the world as a legitimate autocrat and revolutionary creator rolled into one—even though he never sympathized with Peter's philistine brutality and inconsiderate haste. Like almost all his educated compatriots, Leontiev was first carried away by a youthful phase of destructive revolutionary ardour. But having moved beyond it, he gradually became convinced, not only that modern political revolution was doomed to suicidal results—by achieving the reverse of what it set out to do—but that even the 'liberal-egalitarian' progress of Western Europe, despite its self-assured and moderate gradualness, was dragging her treacherously down towards a bottomless abyss.

The ancient Russian Empire, after becoming the keen and assiduous pupil of seventeenth- and eighteenth-century Europe, had risen with almost lightning rapidity into the front rank of political power and simultaneously achieved a high degree of culture, none the less brilliant for its complex derivation. By continuing to steer a persevering course in the wake of the post-1789 European democratic doctrines, the Russian intelligentsia first took it for granted that, by so doing, their country would reap the same substantial benefits as she had visibly reaped from European civilization in the preceding centuries. But soon a small minority observed with apprehension that widening cracks were running through the European edifice. They raised their warning voices to explain these symptoms, and thence to demonstrate that a Russia, which persisted in following Europe's current example or advice, could not expect to escape a similar

KONSTANTIN LEONTIEV

From a photograph

doom to hers, was courting, perhaps, an even more hopeless chaos.

Leontiev therefore taught—and he was not the first to do so—that modern Russian citizens had a new duty to fulfil, namely to resist with all their might the latest moral epidemic, spreading insidiously through Europe, and from Europe through the world. This potent idea, so wounding to European self-esteem, but still so flattering to many Russian pretensions, had already been most vigorously expressed by Fyodor Tyutchev in his *Russia and Europe* (1848). But Leontiev carried it further. Though he shared the conservative tenacity of his distinguished predecessor, he did far less than Tyutchev to extenuate the stuffy prison-house of Nicolas I. For both, but more indubitably for Leontiev, the unstable Russian Empire in which they lived was scarcely more than a groping but necessary prelude to the birth of a more highly civilized Orthodox Empire into which Russia must expand.

Such was the dubious alternative which Leontiev and a few kindred spirits prescribed as the sole reliable Eastern antidote to Western poisons. It presented a cloudy fanatical vision of the future—which none the less moved Russian hearts by its grandiose promise and stirred up thwarted ambitions in every class. Since all that was best in Russia either opposed or ignored the Russian Government, it is hard to explain what led Leontiev to imagine that the cruel and exasperating Petersburg Empire could develop organically into a bigger and better Empire, rich in civilizing virtues which its predecessor so conspicuously lacked. History abounded in examples to the contrary, showing Empires which expanded in wealth and power while declining *pari passu* in spiritual quality. The strident, sabre-rattling united Germany of Bismarck compared unfavourably with the politically weak decentralized earlier Germany, blessed by the genius of Goethe and Bach. And Leontiev himself used this particular illustration of decline. Yet it failed to deter him from thinking, or rather desiring to believe, that 'Holy Russia', the 'Third Rome', must prove a miraculous exception to the general historical rule.

Both now and in the past, Russian intellectuals, blamelessly ignorant of what life is like under a government with limited powers, habitually attempt to justify their own totalitarian rule by arguments which pay tribute to its civilizing discipline. They are genuinely puzzled by the almost callous indifference shown to the moral welfare of its subjects by a liberal democratic government. When they see a government so liberal, that it tolerates opinion and behaviour tending to undermine its very existence, they throw up their hands in contemptuous horror at what seems to them a sickly and spineless abdication of leadership. According to Leontiev's standards, a government which shelved major responsibilities by passing them over to the conscience (or lack of conscience) of every individual subject, absolved from every obligation except to keep within written laws (which a sufficiently cunning man could evade with impunity) was not a government at all. How could it command respect or inculcate obedience, when it passively allowed its misguided citizens to sink into unrestrained bestiality, if such was their desire?

The 'Russian alternative' recommended by Leontiev by no means follows from his diagnosis of the *impasse* in European history. But we must admit that the former, though in a startlingly unexpected shape, seems to have moved many steps nearer to realization than seemed probable in his day. And his diagnosis of the European disease, however shocking to the average European mind, contains undeniable elements of disturbing truth. Leontiev was the first Russian thinker to question the scientific and factual evidence supporting the prevalent Western faith in the all-round social progress and gradual perfectibility of human beings. In this respect, especially in his bold application of judgements of value to large-scale comparative studies of historical civilizations, he deserves to be recognized as a worthy precursor of Oswald Spengler and Arnold Toynbee.

Most thinking Europeans in the nineteenth century took it for granted that the French Revolution, fortified by the ethical teaching of Kant and the Utilitarians, heralded the dawn of a brighter and more progressive era in political organization and human conduct. Leontiev, after due consideration, decided that the importance and originality of these events had been wildly exaggerated. It was all very well for Kant to proclaim 'The starry heavens above me and the moral law within me fill my soul with awe', but what did his categorical imperative mean in practice to the multitude? As for the French Revolution, whatever its good intentions, its political consequences had proved to be a menace and a negation of its aims. It had brought Europe to a fatal turning-point, after which she sank into a feverish wasting sickness, all the more dangerous because it was still unrecognized. For the most vocal Europeans continued to exercise their arts of eloquence in order to persuade themselves —and the outside world—that their chronic illness was no illness at all, but only a drastic course of up-to-date hygiene. They treated Europe's festering self-inflicted wounds as if they were nothing but growing pains, symptoms of sturdy progress towards a healthier social state. 'Since that period,' wrote Leontiev, 'European thought bows down to the human being merely because he is a man. It does not want to honour him because he is a hero or a prophet, an Emperor or a genius. It no longer reveres any rare and high development of human personality, but merely the personality of anyone and everyone, and it endeavours to make everyone happy (here on earth) with equal rights and security, self-satisfied with his own honesty and freedom compressed within the limits of a narrow moral code.' ('The Average European as the Ideal and Instrument of Universal Destruction', 1884.)

The visible social consequences of such a petty, negative and aimless liberty appalled Leontiev. Throughout the whole world he saw the complacent liberal intellect, which held nothing sacred outside itself, quietly spreading its tentacles, or moving forward like a poisonous grey vapour, which enveloped and gradually stifled the vital sense of inner obligation, and obliterated the sharp distinctions of spontaneous and original style. 'Why is it', he asked, 'that Western people are now so fascinated by even the most improbable travellers' tales about the picturesque East? Is it not because they have grown sick of themselves, because European civilization is so busy burying all that is beautiful and inspiring in tomb-like museums or in the shadowy pages of books, whereas to life itself it brings nothing but more and more drabness, physical ugliness, tedious monotony and inward death?' ('The Egyptian Dove', 1881.) 'Both Christian doctrinaires and European progressives, by their united efforts, do all they can to kill the beauty of life on earth—that is life itself.' (Letter to Rozanov, 1891.)

Leontiev's diagnosis of social decline has one rare redeeming merit. It is undefiled by that strain of vulgar class-conscious arrogance with which the champions of proletarians, plutocrats, and other ruling aristocracies and cliques have so persistently plagued us. Indeed he felt so acutely the exacting responsibilities of leadership that he condemns the laxity of rulers and privileged individuals far more severely than he blames the corruption and inertia of the ruled. Since the former had neglected their duty they had allowed the rot to spread unchecked. Having thus forfeited the respect and obedience which had formerly been their due, their blood was on their own heads.

A ray of hope remained to brighten the future of Russian society, so long as the revolutionary darkness from Europe had not spread far enough to overshadow or blot out its Russian source of light. Leontiev was not blind to the many glaring defects of the Tsarist bureaucracy which he had served for several years. But he could never bring himself to condemn organic institutions on the slender pretext that those who represented them were personally unworthy. As a living symbol higher than the state, the Tsar crowned a majestic pyramid, safeguarded an immutable morality of values, impervious to the changing winds of public opinion and to fickle popular votes, and uncontaminated by prevailing calculations of commercial gain. Although he recognized that the ugly social reality fell short of this ideal by an immeasurable distance, he pictured the Emperor and his advisers, resolutely bearing 'the White Man's Burden' of a wise and vigorous administration, promoting the growth of virtue and culture among the inchoate half-savage masses of the Russian Empire.

In this hieratic picture, Russian society, for long naturally stratified into a functional Byzantine hierarchy, moved slowly forward in a solemn religious procession bearing aloft sacred images and banners with inspiring inscriptions. Unless this picture was a fleeting mirage, a mere phantom of wish-fulfilment, might it not—however imperfectly realized—lead Russia towards a healthier future than the slippery road down which all other Western nations seemed to be sliding? Leontiev summed up his warning to revolutionary Westernizers in the following words: 'Wherever the lawful and sacred right of coercion over our will has grown weak, both in the consciousness of those who coerce and in the hearts of those who are coerced, wherever both the ability to govern boldly and the capacity for submitting with love and fear have been undermined, there can be no vital strength, no duration, no stable or lasting order.'

We should pause to consider how Leontiev's strange but sincere faith evolved from the peculiar stress of Russian circumstances, for he would be an inconceivable phenomenon in any other country. The most influential Russian minds of his time had divided into two main rival camps, perpetually scrapping with one another. At one extreme stood those who held the state to be the natural fountain-head and regulator of every social activity, including the citizen's spiritual life; at the other, stood those who, like Bakunin and some Slavophils, relentlessly opposed any form of state, whether monarchical or socialist, as the most potent source of human misery. Leontiev never belonged wholeheartedly to either camp. While his formal principles attached him to the first one, his traditional sympathies drew him towards the second, for Russian culture had always been a heartfelt cry of protest against the Russian state or an imaginative escape from it.

Apart from a small group of Slavophils which crystallized in the forties, most of the intellectually outstanding Russians were confirmed political radicals and religious heretics, if not candid and militant agnostics. They still looked almost exclusively to Western Europe for guidance in their own country's development. Many of them studied in German universities, where they enthusiastically embraced or violently rejected the latest German philosophic systems, especially Hegel's; but they were equally ready to devour and assimilate the soberer products of the English classical economists, together with the more charming and stimulating French Socialists, like Saint-Simon and Fourier. Moreover, these eager assiduous young men were combing the fields of Europe, not as an idle distraction, but in deadly earnest and with a single-minded purpose— to pick out and grasp those seeds which they found best suited for transplanting into Russian soil. To suggest that the leading Westernizers gaped in uncritical admiration at any and every European institution is as crudely exaggerated as to suppose that the Slavophils were ignorant of Europe or hostile to her culture.

Both groups (but the Slavophils less superficially) were saturated with European education, and both, despite their family feuds and quarrels, held one prevailing article of faith in

common. They remained first and foremost fervent Russian patriots, but not in a positive political sense; for they could never
reconcile their purely moral patriotism with loyalty to that
crushing bureaucratic tyranny into which Peter had moulded
the Russian Empire. As Herzen said of them: 'We both had a
single love, though not an identical one, and like Janus, or the
double-headed eagle, we gazed in opposite directions, though
our hearts beat in unison.' Though Herzen does not stress it here,
a strong tincture of hatred contributed to these loving heart-
beats. Burning hatred of Nicolas I's régime was undoubtedly
the first uniting link which drew these turbulent groups together. Uncertainty of driving purpose, further confused by
faulty diagnosis of their country's ailments, remained the
worst stumbling blocks of both. Neither could formulate a line
of thought, realistic enough to include the Empire as a given
source of accumulated Russian characteristics—however deplorable they might be—and simultaneously imaginative
enough to re-vitalize that Empire for a better future.

Leontiev resolved the dilemma by accepting the dynamic
movement of the Empire for what it was, and by foreseeing
how malleable it might become, guided by wiser and abler
hands. He discerned fresh potentialities in the despotism of
intelligent inward impulse imposing a new shape on a weakening disintegrating process. His bold incursion first filled a
puzzling gap in Russian thought, and this feat of interpretation
and forecast constitutes his major title to fame.

II

The accident of his parents' poverty saved Leontiev from being
sent to learn wisdom at a German university. His consular posts
taught him more about South-Eastern Europe than about the
West. He partly admired (with clearly stated reservations) the
Turkish Empire, and he loved the few surviving pagan beauties
of Constantinople and Greece. Conventional critics have found
this eastward-looking Russian embarrassing to pigeon-hole, and
they have in turn described him as a progressive conservative, an inspired prophet, and a wild Byzantine reactionary—
the few condescending words assigned to him by the Soviet
Encyclopaedia follow this last interpretation.

Any study of his writings and career compels us to admit that not a single one of these labels can stick to him securely. He repeatedly attacked the stagnant official conservative point of view, disliked Pobyedonostsev, Alexander III's *éminence grise*, and called him 'not a creator, nor even a reactionary, but a mere conservative in the narrowest sense of the word. He can stop further decay like a frost, but he will never help anything to grow'. As for being a reactionary, if that means a nostalgic determination to put the clock back, Leontiev refused to waste his time in playing with such silly notions. 'However much we may love the past', he wrote curtly, 'it would be absurd to try to bring back its institutions, even approximately'. Of his student days he observed later that the struggle and excitement of revolution appealed to his adventurous temperament, at a time when he had thought too little about the real harm or usefulness of revolutionary action and its later consequences.

During these restless formative years he confined his written work to novels and imaginative stories. He was still a poverty-stricken medical student at Moscow University when the Crimean War broke out. He volunteered, and served throughout the campaign as a military surgeon. Then, after a short period as a doctor in civilian life, he entered the Russian Consular Service where he remained till 1872, filling successive posts in Crete, Adrianople and Salonika. He was obliged to leave Crete because in a heated dispute with the French Consul he struck him with a whip in his own Chancery—an incident which did not hinder his rapid promotion, and which he recalled later as one of his happier moments. In 1869 his wife became mentally deranged—a shadow which darkened the rest of his life. He first started to write seriously on political and social themes after he left the Consular Service, and his most substantial essay 'Byzantinism and Slavdom' was conceived in Constantinople, where he spent a year in 1872–3. By that time his mind and outlook had matured, and he wrote with a sharp clarity and consistent personal conviction quite rare among Russian political thinkers, who so often failed to recover from their chilly plunge into the turbid grey ocean of German philosophy.

Furthermore, Leontiev's long and intimate experience of Russian foreign policy and of the entangled 'Eastern question,' seen from inside the Ottoman Empire, imparts an unforgettably vivid local colour to many of his observations. In 1879 he became Assistant Editor of the newspaper *Warsaw Diary*, and a year later he joined the staff of the Moscow censorship department. Ill-health obliged him to retire in 1887, when he settled down in a small house near the Optina Monastery where he died in 1891, after secretly taking monastic vows, but without having lived under strict monastic discipline.

By upbringing a tradition-loving landowner, by temperament a full-blooded but discerning pagan, in turn a professional surgeon, consular official, religious-minded journalist, and most un-Christian monk, Leontiev enriched the texture of his paradoxical thought by gathering from a storehouse of strange encounters, hardly comprehensible to many of his desk-bound academic critics. That is why the more one-track-minded intellectuals have been reluctant to acknowledge how far he went in elucidating those same problems which tormented his opponents—and which plague the world of today on a larger scale.

Uppermost in his mind floated the fantastic and always cloudy vision of a vigorous and universal Russian civilization, a crowning synthesis of the best that had gone before. Through its sustaining medium, mutually exclusive sovereignties, proud but enfeebled 'national characters', clashing in suicidal competition with one another's claims to final loyalty, would reach fresh guidance and purpose under a multi-national Russo-Byzantine world Empire. Hence, secondly, his laudable concern for the unprecedented spiritual quality indispensable to make such an arduous Empire worth fighting for, his emphasis on the immense civilizing benefits it must confer in order to qualify as a worthy alternative, superior to the commercial-minded democratic West. Finally, he sought to unravel the future course of relations between this incipient Eurasian Orthodox Empire and the older declining Empires and nation-states of Europe. He thought the Asiatic countries hardly counted on their own, since their weakness had already drawn them under the European system. Or rather, they would only start to count if Russia failed, as Europe was doing, by allowing within herself an indiscriminate debilitating mixture of races, religions, classes and customs. 'I suppose', Leontiev tartly observed, 'that the Chinese may conquer Russia if our dilution with Europeans reaches such a saturation point. That is the only road—*for such a Russia!*'

Indeed Leontiev parted company from all his social-revolu-
tionary and reformist contemporaries in that he saw no valid
raison d'être for the future Russian state, unless it was solidly
built on the foundations of the existing one. If it went the same
way as revolutionary Europe, it would do better to crumble into
dust, because in that guise it would benefit nobody, least of all
itself. What did Leontiev mean by the unique foundations of the
Russian state? Clearly he did not seek them in immutable forms
of government or in sacrosanct and static laws. For him all
institutions and laws were transitory. He pointed to more
deeply embedded underlying characteristics, to the impulse
imparted by a harsh and stormy national history, moulding
the character of the Russian people, but most of all, to the
Byzantine tradition of government as a sacred civilizing force,
standing above the prosaic administrative machinery of the
state.

European political thinkers have normally taken for granted
that the Tsars never accepted any legal authority or overriding
religious sanction, which their own arbitrary fiats could not
defy. This judgement harps overmuch on the effects of Tartar
despotism, which during two and a half centuries undoubtedly
hardened the average Russian to endure the most brutal and
capricious tyranny. It does less justice to the Kiev period, which
revered Byzantine laws, and it slurs over national factors which
subsequently defeated the Tartars.

Byzantine versions of Roman statute books stated, though
ambiguously, that the sovereign's power was strictly limited by
conformity to Christian injunctions. In practice this oriental
and Erastian divine right of kings was flexible enough to justify
most sovereign dictates. But the capture of Constantinople by
the Turks (1453) transformed the situation. It simultaneously
magnified the new moral responsibilities of the Russian Empire
and widened the scope of its arbitrary character. The Orthodox
Church began to preach the sanctity of Moscow as the Third
Rome, and of the Tsar as the only legitimate heir of the extinct
Byzantine Emperors, the chief defender of Christendom from
heathen barbarians. When Ivan III married Sophia Paleologus,
the daughter of the last Byzantine Emperor, he visibly invested
Holy Russia with the full Byzantine heritage. The letters
written to him by the Greek Abbot Philotheus address him as
'Sole Autocrat of the Universe, only Tsar of the Christians'

and exhort him dutifully to maintain true orthodoxy intact until the Second Coming of Christ. 'Two Romes have fallen, but the Third stands, and a Fourth there will never be.'

Thus fortified by priestly adulation and popular faith, the Tsar rose to the sacred majesty of a universal priest-king, wielding absolute authority in God's name. Even if he were a brutal tyrant, a usurper, or a useless weakling, he became as Tsar the divinely appointed ruler whom Christians must dutifully obey. His victims should patiently endure their ruler's errors and crimes as a scourge sent by God to punish people for their many sins. Good and bad rulers, like good and bad harvests, came from the inscrutable judgement of God. After Peter the Great abolished the autonomous Patriarchate and replaced it by the state-appointed Holy Synod, the narrow surviving margin between temporal and spiritual power was finally obliterated. Both merged in a theocratic autocracy, incarnate in the personally responsible Emperor.

III

During Leontiev's lifetime this medieval and Asiatic mixture played its part in moulding the stern régime of Nicolas I and in producing the famous official formula—Orthodoxy, Autocracy and National Character (*Narodnost'*). But the hard ingredients had not yet petrified into a motionless rock. Life in Russia, even official life, had not entirely lost the savour of personal aspiration. On the contrary, the final item in this triad stood for a newly discovered faith, And it showed that the Empire had aptly unfolded its own banner of national character at a most apposite moment, when European upheavals threatened to lead astray the inarticulate popular feelings of all countries left without clear governmental guidance.

The report which his Minister of Public Education (Count Uvarov) presented to Nicolas I in 1843 throws a sharp light on the more constructive ideas of the Russian government at that time. 'The redeeming conviction', wrote Uvarov, 'that Russia lives and preserves herself through the spirit of a strong, humane, enlightened autocracy must penetrate our whole popular education and develop in harmony with it . . . National character does not force us either to go backwards or to stand still;

it does not demand immutability of ideas. The framework of the state, like a human body, changes its outward appearance according to its growth . . . It is enough if we preserve the inviolable sanctuary of our national qualities.' Although Uvarov's words verge on the supremely polished condescension of a Chinese Imperial rescript, they cannot be dismissed as empty official hypocrisy. That they had some practical bearing on educational policy is clear from the following statement in the same report. 'Without excluding people of the serf class from participating in the beneficial fruits of knowledge and enlightenment, the Ministry has considered it indispensable to do so according to the measure of the genuine needs and the direct mental and moral benefit which could be derived by people of that class. The education of serfs is therefore confined to the parish and district schools.' In fact serfs were also admitted to the higher schools, but only if their masters gave them their freedom.

Leontiev analysed acutely the effect of some of the major internal reforms of Alexander II, especially the educational ones, on the quality of Russian society. He argued with some justice that, although these reforms were acclaimed by the liberals as steps along the upward path of Europeanization, their impact had awoken sleeping Russian instincts, and provoked them more and more into asserting their own essentially un-European national consciousness. The emancipation of the serfs, for instance, focused public attention for the first time on the ancient peasant commune as the corner-stone of agricultural organization. Consequently the peculiarly Russian *mir*, as an administrative organ and centre, became under the new legal settlements much more prominent than it had been before 1861. Even the propaganda of the *Sovremennik* group, applauding every foreign innovation so long as it took a Socialist shape, cooled down in the sixties. Their attitude to European institutions became more guarded, less indiscriminate, more selectively utilitarian (good or bad *for Russia*)—reflecting some of Herzen's bitter disappointment in Europe after 1848. They shared in that fleeting revival of self-confidence in native Russian integrity and enterprise—a mood which brightened the early reform period of Alexander II. Western Europe, by comparison, especially when it was seen at close quarters in the sober light of day, failed to fulfil those sanguine expectations which so many progressive-minded Russians liked to forecast. After 1848 only a fading dream survived of that European example and initiative which Russia had accepted and followed without question throughout the eighteenth century.

On the same score Leontiev expressed grave misgivings about the sweeping extension of primary and secondary education in European style, which took place under Alexander II from 1864 onwards. The illiterate Russian masses with their ancient peasant wisdom seemed to him the last unspoiled reserve of spontaneous national character capable of saving Russia from dissolving into an insipid cosmopolitan jelly. Leontiev said that Russian silence in the face of European taunts about her mass illiteracy was wrongly understood as embarrassment in admitting a bitter truth. But, he rejoined: 'I do not find this truth is bitter. It is rather our merit than our misfortune.' While he was living in the Danubian towns, he observed: 'I felt ashamed, not for the Russians with their illiterate simplicity, but for the Greeks with their literate ignorance. The Greeks, Moldavians, etc., admire us only to the extent that we are European; it does not enter their heads to admire us for our Russian qualities. . . . What is that mass, that ocean, the Russian people, which they regard as dumb and brutal, because it stands remote from their petty and dry demagogic movements? That they cannot know and cannot learn so long as we ourselves are higher than they.' (*Gramotnost' i Narodnost'*, 1870.) He was far from advocating illiteracy or blissful ignorance as virtues for their own sake. He merely argued that the educated section of the Russian people ought not to start extending their instruction to the uneducated part, until it (the educated part) had grown more mature, more certain of its own aims. Widespread school education could bear good fruit only when landowners, officials, teachers, etc., people of mixed, hazy, German or Anglo-French ideas, had all become much more *Russian* than they were under the influence of the latest European theories. 'We should be glad', wrote Leontiev, 'that our common people dislike and distrust our intelligentsia. The ideas and political tastes of our intelligentsia are all borrowed, but our people (*narod*) have their own ideas and tastes. If we draw too close to the people we only injure them; we injure them not in that coarse sense of depriving them of some material gain, but in the far more important sense that we almost unconsciously teach them

European ways, and cannot avoid doing so, because we ourselves up till now have proved incapable of inventing anything of our own, and so far as national creativeness goes, we stand lower than Asiatic people, Indians, Chinese or Moslems, who have almost entirely created their own mode of life.' (*Gramotnost' i Narodnost'*, 1870.)

In paying this just tribute to the greater integrity of the uneducated Russian, Leontiev cherished no rosy Rousseauesque illusions about the 'noble savagery' of the Russian people *en masse*. For him the fact that they were simple peasant folk or members of the Slav race conferred on them no marks of superior merit. Those national qualities which they preserved, and which he singled out for admiration had even less to do with class than with race—except in so far as class distinctions, corresponding to distinctions of function, remained an immutable element in the Byzantine hierarchy. A peasant might have admirable qualities, but a peasant without a master became a fish out of water, if not a more dangerously destructive animal. Leontiev referred to the Pugachëv revolt as 'one of those bestial atrocities to which our God-fearing people are only too prone when the government whip is not raised over them'. Indeed he found fault with the muddle-headed sentimentality of the whole *Narodnik* Movement. 'In these words, humble yourself in front of the people—especially in front of the peasant—there is confusion and partial falsehood. Why should we humble ourselves before the common people? Out of respect for their physical labour? That respect, everyone knows, can be taken for granted, and many of our serf-owners understood it long ago. Is it then in order to imitate their moral qualities? They have, of course, some admirable ones. But I do not think that the family, social and personal qualities of our common people are on the whole so worthy of imitation. It is hardly necessary to imitate their harsh treatment of the sick and feeble, their wild cruelty when they are angry, their drunkenness, their disposition to cunning trickery, and even to fraud.' And writing of the Crimean War, in which he had fought, Leontiev remarked: 'Some members of the nobility at that time certainly bowed down to the Karatayevs, but not the Nicolas Vronskys of Rostovs of the forties, who, while they loved the Karatayevs, were ready to give them a beating on necessary occasions.' (*Analysis, Style, and Trend*, 1890.)

IV

A healthy and more fruitful co-operation between the dominant minority and the masses could only be restored if the former strengthened their flagging leadership and thereby recovered respect for their authority. Leontiev frankly declared that he thought the majority of Russians were by nature wholly incapable of benefiting from any higher degree of personal freedom and initiative. Hence European education would do them more harm than good. Unless they were perpetually pricked by the spur of coercion and fear, not only would they stagnate individually, but they would let everything around them fall to rack and ruin. For the same reason Leontiev was sceptical about the ruling capacity of the Europeanized Russian upper class, since their convictions and self-confidence had been too much shaken by imported notions about human equality. 'These Russian Europeans', he said, 'are often very loyal; they are ready to send their sons to death for the Tsar, and they are not afraid to sacrifice their property.' He thought that the Russian nobility, with all their faults, contained more generous-hearted, honest and trustworthy people than any other class of Russian society. But their virtues were much more personal than civic; they were too unstable, too easily carried away by new impressions, and they lacked a strict organizing political quality. The clumsy philanthropic innovations of the more 'advanced' landowners and officials were neither appreciated nor understood by the ordinary peasants, who preferred firm, severe but 'Russian' masters and responded most readily to strong and even ruthless leadership. Readers of Turgenev will recall with a smile, among his portrait gallery of well-meaning eccentrics, the improving landowner who satisfied his agricultural conscience by ordering an expensive threshing-machine from Germany, then locked it away in his barn and conveniently forgot about it for the rest of his life, because the peasants disliked the idea of using such an infernal foreign machine.

Half-savage vigour, undisciplined but enterprising ardour to learn (the fatal attraction to Europe was itself a symptom of this ardour), innate fear of sin, love for the principle of coercive power—these were the elemental constructive qualities, more social than personal, which for Leontiev most clearly distinguished Russians from Europeans. Russian Westernizers, *i.e.* all liberals or socialists of either French or German schools, proved themselves to be blind or hypocritical when they refused to reckon with these basic Russian qualities, especially when they babbled that new and better Russians could be fabricated out of Western moulds. Their case was further weakened by the latest evidence from Europe itself. Had not those same Western nations, which had achieved the fullest range of civil liberties and economic prosperity, pitifully failed to win those more ultimate *civilizing* benefits which the people who preached and fought for them foretold?

From what present impediments could European democratic progress free us, Leontiev went on to ask, and in return for what positive future gain? He elaborated his analysis and his negative answer in a number of remarkable essays, the most substantial of which are 'Byzantinism and Slavdom' (1875), 'The Average European as the Ideal and Instrument of Universal Destruction' (1884), 'Racial Politics as a Weapon of World Revolution' (1888). The upshot of Leontiev's argument is that the *recent* social development of the West, far from providing the East with an example of what to follow, is the grimmest warning of a landslide, to be avoided at any cost. 'In abandoning their former social order Europeans have become neither better, nor wiser nor happier. They have grown pettier, more uniformly insignificant, less talented. True, there is mass education, but it is stupider than before. Is it not stupid to believe so blindly as most European-educated people do today, in something utterly impossible, in the final triumph of justice and well-being on earth, in a colourless, impersonal bourgeois or workers' earthly paradise, lit by electric light and talking by telephone from Kamchatka to the Cape of Good Hope? . . . It is ridiculous to serve such an ideal, which fails to correspond either to the experience of history or to any of the laws and examples of natural science. Organic nature lives by diversity, antagonism and struggle : it reveals its harmony in that antagonism and not in any shallow unison.' (*Russkii Vyestnik*, January 1896.)

The technical progress of exact science had fostered pathetic illusions of a corresponding spiritual advance. Only in Russia had the tree of knowledge not yet sucked dry the tree of life. For only there society had remained hierarchical without fossilizing into oriental immobility. The Russian state (though perilously near) had not yet turned into a satellite revolving round the sun of Europe; it moved more slowly, but round its own centre of gravity. For it differed from all Western states, not only in degree but in kind. Its unique body-politic, so unlike prosaic Western governmental machinery, functioned like a complex organism, deriving motive force neither through reforms extorted by threats from below, nor through governmental repressions and severity alone, but through the interaction of faith, power, laws and traditions, together with that inward freedom of personality which remains possible even under torture.

Above all, Russia never was, and never could be, a purely racial Slavonic Empire. By her history, by her social stratification, by her racial complexity alone, she had grown into the most un-Slavonic of all the Slav nations. She suffered far less from racial or national fixation than either the Poles, the Czechs or even the Southern Slavs. A Russian peasant would describe himself as 'pravoslavny' (Orthodox), but the epithet 'Russian', he applied only to the language which he spoke. Indeed, it is very much to Leontiev's credit that, with all his anti-European prejudices, he cherished none of the morbidly exalted Narcissus-like pan-Slav love for Slavs. He did not shrink from wounding national vanities when he pointed out that the Russian state was a mixed product of influences entirely foreign to any basic Slav qualities. 'A purely Slavonic content is much too poor for its universal spirit.' Its strong spiritual discipline was of Byzantine origin; order and accuracy in administration had been taught by the largely German bureaucracy of Peter the Great; mixed blood (much of it Tartar) flowed in the veins of Russian nobles who provided so many of the most vigorous national leaders.

But the keystone of the state arch Leontiev found in Byzantium, its sacred autocracy, in its peculiar Eastern Christianity, irreconcilable with any Western churches or sects. As for Slavdom, it remained for him an enigmatic sphinx, something confused and shapeless, a vague floating ethnographical expression and sentiment, linking Great Russians and other Slavs only by related languages and by similar though indescribably mixed blood. Byzantium, on the contrary, as taken over by Russia, stood for clear-cut intelligible principles, firmly embodied in government institutions, religious ritual and personal habit, as well as in tangible and inspiring artistic forms. Without the organizing moral force of Byzantium, how could the Russian state have survived Tartar misrule? Did it not equally sustain Russian unity in her long battles with Poland, with the Swedes, with France and Turkey? 'Reverence for the church and obedience to the Emperor saved Russia in 1812!' 'Under this banner, if we are true to it, we shall be powerful enough to withstand the onslaught of the whole of international Europe, if after destroying everything noble within herself, she dares at any time to invade us with the decay and shame of her new laws and petty material well-being.' (*Russkii Vyestnik*, January 1896.)

IV

Leontiev felt convinced that the democratic republics of Europe would be more bitterly hostile to the Russian Empire than monarchical Europe had ever been. The Soviet Union is only intensifying a traditional policy when she stands on guard against what is now termed 'capitalist encirclement'. For those who believe that psychological as well as economic motives underlie Russian foreign policy—always so puzzling to foreigners but so crystal-clear to themselves—Leontiev's picture of long-term national objectives is vivid and (for that period) plausible. But he goes further than analysis of past and present motives in state policy. He boldly predicts—and here he is at one with Danilevsky—that the Russian Empire had not yet reached its highest stage of flowering complexity. If the historical beginning of any state always marks with an indelible imprint the whole unfolding movement of its people, then certain innate features, not so visibly important at first, will thrust themselves most emphatically to the fore, as the state approaches maturity.

His faith in the imperial shape of Russian fulfilment fully explains why Leontiev hated Russian liberals even more than he hated revolutionaries. The latter (unless they belonged to a European intellectual school) could be excused as unhappy victims of mad impulse and despair; but the former, who deliberately made a fetish of alien European ways, without observing that these were hastening Europe's downfall, betrayed a criminal ignorance of the innermost essence of the Russian state. Not content with pitifully aping a Europe which they did not understand, they surreptitiously undermined all that had formed the unique thousand-year-old foundation of the original Kiev and Moscow Russia. Yet in spite of his passionate concern to save the Russian Empire, one terrible misgiving racked Leontiev's mind. Could it be that the undeniable decline of his contemporary Petersburg Russia was due, less to the subtle poison spreading through its limbs from a decadent Europe, than to its own organic enfeeblement and ripe old age? He could find no conclusive answer. 'Whether we begin our history with Rurik (862) or with the baptism of Vladimir (988) we are very little younger than Europe, whose social history should be reckoned from the ninth century (the reign of Charlemagne). Not all states have continued for a thousand years. It is hard to survive longer, easy to vanish earlier.' (*Russkii Vyestnik*, January 1896.)

At other times he seemed to believe with Herzen that the Slav world was still much younger and fresher than the European, because Slav childhood had lasted longer, because their history had remained nearly stationary, through not having grown and changed with the passage of time. People might hate Russia, but they could not say of her as they said of France, that she was senile or decrepit. He faced the issue most squarely when he wrote in 1880 : 'Russia is now in the grip of a quiet, slow decay, one of those Great Russian processes is taking place, which with us always precedes a profound historic upheaval—the baptism of the Kiev people in the Dnieper, Peter's destruction of national traditions, and finally the present state of affairs, essentially a transition towards something different.'

Russia might still save herself, if she stood firm and acted energetically on her own initiative, after casting off the cramping tutelage of democratic Europe. Her only alternative was to merge and sink her national identity by joining the grey amorphous republicanism of Europe, but that step would be equivalent to her death. Meanwhile Byzantium remained the clearly drawn ground-plan of a spacious building, in which the upper stories had not yet been started. Only a Russian Empire revived from its own original sources of strength could continue to build them. Woe to Russia and to the world if this effort failed ! 'Russia's internal decay should lead to action which must be

spontaneous and creative, in order to avoid becoming wholly
destructive (I do not mean in the European sense, but infinitely
more destructive).' (*Letters on the Eastern Question, Grajdanin,*
1882–1883.)

Moreover, Russian governmental power provided for Leontiev the only trustworthy guide into an otherwise shapeless
future. Without superior power, how would she be able either
to resist a disintegrating Europe, or to preserve the smaller
Slav countries, still more prone than Russia herself to imitate
Europe, weaker and more politically fluid? Byzantine elements
were indispensable to Russian power. Once they fell into discredit, the centrifugal forces of the vast heterogeneous Empire
would quickly gain the upper hand, the whole top-heavy structure would crack, totter, and finally split into its multifarious
national and racial constituent parts.

Leontiev showed scant sympathy with what he called the
'tribal nationalism' of insignificant or second-rate peoples. He
judged 'cosmopolitan democracy and political nationalism
(without any principles of culture or spontaneous force)' to be
merely two distinct aspects of the same decaying process. 'For
the French, *who started it,* this cosmopolitan ideal was patriotic
and national. For other nations the national question turned
into naked racial politics. . . . This was so deceptive, and people
were so blinded by it, that many thinking patriots (even our
Slavophils) failed to recognize in the so-called national movement their worst enemy—the cosmopolitan revolution! It
spread everywhere, beginning in 1821 with the Greek uprising.
Its result was everywhere the same—liberal democracy and
dreary cosmopolitan uniformity of ideas, tastes, desires and outward appearances. *Had it not been for Russia,* this blending and
debasement would have been worst of all among the Slavs,
owing to their proneness to imitate, their political weakness and
poverty of thought.' (*Letters on the Eastern Question, Grajdanin,*
1882.)

This same conception of Russia as a supernational civilizing
force can be used to justify that high-handed attitude to smaller
nations, which is such a familiar ingredient of Russian political
practice. Even the most enlightened Russian patriotism has
seldom been compatible with respect for the patriotic feelings
of smaller nations, unless they are weak enough to be meekly
subservient to Russia. Leontiev's contempt is eminently sincere,

especially for the Slav countries 'liberating' themselves from
Turkish rule. 'What would happen?' he asked, 'to all those
learned and liberal Slavs with all their orators, professors,
doctors and petty national pride, if in the distant background of
the picture there was not visible the expanse of Great Russian
snow, the Cossack lances, and the axe of the bearded Orthodox
peasant, calmly and firmly guided by our half Byzantine
Tsar?'

Occasionally in his more exalted passages Leontiev approached the pan-Slav Danilevsky in proclaiming the Russian
mission to lead a new original independent civilization, not
only through uniting the Slavs politically—but by swallowing
up and transforming the whole of Europe, even as Europe had
swallowed up and transformed Roman, ancient Greek and in
part Byzantine civilization. In 1882 he wrote: 'Pan-Slavism may
be inevitable—But Orthodox pan-Slavism is salvation, whereas
liberal pan-Slavism means ruin, most of all for Russia.' But, to
do him justice, he more often revealed how sceptical he felt
about the realization, and even more about the practical value,
of such boundless political ambitions. Past history seemed to
demonstrate that no single state could last much longer than a
thousand years—and the Russian state was only slightly
younger than the 'senile' European ones, who had reached
their third and final phase of dissolution. Moreover, Leontiev
was honest enough to admit that—hard as he tried—he could
find in Russians no encouraging signs (except in literature) of
original constructive genius—and still less in other Slav peoples.
He had the highest respect and even love for traditional European civilization. He only condemned its final contemporary
phase because it was rotting away and infecting healthier
neighbours. Russian civilization, though it was bound to be
different, might still prove to be inferior to Europe at her best.
Most of the Slavophils liked to think that the curious lack of
mental fertility and inventiveness among Russians in the past
provided proof of their immaturity and youthfulness, and were
signs of tremendous budding potentialities only waiting to be
released from bondage. But Leontiev reasonably questioned
whether so many centuries of monotonous poverty, in spite of
endless borrowing from other countries, gave any guarantee
that native talent would burst into sudden luxuriant bloom in
the immediate future. Even the Slavophil Khomyakov observed

plaintively on one occasion that all Russian science had so far failed to invent so much as a decent mouse-trap.

In comparing Russia with European states, Leontiev contended that no nation or civilization could survive for long if the state containing them was built on soft or shifting foundations. History showed him that democratic republics were more unstable than aristocratic ones, while hierarchical monarchies (like Egypt or Byzantium) lasted much longer than either. And he hated the plutocratic liberal form of democracy as the most empty, futile and unprincipled of all human societies. 'There is reason to hope,' he said, 'that the present agrarian and labour problems will resolve themselves into nothing other than a new form of feudalism—a new special kind of compulsory attachment to organizations, classes and communities, and in part of individuals to other individuals placed above them in career and function.' (*Temple and Church, Grajdanin*, 1878). Meanwhile, European democracy had betrayed the heritage of European culture; by corrupting both her own people and outsiders who fell under her sway, Europe was leading the world to universal disintegration. In his essay 'Why is Liberalism harmful to us?' (*Warsaw Diary*, 1880) he wrote: 'The system of democratic liberalism is the absence of any system, a denial of any absolute values, a fear of everything consistent and bold. In the thirties and forties it was noble and even brave to be liberal. Now it is so easy, and demands so little intelligence, knowledge or effort . . . I prefer to stick to 'The Tsar and Russia', for I confess I cannot understand the French who are able to love any France and are ready to serve any kind of French Government. I want my country to be worthy of my respect.'

Apart from the instinctive personal disgust which Leontiev felt against the prevailing ethos of the new democratic states, he considered them to be hopelessly fluid and unstable, drifting rudderless towards some dark abyss in the future, an abyss which was not yet clearly visible, but whose proximity had already begun to fill thoughtful people with deep apprehension or despair.

During Leontiev's lifetime the various brands of anarchic, syndicalist or state socialism were far from being so sharply distinguished from liberal democracy as they are, both in theory and practice, today. In any case the classical liberal doctrine of a state with strictly limited authority, relying on a sound individual conscience to do the most important things, was being step by step abandoned during this period even by liberals themselves. The Western type of social democracy had developed from below through the successful agitation of organized labour groups, and from above through governmental programmes of gradual reform, both involving an extension of the government's sphere of action. This process inevitably widened the state's functions and increased its power, while it gave ample evidence of fusion in practice between Liberal and Socialist movements. Therefore, although Leontiev's judgements sound far too sweeping to be accurate in detail, the march of events compels us to admit that he was right in principle when he identified the supporters of both movements as 'believers in liberal egalitarian progress'.

V

Indeed, if enlightened autocracy failed to rise to the occasion by providing bold leadership on its own initiative, Leontiev seemed ready to back the avowed revolutionaries against the moderate and cautious reformers. 'Revolutionaries', he wrote, 'everywhere despise our moderate liberals—and they are right in despising them. Though these extremists may fight genuine conservatives to the death, yet they will find all the essential conservative doctrines indispensable to themselves. They too will need fear. They too will need discipline, hardened by a tradition of obedience to orders and habitual acceptance; and nations (let us suppose) who have successfully reshaped their economic system, but who are none the less dissatisfied with everything on earth, will start to burn again with mystic fires. . . . Social organisms, including Western ones, may lose the strength to resist de-stratification, or those chronic cruelties without which it is impossible to build anything durable out of human material. Perhaps the alliance of socialism (the slavery of the future, as the liberal Spencer called it) with Russian autocracy and with a fiery mysticism (which philosophy will serve like a faithful dog) is still a possible outcome, but this will be a horrible thing for a great number of people.' (Letter to V. Rozanov, written in 1890; pub. *Russian Messenger*, May, 1903.)

Leontiev accused all liberals either of blind stupidity or sheer deliberate deceit. Either they were too short-sighted to see more than one step ahead, or they persisted in pursuing an obviously impossible goal. For him a true belief in progress could only be a pessimistic one—destroying absurd and puerile illusions about any approaching paradise on earth. The way to belief lay through unbelief. Such a qualified pessimism of general outlook, far from amounting to defeatism, was no more than a healthy and honest admission of human fallibility. Pessimists, who relinquished that crazy belief in the possibility of universal human well-being or happiness, would achieve more optimistic results in personal life. They would not expect too much from people, they would be more wisely tolerant, humane and well-balanced than restless agitators for a future golden age, to be attained by equalizing reforms, or by extraordinary discoveries in physics and chemistry.

Furthermore, had liberals been less short-sighted, they would surely have admitted that, whatever else the new state forms in Europe might eventually become, they could not possibly remain much longer peaceful, liberal or mild. Leontiev rightly foretold that increasingly complicated world-wide politico-economic problems, imposing themselves on future national governments, would prove terrific obstacles to the retention of any kindly and moderate liberal faith. In 1880 he already wrote that socialism as a profound and to some extent violent economic upheaval might be unavoidable, at least for part of the human race. 'Without dwelling', he remarked, 'on the amount of suffering and humiliation which this upheaval will inflict on the conquered, even the conquerors will soon understand that they are very far from having reached well-being and peace. These coming conquerors would either organize more freely, more liberally than we do, in which case the new society would be stricken by a kind of chronic legalized anarchy, like certain South American republics or some of the ancient Greek city democracies. Alternatively, their laws and requirements would be infinitely severer than ours, more exacting, more cramping, more ruthless and fierce. In the latter case, people's lives will be much harder and less healthy than are now the lives of good conscientious monks in strict Orthodox monasteries. Thus after trying every experiment, even the bitter extreme of socialist organization, the leaders themselves of these new societies are bound to grow deeply disillusioned.

U

. . . It will never be better for everybody, it may be better for some, but it will be worse for others.' ('On Dostoevsky's Speech at the Pushkin Festival', *Warsaw Diary*, 1880.)

VI

Leontiev seems to have sincerely believed that we might all escape such a dismal fate if the Russian Empire took on a new lease of life. In order to make sure of this, the most important political change he advocated was a bold solution of the Eastern Question, enabling Russia to place herself at the head of a new Orthodox Eastern Empire, which would then become the leader of a completely anti-European movement. 'We should prefer the traumatic shock of a great war to slow chemical poisoning through contact with Europe', he frankly announced. That ambition was very nearly achieved in 1878, but the full fruits of her victory over Turkey were promptly and resolutely snatched from Russia by the united European powers at the Congress of Berlin. Leontiev wrote in that year: 'How comforting it would have been to read about the triumphant march of our victorious bodyguard with music and flying banners through the motley streets of Istanbul, majestic even in its squalor. How terrible to think that what is most indispensable to us—Tsargrad and the Straits—is slipping once more out of our hands. . . . Our own moral need to achieve a clear and visible triumph is something far removed from Chauvinism. That stupid word, invented by pacifist liberals, was then applied to French ambition, which merely pursued glory to gratify its vanity, without any beneficial concrete result!' (*Temple and Church*, *Grajdanin*, 1878.)

During his term of service as Russian Consul in Turkey, Leontiev had scope to observe and comment on the brutal side of Turkish rule over the Balkan Christians. He none the less maintained that, chiefly owing to Ottoman severity, genuine Orthodox religion and Slav feeling had been stimulated and kept alive. 'Living in Turkey I soon understood, though with horror and grief, that thanks only to the Turks, Orthodox and Slav sentiment had survived in the Balkans.' (*A Hermit's Letter*, *Vostok*, 1879.) The old Slavophils had fondly imagined that the eclipse of the Turkish crescent would be followed immediately by the rising of a brilliant Orthodox sun in the Christian East.

But, instead of that, the weakening Turkish grip over the Balkans exposed the Balkan Slavs to the infiltration of a petty provincial nationalism from the West. Consequently Leontiev began to fear that the Russian Empire might step in too late to replace Ottoman discipline by its own superior organizing power. 'How could we not foresee that a Bulgarian schoolmaster, merchant, doctor or shopkeeper, even a political leader of peasant or shopkeeper origin, would find quite inaccessible and undesirable all that was so clear and eminently desirable to Kireyevsky, Khomyakov and Aksakov? For were not these all Russian aristocrats, gifted, learned, enlightened, moved by strong ideals, saturated in European culture? That is why our disappointment is now so deep, so shameful . . . I say 'our', because I too went fifteen years ago to the Near East, a pupil, a follower of that cultural Slavophilism, which was intended to spring up and flower so luxuriantly on the indestructible ancient roots of Orthodoxy.'

Leontiev felt disgusted that the Slavophils had started to grow famous and influential only at the cost of abandoning their most valuable belief in an independent and original Russian civilization, and after they had degenerated into strident propagandists for the mere liberation of the Balkan Slavs from all that till then had prevented them from turning into the most commonplace European petty bourgeois. But he did not abandon all sense of proportion; he never claimed that his own forecast of Russia's brilliant civilizing future revealed an emergent law of nature. Moreover, while it was bound to be different, he did not rule out the possibility that the new Russian civilization might be, not better, but infinitely worse than Western Europe, or might fail to materialize altogether.

Nor did he favour destroying the Ottoman Empire by war. He contented himself with urging that its capital should be removed from Constantinople to Asia Minor. It is far-fetched to infer that he dreamed of world-conquest. In retrospect he surveyed more calmly and deliberately the climax of the Eastern Question in 1878. 'We should think less about the liberation of the Balkans than about their re-organization. The weakened Sultanate was unable to resist being Europeanized. *But we can, if we want to.* . . . We showed we could in the last war, and, far more important, we showed it in the realm of political thought by the manifesto of April 29, 1881.

'In the face of constitutional Europe and of all republican America, we then announced that we did not intend to live any longer on foreign minds, but would put all our strength into making autocracy effective and stern. Turning away sharply (and God grant for ever) from the course of emancipating society and individuals, we started on the course of emancipating our own thought; we changed from the pursuit of gradual but certain destruction to the pursuit of well-organized and creative life. Through this action we decided for the first time since Peter the Great to be original, not only in the sense of asserting our authority as a strong state among other states, but in formulating a unique political and cultural ideal, bold, independent and clear.' (*Letters on the Eastern Question, Grajdanin*, 1882.)

Leontiev's horror of contemporary Europe is unlikely to endear him to many European hearts. In its agitated intensity it verges on the pathological. And his downright condemnation of nineteenth-century liberalism failed to draw any distinction between the English, French, German and Russian brands. Not only the Manchester liberals, but the aristocratic Whig liberals of England (who impressed Khomyakov and Koshelëv and might therefore have found some echo in Leontiev's fastidious temperament) were indiscriminately lumped together with the glib French bourgeois and the coarse German demagogue. What mattered to him was that they all *seemed* then to be moving in a similar direction, and through this disintegrating flux of democratic progress their former vital distinctions and varieties would eventually merge into a single featureless uniformity—(the exact reverse of civilized development, which Leontiev defined as 'an increase in disciplined variety').

Leontiev hated the new Europe platonically and on principle, and not through any sense of personal spite, for he had never lived there except in the almost oriental south-east. 'Can we either pity or admire the majority of contemporary Europeans? How could we pity them? They are so self-satisfied and impudent, they are so far ahead of us and the Asiatics in many technical and material advantages. Even the poor European artisan of our day is so conceited, without a trace of spiritual humility, so absorbed in his vaunted personal dignity and petty personal welfare, that one could hardly feel much spontaneous sympathy for him; and what could one feel through cold reflection, by straining oneself to picture him as a victim of hard economic circumstances? It seems to me that in order to feel any influx to the heart of that moral love or disinterested admiration, we should first need to see the contemporary European humbled, conquered, wounded or imprisoned. ('On Dostoevsky's Speech at the Pushkin Festival', *Warsaw Diary*, 1880.)

It is all the more remarkable that Herzen, who spent so many years of exile in France and England, and whose political views in other ways were poles apart from Leontiev's, reached identical conclusions about the future of European democratic states. Like Leontiev he could find in the *average* European citizen little to admire and nothing to emulate. And he knew the mentality of Western Europeans far better than Leontiev did. Even French civilization, so great in the past, seemed to him to be fading away on an exhausted soil. And France was, for Russians, the leading nation of Europe, because culture still meant more to them than economic strength.

Would Europe settle down for long in its republican form, which meant nothing less than the destruction of all the individual European states, or would it collapse into anarchy? Leontiev asked. 'In either case Russia needs organized strength and discipline, to save herself from infection, and to save in Europe whatever is worth saving, especially those things which made her former greatness'. (*Byzantinism and Slavdom*, 1875.)

History has not fulfilled Leontiev's grandiose plans for the revival of the Russian Empire, and the salvaging of ancient European civilization is far from being a conspicuous feature of Soviet policy. But some of his gloomier predictions about the future of Russia and Europe have come true. In spite of his passionate prejudices, he foresaw the main course of events far more accurately than either the rationally hopeful Russian liberals or the more destructive revolutionary anarchists. The Russian colossus, physically weakened by wars, was spiritually undermined and overwhelmed by a violent fever which originated in Europe. Byzantine Russian civilization seemed to perish together with the Russian Empire, poisoned at its roots. Nevertheless, though the entire theoretical basis of the Russian Empire has been twisted and turned upside down by the Soviet interpretation of Marx, the underlying motive forces of the re-integrated Soviet state are now readily compared with the older pattern of the Germanized Byzantine autocracy. People who talk about the Soviet régime as inverted Tsarism need to distinguish the despotic—and within their limits successful— Empires of Peter the Great and Ivan the Terrible, from the semi-liberal reformist Empire of Alexander II, which ended in failure, and what is now called 'reaction'. Which kind of Tsarism do they mean? Had Leontiev been alive today, he would have been among the first to understand why the 'Tsar Liberator' is passed over by the Bolsheviks in icy silence, while the cult of his harsher predecessors, Peter and Ivan, has grown into a fervent national ritual. It is uncertain whether this Soviet reaction to the distant despotic past denotes a spiritual affinity more far-reaching than the instinctive urge to justify present actions by historical precedent, however remote it may be. But if we replace a divinely appointed autocratic Tsar by a deified political leader, the moral authority of the Orthodox state-church by a fanatical social creed of German-Jewish origin, compulsory state service under the Tsars by centralized industrial planning and labour-conscription, then a broad picture emerges which bears some formal resemblance to Leontiev's forecast. At least it links intelligibly the old hierarchical society with the even more strictly stratified society of the new Socialist Empire.

Seen in this light the liberal democratic period fades into an unstable interregnum, promoted by noble but short-sighted dreamers like the Decembrists and early Slavophils, brilliant in the arts, moderate in civic construction, but turning ever greyer and dimmer until it finally dissolves in chaos.

Certainly the liberal period from 1856 until the Revolution was marked by a series of military and political disasters for Russia, yet it saw the most splendid outburst of literature and music that she has ever known, before or since. Squalid or arrogant in worldly triumph, individual Russians proved glorious in defeat, and through defeat stronger in imaginative creation. Indeed a successful, proud, aggressive fatherland rarely appealed to intelligent Russians as a civilized ideal. In this respect Leontiev was exceptional, and showed a German streak, though his ideal of national aspiration, and of concrete visible beauty as the criterion of its success, was eminently non-German.

But he was not a voice crying in the wilderness. Several other eminent Russians interpreted Europe's alleged decline as

Russia's golden opportunity. Tyutchev and Dostoevsky both asserted *ad nauseam* that Europe was spiritually rotten to the core. If Russia continued to follow European doctrines she would perish. Liberal laxity and laziness, leading to socialism and revolution, would also ruin the West; in so doing it could at last render a service to the East, but only if the East remained immune. Perhaps this is what Tyutchev meant when he used those ominous words, 'The Red West will be our saviour'. After 'red' Europe's collapse, Russians, for so long 'the world's outcasts', would find themselves leading the world. Herzen developed an equally unreasoning faith in the potentialities of Russian civilization, though the idea of the Russian state itself as a possible civilizing factor always filled him with horror. He hardly considered whether the one could exist without the other. Finally, the historian Klyuchevsky, commenting on the achievements of Alexander II, expressed the soberest misgivings; could liberal seeds imported from Europe ever sprout healthily on that alien semi-Asiatic soil? 'We now begin to think in what way the past can help us, at the moment when we seem to have broken every link with it. But our reflection contains an important oversight. Admiring how reform has changed Russian antiquity, we fail to perceive how Russian antiquity has already transformed reform.'

Some of Leontiev's most important ideas were thus partially confirmed by the independent utterances of such brilliant and diverse contemporaries. In saying this, I am not making a bid for originality; I am merely trying to correct a still current prejudice, in the light of which Leontiev has for long been represented as an almost pitiful eccentric, who stood isolated and obstinately aloof from the most important trends of his day. He may well have been, and quite deliberately chose to be, alien to the changing intellectual fashions embraced by the majority of Russian intellectuals. But he was constantly aware, far more than they, of deeper social undercurrents, and he discerned distinctly whole new situations looming large as life on the horizon, where less penetrating observers caught only fleeting glimpses of clouds and threatening storms.

His imaginative and stylistic qualities would alone entitle him to the position which he is gradually, if grudgingly, being awarded as a classic of Russian thought. And his cast of mind, if not his recommendations, finds far more support throughout the contemporary world than it did in his own century. His political thought exercised some influence on action, since it took root among the anti-Bolshevik Eurasians, who revere him as one of their principal teachers. And Bolshevik minds,[1] with their revengeful sense of inverted intellectual aristocracy, and through their utilization of Soviet anti-European or anti-American policy in order to gain credit with Asiatic nationalists, have also recognized and exploited his acumen.

---

[1] Though public discussion of Leontiev's dominant ideas has naturally enough not been encouraged since the Revolution, some continued Soviet interest in him is revealed by the republication of his autobiographical essays in *Moya Literaturnaya Sud'ba* (*Literaturnoe Naslyedstvo*, Moscow, 1932.)

INDEX